JURISDICTION

JURISDICTION

A COP AND A PASTOR TALK ABOUT LIFE

Jon McNeff
Jim Mcneff

CrossLink Publishing

CrossLink Publishing
601 Mt. Rushmore Rd, Ste 3288
Rapid City, SD 57701
www.crosslinkpublishing.com

Ordering Information:
Quantity sales. Special discounts are available on quantity purchases by corporations, associations, and others. For details, contact the "Special Sales Department" at the address above.

Jurisdiction/McNeff —1st ed.

ISBN 978-1-63357-164-8

Library of Congress Control Number: 2018960544

First edition: 10 9 8 7 6 5 4 3 2 1

All scripture quotations are taken from the NEW AMERICAN STANDARD BIBLE®, Copyright © 1960, 1962, 1963, 1968, 1971, 1972, 1973, 1975, 1977, 1995 by The Lockman Foundation. Used by permission.

What people are saying about . . .

Jurisdiction: A cop and a pastor talk about life

As a retired chief of police and follower of Christ, I found *Jurisdiction* to be the most compelling true-life testimony for the redemptive power of Christ. Authors, Jim and Jon McNeff combine the human depravity seen through the eyes of a cop, with the restorative promise as shared by a pastor. This is one of the most powerful testimonies I've read. It touched my spirit, and I know it will also touch yours.

—**Scott Silverii**, PhD, chief of police (ret.), Thibodaux Police Department, Louisiana, founder, Brick Breakers Men's Ministry, co-founder, Marriage Matters Ministry

Jon and Jim McNeff have crafted a unique approach to describing the ills of our society through stories of the law from the viewpoint of a pastor and a cop. It is only fitting they break it down into criminal activities, because all of us are lawbreakers. But don't be fooled into thinking these are just "detective" stories because they aren't. They mirror the human condition and the wrong thinking that lead to sadness and ultimate defeat. These gentlemen have hit the nail on the head about truth and consequences.

—**Ron DiCianni**, bestselling artist and author

To be able to listen in on the experiences of a cop and pastor as they tackle challenging questions of God's *Jurisdiction* and sovereignty can have wide impact on believers and non-believers alike. This clear, compelling, and thorough offering provides answers for anyone seeking solace, healing, or hope. All you have to do is peel back the cover and start reading.

—**Mike Major**, chief (ret.), Bureau of Investigation, Orange County District Attorney's Office, California

Freedom is not doing what you want but being what God created you to be. According to the Bible, the good life is a life lived in accordance with the will and pleasure of the Creator. In their helpful book, Jon and Jim McNeff remind us that life is God's *Jurisdiction* and therefore a matter of joyful submission on the part of man toward God. May this compelling book remind us all that death not life, bondage not freedom, and despair not joy results from a life that declares autonomy from the Creator. As Jon and Jim will argue, being on top of life requires coming under the rule of Jesus Christ!

—**Philip De Courcy**, senior pastor, Kindred Community Church, Anaheim Hills, California Bible teacher, national radio broadcast Know the Truth

Jurisdiction will lead the reader to traumatic homicide scenes, gruesome traffic collisions, and the reality of death row. The journey's purpose is to discover God is graciously in charge, regardless of our limited perspective. *Jurisdiction* illuminates eternal truth that is undeniable when the Bible is the foundation.

—**Sara Delaney**, JD, inspector (ret.), Marin County District Attorney's Office, California

"As a cop, you work for God" . . . or so you're told. It's truly hard to appreciate when your world is filled with those who claim to be him. *Jurisdiction* clears the muddy waters that keep officers from understanding who God truly is, what he came to do, and the difference it makes. Read it, apply the truth contained in its pages and discover the profession's greatest resource.

—**Jim Bontrager**, national board member,
Fellowship of Christian Peace Officers – USA

Any book written by a cop and a pastor deserves attention, but *Jurisdiction* commands it. Jon and Jim tell the truth about who God is and who we are, compelling us to live for and under the rule of Jesus Christ. Here is a rare combination of hard-hitting narrative and life-giving doctrine that makes for a riveting work I heartily recommend!

—**Dr. Kent Dresdow**, senior pastor,
NorthCreek Church, Walnut Creek, California

As a career cop, I have had the opportunity to see things I would never have been able to see, and the misfortune to see things I wish I'd never seen. This no-nonsense and relatable book has enhanced my abilities in speaking with others about the most compelling and important subject there is, God's *Jurisdiction*.

—**Houston Gass**, chief of police, Fritch, Texas

Jurisdiction answers questions regarding God's sovereignty in creative, yet straightforward ways using illustrations from the criminal justice system and connecting them to biblical doctrine. It is a persuasive and undeniable education.

—**Tina Jaeckle**, Ph.D., L.C.S.W., B.C.E.T.S., F.N.C.C.M.,
Sociology and Criminology Department of Social Sciences,
Flagler College, St. Augustine, Florida

We dedicate this book to our wives, Anne and Jamie. Anyone who knows us knows that we definitely "married up." Their encouragement in the writing of this book is a small part of our marriages that have been marked by unquestioned commitment, undeserving love, constant encouragement, and a true partnership in all of life. We dearly love both of you!

Contents

Foreword

When one man shares the life experiences of a police officer, and his brother, who has pastored for more than forty-years applies biblical answers, it is insightful. These men combine remarkable life stories and solid theological skill in a compelling presentation that moves logically from skepticism to belief.

Truth is always relevant. It is never in need of being updated. And yet it must be presented clearly to bring understanding. *Jurisdiction* presents the seemingly opposing truths of the sovereignty of God and human responsibility in a way that brings clarity and understanding. Along the way they deal with other tough questions that many are afraid to ask, let alone answer. Is man a sinner or just sick? Can Jesus be your Savior without being your Lord and Master? Is there such a thing as hell? What will heaven be like? How can one know that they are going to heaven? These are some of the issues illustrated in life and answered from the Scriptures.

Integrating truth and life into written form is not easy. But these men have done it well. They show the relationship between life and theology in a seamless manner that presents a logical and reasonable worldview. Moreover, it provides a path for skeptics searching for answers and a hope that closes the gap of doubt for believers.

The authors do not offer pat answers or pious platitudes. The story in the last chapter of a woman who lost her husband and two of her sons in the span of a couple of years, will touch your heart. But reading of God's comfort and sustaining power will bring hope. This is where the book shines brightest. The application of theology to the deepest questions of life shows a willingness to wrestle with both in an honest and forthright fashion.

Having been a book addict for most of my life, I found *Jurisdiction* to be well worth my time. The authors have done their homework and lived many years with broken, desperate, and even unlawful people. God's Word has been a lamp unto their feet. They share the light God has shown them. You need not live in quiet desperation if you choose to read this wonderful work and accept the answers offered.

—Dr. Phillip Howard
senior pastor, Valley Bible Church,
Hercules, California

Gratitude and Acknowledgements

Completing *Jurisdiction* with the quality we hoped to achieve would have been a daunting task without the help of Dave McNeff, Lois Gonzenbach, Jim Daggs, Dr. Kent Dresdow, Dr. Phil Howard, and Ron DiCianni. They freely offered their time to provide feedback, insight, editorial assistance, and simply buoyed our effort. We offer our heartfelt gratitude for the gifts they have extended on our behalf.

We appreciate the law enforcement and ministry professionals who took the time to review the manuscript and provide an endorsement. Their stamp of approval convinced us that we were on the right trail.

We also thank Carol Rhodes for writing her story for us to use in this work. Ultimately, her faith in our sovereign God is a reflection of the truth contained in the book. This is especially true of the doctrine of heaven as it appears in the final chapter.

Finally, there are many police-related tales from Jim's career that are used for illustrative purposes in *Jurisdiction*. While the stories are authentic, we have primarily used pseudonyms in lieu of true identities.

Introduction

The term *jurisdiction* might be ambiguous or hold several meanings for people, yet it is defined this way:

1. The power, right, or authority to interpret and apply the law.
2. a. The authority of a sovereign power to govern or legislate
   b. The power or right to exercise authority: control.
3. The limits or territory within which authority may be exercised.[1]

Every law enforcement agency has jurisdiction somewhere. If it had no authority to enforce laws, there would be no need for its existence. Jurisdiction is established between cities, townships, parishes, counties, states, and the federal government.

Criminal and civil cases are funneled into the appropriate court with authority to handle the legal matters before it. Each agency has policies and procedures that further clarify how to perform duties within their specific area of responsibility. Jurisdiction is not restricted to law enforcement agencies. Other organizations within the criminal justice system have defined areas of responsibility and jurisdiction as well.

It sounds simple, but as many working within the system know, it can get confusing and downright confrontational at times. Countless professionals within the law enforcement community

---

[1] *Merriam-Webster's Collegiate Dictionary, eleventh edition,* (Springfield, MA: Merriam-Webster, Inc., 2003).

can share a horror story or two about a confrontation surrounding jurisdictional issues involving a criminal investigation, prosecution, or other function related to duties of justice. When such conflicts exist, we rely upon policies, procedures, and codified law to determine where authority rests as we resolve discord. At times the answers appear clear, at other times they remain vagué. Ultimately, someone is required to determine jurisdiction and take action to provide the service required to fulfill professional obligations.

Many parallels can be seen in life. Most people naively believe they have ultimate jurisdiction over their lives. In our selfie generation we are repeatedly told that man is the master of his fate and personal opinion is the ultimate authority. Of course, that view implodes when confronted by the realities of broken relationships, financial reversals, sickness and disease, and ultimately, death.

Jurisdiction was written using police stories to illustrate and connect biblical principles to practical use—to help the reader understand God's jurisdiction. The stories at the beginning of each chapter provide powerful evidence of the need for the content that follows each story. If all we had in life were stories like this, we would be completely lost with no hope of meaning or redemption.

But the undeniable realities contained in the stories are complemented in the theological section that follows. Please don't let the word theological intimidate you. In its most simple form the word means "God's word." As we present the stories of the heartbreak, pain, and suffering of this world, doesn't it seem fitting to at least see how God views them?

This book is written for the skeptic who questions the existence of God and thus rejects the concept of His control over the world. But the flow of the book will show the objective reader that the realities of life dictate a different worldview. Read with an open mind, this book will show that the pain and suffering endemic to our world can only logically be explained through the lens of a loving and just God who is the author of the only approach to life that is coherent, just, and true. In the end, it is the only way that the soul of man can be truly satisfied, as he is made right with God and enabled to enjoy His presence forever.

But the one who believes in God's sovereign control over this world will also profit from this book. The arguments presented are logical and truthful. They are presented in such a way that they will instill a greater awareness of the truthfulness of God's existence and His loving and just control of the affairs of man. God does not exercise His rule as an absentee landlord who cares about nothing except collecting the rent or a tyrannical dictator who squashes all dissent under His oversized thumb. The arguments given for the jurisdiction of God will bring confidence and encouragement to one who already believes them.

The design of this book is to trace the trajectory of God's sovereign jurisdiction from initial skepticism and unbelief, through man's efforts to find meaning in life, to God's response. Along the way, we will attempt to answer the questions that confront everyone in the journey of life. We will provide logical, coherent answers to troubling questions. "Does God exist?" "Has He revealed Himself to man?" "What did He say?" These questions are not incompatible with truth or faith. As you will see, even the most brilliant scientists and philosophers of our world cannot provide convincing arguments that cause one to answer these questions negatively.

The book is divided into three sections that move from skepticism to resolution. The first section focuses on man's basic problem in life. If you don't know what the problem is, you will never figure out how to fix it. In chapter one we will argue that the undeniable force in mankind that causes bad things to happen is moral in nature. It is sin, not sickness. Given the drastic nature of the problem, the next chapter will examine man's haunting search to find an answer for his problem. Chapters three and four will expose man's inevitable awareness that God is watching what we do and yet our natural propensity is to run from Him. The last chapter in this section will introduce the subject of free will as man's attempt to solve his problem.

Section two introduces God's solution to man's problem. Chapter six does this by providing compelling evidence for the existence of God, and chapter seven shows how God has revealed Himself in His divine book, the Bible. The sovereign decree of God is explained in chapter eight, while chapter nine tackles the conundrum of merging God's decree with the free will of man.

The last section of the book begins in chapter ten by presenting the inevitable conclusion of God's jurisdiction for those who reject it. Chapters eleven and twelve clarify God's solution for addressing the problem of man by asserting that man can do nothing on his own to save himself because it is only through God's grace that the sin problem of man can be solved. The last chapter of the book presents the beauty and glory of heaven as the end of all human suffering and the eternal destination for all who respond to God's sovereign claims on their lives.

A final word of introduction might be helpful. One might ask, "Why are you writing this book?" That question reminds us of the ancient words of King Solomon in the book of Ecclesiastes when he wrote, *"the writing of many books is endless, and excessive devotion to books is wearying to the body."*[2] One might infer from that statement that the writing of another book is merely more yammering about something that's been written before or is completely unnecessary.

While we acknowledge that the content of this book has certainly been written about before by more able authors, we feel it is appropriate to write about it again because it is so needed. In that same section of Ecclesiastes quoted above, Solomon also said, *"The words of wise men are like goads, and masters of these*

---

[2] Ecclesiastes 12:12

collections are like well-driven nails; they are given by one Shepherd."[3] Our hope and prayer is that the words of this book will serve as goads that provoke critical thinking, and well-driven nails that hold together a well-constructed argument about life from the Author of Life.

There are two primary reasons for the writing of this book. The first reason is to counter the prevalent worldview that there is no credible reason to believe in God and the Bible. Dostoevsky said, "If there is no God, then all things are permissible."[4] That is a true statement, but no one can truly live like that. Those who claim God does not exist want to maintain a system of morality and order that defies their atheistic beliefs. Those beliefs need to be countered by logical, coherent thinking that reflects the reality of human relationships. Leaving everything up to chance, even over billions of years, is simply not a viable option.

Tim Keller quotes Alvin Plantinga in offering an illustration on a smaller scale that shows how vast numerical odds still do not add credibility.

> Imagine a man playing poker and dealing himself twenty straight hands of four aces in the same game. Would you think he was cheating? What if he claimed that there were an infinite number of parallel universes so that in any one universe at any given time it would be mathematically possible to deal yourself four aces in twenty straight hands in the same game, and he just happened to be living in that universe?[5]

---

[3] Ecclesiastes 12:11

[4] Fyodor Dostoevsky, Constance Garnett, trans., *The Brothers Karamazov* (repr., 1880, Digireads.com Publishing, 2017), 635.

[5] Timothy Keller, *The Reason For God: Belief in an Age of Skepticism* (New York, New York: Penguin Random House, 2008), 131.

Would you believe him then? I'm not a poker player, but I think that would still stretch the credibility for anyone, despite the appeal to vast mathematical odds.

We will show that the strident atheistic worldview is inherently inconsistent and cannot be logically defended. There are better answers to life than to believe that everything came about by mere chance with no reason or meaning.

A second reason for the writing of this book is to offer a positive, healthy alternative to the toxic worldview that permeates our culture. Tragically, it seems that many in our world are living with an incoherent worldview that offers no reason or hope for life. But merely going through the motions of life doesn't bring fulfillment. There are also many others who live in the poisonous cesspool that is the result of a worldview that offers nothing but more of the same. This demands a response.

An observation by Tim Challies illustrates the need to address this. In 1910 an educator named Abraham Flexner wrote a report entitled *Medical Education in the United States and Canada* that was released by the Carnegie Foundation. This report offered a number of recommendations on how to educate doctors. Many of these recommendations brought about changes in health care in America that continue to be felt today.

One of Flexner's most significant recommendations involved the proper order of classes in medical school. Flexner recommended four years of intense medical training, the first two devoted to basic science and the last two given to clinical training. The first section was broken into two blocks of science, "the first year being devoted to learning normal human anatomy and physiology and the second year focusing on abnormal physiology and the disruptions of disease." The idea was to focus on what is normal first, so the students would have a good basis of comparison before they moved on to study disease and abnormality.[6]

---

[6] Tim Challies, *The Discipline of Spiritual Discernment* (Wheaton, Illinois: Crossway Books, 2007), 100-101.

It seems obvious to any objective observer that our world is increasingly fascinated with the abnormal, corrosive events of life, not the healthy ones. Russian-born Pitirim Sorokin, the first professor and chairman of the Sociology Department at Harvard, made this observation over sixty years ago. His book, *American Sex Revolution* pulls no punches as he observes:

> There has been a growing preoccupation of our writers with the social sewers, the broken homes of disloyal parents and un-loved children, the bedroom of the prostitute, a cannery row brothel, a den of criminals, a ward of the insane, a club of dis-honest politicians, a street corner gang of teenage delinquents, a hate-laden prison, a crime-ridden waterfront, the courtroom of a dishonest judge, the sex adventures of urbanized cavemen and rapists, the loves of adulterers and fornicators, of masoch-ists, sadists, prostitutes, mistresses, playboys. Juicy loves, ids, orgasms, and libidos are seductively prepared and served with all the trimmings.[7]

That was over sixty years ago. Think of how far we have fallen since then. We need more than a mid-course correction. We need a new playbook that ensures emotional and spiritual health. Without this, Thoreau's statement is accurate. He said, "The mass of men lead lives of quiet desperation. From the desperate city you go into the desperate country. A stereotyped but unconscious despair is concealed even under what are called the games and amusements of mankind."[8] Thoreau's caustic evaluation seems to be even truer today.

Dietrich Bonhoeffer, a Lutheran pastor who was imprisoned and eventually hanged for plotting the assassination of Adolph Hitler in WWII said, "If you board the wrong train, it's no use

---

[7] Pitirim Sorokin, *The American Sexual Revolution* (Boston: Porter Sargent Publisher, 1956), 58.

[8] Henry David Thoreau, *Walden* (repr., 1854, USA: Sam Torode, 2009), 8.

running along the corridor in the opposite direction."[9] If you are doing this, maybe it's time you stop long enough to understand your plight and change trains. Even though we ultimately come to this position by faith, it is our hope and prayer that this book will lead you to faith and convince you that recognizing God's jurisdiction is not only logical and reasonable, it is the only way to live a healthy, fulfilling life and find peace with God.

---

[9] Eric Metaxas, *Bonhoeffer: Pastor, Martyr, Prophet, Spy* (Nashville, Tennessee: Thomas Nelson, 2010), 187.

OUR UNIVERSAL PROBLEM

"I do not know what the heart of a bad man is like. But I do know what the heart of a good man is like. And it is terrible."[10]
—Ivan Turgenev, 19th century Russian novelist

Houston, We Have a Problem!

What's wrong with us?

"Houston, we have a problem" has become synonymous with a crisis. It is frequently used when events have tumbled out of control. On April 14, 1970, each astronaut aboard the Apollo 13 command module Odyssey contributed to what morphed into the famous phrase when they experienced a major explosion in their service module while 200,000 miles from earth.

> Fred Haise: "Okay, Houston—"
> Jack Swigert: "I believe we've had a problem here."
> Jack Lousma: This is Houston. Say again please."
> Jim Lovell: "Houston, we've had a problem. We've had a main B bus undervolt."[11]

---

[10] R. Kent Hughes, *Are Evangelicals Born Again?: The Character Traits of True Faith*, (Wheaton, Illinois: Crossway Books, 1995), 75.

[11] Transcript from http://apollo13.spacelog.org/page/02:07:55:19, (accessed July 3, 2014).

Mission control in Houston was faced with an enormous problem that almost ended in tragedy for the Apollo 13 astronauts. In a similar way, we could say the same thing about humanity.

"You can't make this stuff up." Law enforcement officers often repeat this phrase when they come across a scene that is bizarre and twisted. When analyzing the evidence, they shake their head and ask, "What in the world is going on?"

BRUTAL CRIMES

My police agency had such a case in March of 2009. I was the Detective Bureau commander and responded to the scene of an attempted murder. The forty-seven-year-old male victim looked like he had been run over with a lawn mower. But, in reality, he had been bludgeoned with a machete that severed most of his nose, some of his scalp, and several fingers. His skull was cracked, and he had defensive wounds consistent with someone who desperately tried to ward off his attacker. He was left for dead, lying in a pool of blood in the alley behind his apartment—but he did not die.

The paramedics skillfully collected Tom and his body parts, rushed him to the University of California Irvine Medical Center where over the course of the next few days, doctors worked hard to put him back together. Plastic surgeons successfully reconstructed his nose and face, but one hand remained permanently maimed, as three fingers could not be saved.

Investigative process

As the investigative process began, our detectives collected evidence and interviewed family members and neighbors. Unfortunately, we had no eyewitness who could describe the attacker other than he was dressed like "the grim reaper." Since the viscous assault occurred at dawn, one witness described "sparks flying" when the machete ricocheted off the victim and scraped the asphalt. We had no apparent motivation, as robbery was ruled out since no property was taken. The attack seemed to be personal. Someone wanted Tom dead, but why?

The man sliced and diced by a machete was a dutiful FedEx driver. The heinous crime occurred as he departed his apartment, fitfully adorned in his black and purple work uniform, clothing that was now stained crimson red.

We interviewed co-workers but came up empty on theories related to his employment. They each seemed to provide similar details regarding "Ordinary Tom," . . . no highs nor lows, a few friends, but no known enemies.

Behavior analysis is a dynamic tool when investigating crime. For instance, how was the eye contact? Were there unnecessary grooming techniques used? Was the body language consistent with the spoken word? Did the person divert attention during direct questions? . . . and so on.

Analyzing behavior can be fragile if solely relied upon for evidence, but it is a goldmine when determining where the focus of the investigation should be directed. In this case, the focal point shined brightest on the family and a live-in acquaintance—a very quirky man.

Tom was married and living with his wife, Hilda, and their three children, ages sixteen, eleven, and ten. Tom and Hilda had a friend who appeared to be down on his luck and lived with them. We found it creepy that Herbert, their mid-30s friend, slept in the same bedroom with Kayla, the sixteen-year-old daughter. Hilda and Kayla were each protective of Herbert steering us away from allegations of any kind.

Herbert was a tall, chunky man, with pale skin, and dark greasy hair. His sunken eyes spoke words that were not uttered by his lips. *Untrustworthy-stooge* was the unanimous perception by each investigator on our team.

Unkempt and portly Hilda was also far more concerned with their finances than Tom's welfare. Once upon a time, this woman had some appealing glamour shots, but those days were long ago.

She waddled when she walked, and her droopy face matched her somber disposition. Think of *Eeyore*, the pessimistic, gloomy, depressed, donkey who is a friend of Winnie-the-Pooh, when trying to understand the individual we encountered.

At one point, Hilda stopped by the hospital in her attempt to collect Tom's ATM card without even asking about his well-being—like whether his nose or fingers would ever work again. After he came out of a coma she tried to convince him to sign a power of attorney giving her access to one of his investment accounts. Everything she did or didn't do pointed toward guilt, not the grieving spouse she pretended to be.

Neighbors said Herbert and another friend frequently wore black trench coats and dueled in the courtyard with swords.

Really, we pondered? Grown adults dressed in Gothic garb jousting in the apartment complex? Consequently, we theorized that Hilda and Herbert were having an affair and conspired with another friend to kill Tom. Now we needed to identify Herbert's jousting partner and hope that DNA evidence would place him at the scene of the crime.

Barboza the butcher

We interviewed more friends and conducted surveillance. Finally, we identified Herbert's ally as Barboza who worked as a butcher in a local grocery store.

Our detectives followed Barboza from a distance for days hoping for a chance to surreptitiously collect DNA left behind. After much anticipation, an opportunity presented itself.

Barboza drove into a parking lot, got out of his car, and hawked a gob of spit onto the ground. While we preferred a discarded soda or beer bottle, the spit would do. Now the shortest tenured detective on the surveillance team was tasked with collecting the nastiness from the asphalt in the parking lot.

A few days after submitting the sample to the crime lab, we had the results. Bingo! It was a match. The DNA from his saliva matched DNA from drops of blood, which had been found leading away from the scene of the crime. Now we had our suspect identified.

When detectives served the search warrant at Barboza's home, they also interviewed his girlfriend, Brittney Mae.

Brittney was loyal to a point, but she wasn't going to jail for the butcher. She quickly confirmed that Barboza was absent from his residence at the time of the attack. She also admitted to helping him burn his clothes in a backyard fire pit when he returned.

Moreover, a personal check from Hilda was located in Barboza's car, as was Tom's schedule. Finally, Brittney led us to the machete used to disfigure Tom. It was securely taped to the backside of a dresser in his bedroom.

As a result, we arrested Barboza. However, the butcher was resilient as he resisted all methods of interrogation and never confessed.

Meanwhile, our investigators re-interviewed Hilda and Herbert. I watched their stories crack via closed circuit TV. There is a time to play nice during the interview process, and a time when pleasantries are thrown out the window and the true interrogation begins. It was time to "go for the jugular" in an effort to break through the lies and deceit. Now was the time, and our detectives were good at it. We drove a truck through their testimonial inconsistencies and behavioral irregularities.

Eventually, both Hilda and Herbert confessed. They had been planning Tom's demise for more than six months. Even Hilda and Tom's 16-year-old daughter, Kayla, had been privy to the plan—which included hiring Barboza for a modest fee of $5,000 to "butcher Tom to death."

A band of scoundrels

The band of scoundrels mistakenly believed killing Tom, while leaving for work, would net them a life insurance settlement from FedEx, and they would be able to live happily ever after on a ranch in Wyoming. The murderous plot was justified in their minds because of Tom's excessive drinking and violent behavior, even though neither had been documented in local police files. Self-righteous, co-conspirator Herbert said he asked God how an undeserving man like Tom deserved to have a wife and kids.

As the case progressed through the criminal justice system, Hilda, Herbert, and Barboza each pled guilty to attempted murder and mayhem in 2013. Hilda and Herbert received a fourteen-year prison sentence, while Barboza the butcher received twenty-five to life as his punishment.

Several years later, Tom suffers from post-traumatic stress and has trouble using a walker to get around. There are also three children whose mother is in prison for conspiring to murder their father.

Unfortunately, this case is all too common in our culture today. What should be the safest place of all—the home—can be more volatile than a building demolition. Why is that? A more difficult question is why did Herbert and Hilda devise a plan to kill her husband? Most people would say they were "sick," thus insulating themselves from ever thinking that they could fall prey to the same problem.

WHAT'S WRONG WITH US?

But what if they were not sick. What if they were just normal people who made some "wrong" decisions? And what if we have that same "ability"? What if it is part of who we are as members of the human race? What if we are all "sick"? What if "normal" people are capable of doing really bad things? Upon further examination, this seems to be true. A story from WWII illustrates this possibility.

At the end of WWII, many of the war criminals were brought to trial. In 1960, Israeli undercover agents apprehended Adolf Eichmann, one of the most notorious masterminds of the

Holocaust in a daring raid on his South American hideout. He was returned to Germany for trial. When he was brought before his accusers a string of concentration camp survivors were called as witnesses. One of them was a man named Yehiel Dinur, who had escaped death at Auschwitz.

The YouTube video of this trial is gripping. Dinur is ushered into the witness box. Facing him, behind a bulletproof glass shield, is Eichmann, who had personally executed many Jews and had ordered the extermination of millions of others. Dinur hadn't seen him in eighteen years.

The presiding judge asks Dinur to place a skullcap on his head, and place his hand on the Bible as he is sworn in. He seemed shaken. Mortified might be a better word. Dinur answers a few simple questions about his birthplace, his occupation, and his two years in Auschwitz. Nine minutes into his testimony Dinur attempts to stand in the witness box but begins sobbing uncontrollably as he faints and collapses onto the floor in a heap. The judge declares a recess because it is apparent Dinur cannot continue his testimony.

Why did he collapse? Was he overcome by grief? Hatred? The heinous nature of the crimes Eichmann committed? The mere presence of this madman in front of him? No. In an interview on 60 Minutes that aired on February 16, 1983, host Mike Wallace asked Dinur about his response that day.

Dinur replied that, as he looked into the face of Eichmann, he did not see the personification of evil he had expected. Instead he saw an ordinary man. In that one moment when time stood still, Dinur came to the realization that whatever was in Eichmann is part of the human condition. "I was afraid about myself," Dinur explained. "I saw that I am capable to do this . . . exactly like he."

Wallace then faces the camera and asks several poignant questions. "How is it possible . . . for a man to act as Eichmann acted? Was he a monster? A madman? Or was he perhaps something even more terrifying: was he normal?"

Yehiel Dinur concluded, "Eichmann is in all of us."[12]

Is that true? Do "normal" people do these kinds of things? Many people would contest this, saying that it's only the really "bad" people who do these appalling crimes. The rationale is that people like Eichmann and his madman boss, Adolph Hitler, and other lunatics like them, are the ones who are really "sick." But is that true? A more contemporary story suggests it's not only the Eichmanns and Hitlers of this world who are capable of heinous acts.

HIDING AMONG US

In 1999 Sara Jane Olson was living an idyllic life in Minneapolis. She was married to a physician, lived in an upscale part of town, and played the part of a doting soccer mom to her three daughters. Involved in her community, she was a lay minister at the Minnehaha United Methodist Church, narrated the Christmas pageant, read to the blind, prepared meals for the homeless, and taught English as a second language. Nice lady.

She was also a criminal. On June 19, 1999 the FBI arrested her. Unknown to her husband and daughters, her real name was Kathleen Soliah. She had been a fugitive for the past twenty-three years after fleeing Los Angeles in the wake of her participation in a crime spree while she was involved with the Symbionese Liberation Army, the group that rose to fame with the kidnapping of newspaper heiress, Patty Hearst. Soliah was involved in several bank robberies. One that occurred in Carmichael, California, resulted in an innocent victim, Myrna Opsahl, being killed. Four months later, Soliah planted bombs beneath two police cruisers, attempting to kill the officers in them. Fortunately, the explosives were discovered and defused before they could detonate.

---

[12] Transcript from *60 Minutes*, 15, no. 21, as broadcast over the CBS television network, 6 February, 1983, quoted in Charles Colson and Ellen Vaughn, *Being the Body* (Nashville, Tennessee: W Publishing Group, 2003), 205-206.

What part of that is "normal"? What part is "sick"? What part is something else? Were her actions mistakes or oversights? It doesn't seem so. A mistake is when you miss a freeway exit. An oversight is when you forget to carry the five on your income tax return. Some would argue that she gets a pass because her political views were justified. Tell that to the family of Mrs. Opsahl or to the police officers she intended to kill. It is apparent that something much darker lies beneath the surface of Mrs. Olson/Soliah. This was something deeper than "sick." "Normal" people don't do these types of things. Or do they?

GROUPTHINK

We can also see the results of "normal" people committing heinous acts against humanity in large groups. This is often called the power of *groupthink*. The events that happened in Jedwabne, Poland, in 1941 serve as an example of this. For three hundred years Jews and non-Jews existed peacefully in Jedwabne. They lived next to each other. They went to school together. They sold goods to one another. In short, they coexisted peacefully with each other.

But all of that changed in the course of a single day. On July 10, 1941, by the order of Mayor Marian Karolak and the occupying German military, forty Jews were rounded up by their fellow citizens, herded into a pre-arranged empty barn and shot. Later the same day, most of the remaining Jews, around 250, were also rounded up and herded into the same barn before it was set on fire. Anyone attempting to escape was shot.[13]

What caused former neighbors to turn on their fellow citizens and kill them? Was it anti-Semitism? Hate? Resentment? We get some clue by noting that the German soldiers who occupied

---

[13] (Polish) *The 90th session of the Senate the Republic of Poland.* Stenograph, part 2.2. A Report by Leon Kieres, president of the Institute of National Remembrance, for the period from July 1, 2000 to June 30, 2001. Donald Tusk presiding.

Jedwabne told the non-Jewish citizens that the Jews were the cause of their problems. They told them, "You can kill them if you want and take their land, their farms, and their possessions."[14] So maybe their heinous actions were motivated by nothing more than old-fashioned greed. But is this the cause or merely a symptom of something deeper? Worse yet, were these "normal" people?

NORMAL PEOPLE

If we probe deeper, we can see that criminals and certain neighbors are not the only ones who have a dark side. We are all aware, for instance, that people can steal without ever being labeled a criminal. Not only are they not identified as criminals; many don't even look like thieves. Many of them are white-collared, BMW driving, respectable members of their golf club.

But they can also be affected with the same problem as war criminals and convicted murderers. They might look respectable, but they are also evil. As C.S. Lewis wrote:

> The greatest evil is not done in those sordid 'dens of crime' that Dickens loved to paint . . . it is conceived and . . . moved, seconded, carried, and minuted . . . in clean, carpeted, warmed, and well-lighted offices, by quiet men with white collars and cut fingernails and smooth-shaven cheeks who do not need to raise their voices.[15]

Noted psychiatrist M. Scott Peck wrote of the insidious nature of man over thirty years ago in his book *People of the Lie*. He acknowledged the presence of evil in every person, even the most ordinary.

---

[14] Jan T. Gross, *Neighbors: The Destruction of the Jewish Community in Jedwabne, Poland* (Princeton N.J.: Princeton University, 2001).

[15] C. S. Lewis, *The Screwtape Letters* (New York: Macmillan, 1961), x.

They live down the street—on any street. They may be rich or poor, educated or uneducated. There is little that is dramatic about them. They are not designated criminals. More often than not they will be "solid citizens"—Sunday school teachers, police officers, or bankers, and active in the PTA.[16]

Peck makes a valuable distinction between the "bad" people like Hitler and "normal" people who are also evil. In discussing the common thread of evil that runs through everyone he asks,

How can this be? How can they be evil and not designated as criminals? The key lies in the word "designated." They are criminals in that they commit "crimes" against life and liveliness. But except in rare instances—such as the case of a Hitler—when they might achieve extraordinary degrees of political power that remove them from ordinary restraints, their "crimes" are so subtle and covert that they cannot clearly be designated as crimes.[17]

And what are the subtle and covert crimes that go undesignated. We all know what they are. You lie about taking a "sick" day from work or use your company car for personal business. No harm, no foul, right? But what about finding out your husband has cheated on you with your best friend, or your 16-year-old son comes home drunk, or your high school daughter tells you she's pregnant? Issues like these are not crimes, but we intuitively know there is something wrong with them.

And what about the common crimes that we still punish with fines and jail time? We still call the police when our home is burglarized. If someone punches us in the face with his fist, we know this is clearly wrong. And in a land of sexual freedom, everyone

---

[16] M. Scott Peck, *People of the Lie: Hope for Healing Human Evil* (New York: Simon and Schuster Inc., 1983), 69.

[17] Ibid.

still understands that rape is more than just "offensive." It is wrong, clear and simple.

So where does this leave us? In our discussion so far, we have a wife and friend who tried to kill her husband, a war criminal, a soccer mom, and the inhabitants of a whole village who all illustrate the same point. What's wrong with these people? The prevailing opinion seems to be that people like this are "sick."

ARE THEY SICK?

There are a lot of reasons offered to explain the "indiscretions" of life. Some say that a lack of education or our lack of socio-economic standing or the way our mother treated us is the cause of these problems. But we all know of people who had little or no education or came from an impoverished background or a broken home, and yet they never resorted to criminal activity.

So what causes supposedly normal people to do bad things? They are called "sick." But what does this mean? Do they have a temperature? Do they need medical treatment? Do they need to be hospitalized? These are fair questions, since "sick" is a medical term. But I would suggest that "sick" is not an adequate term to be used at all. There are several problems with seeing bad actions merely as sickness.

First, sickness as a term used to describe people's actions is hard to categorize. What kind of sickness is it when you knowingly lie? Is a "little white lie" different than lying to the government on your income tax returns or padding your resume with a degree you don't have? What about someone who murders? Is that a different sickness than one who merely thinks about murdering someone? What about the one who actually carries out an attempt to murder someone but is unsuccessful?

Second, sickness is not an appropriate term to describe behavior because behavior involves choice and sickness does not. Of course, this may be at the heart of why some want to label bad behavior as sickness because that means they are not responsible for the consequences of their actions.

If a man who is drunk smashes the head of his wife in with a baseball bat is sick, then he isn't at fault because he was drunk. But if he chooses to drink a beer, and then a second and third and fourth, knowing all the time of his history of anger and violence when he is drunk, then he is clearly accountable for his actions. If alcoholism is a sickness, then it is the only one that someone chooses to buy in a bottle.

Third, the sickness model is fatally inconsistent. If all the bad things we do are indications of sickness, and we are not responsible for them, then this must also apply to those who have done bad things to us. *After all, if we are not responsible for our acts, neither are they.*

If the leaders of Nazi Germany were sick, then why did the world agree to bring them to trial and execute them when they were found guilty? Why didn't the Nuremburg trials send them off to anger management class or insist that they enter therapy? Why do we call the police and not a therapist when someone breaks into our house? It seems apparent that the problem of bad behavior that we all face as human beings is not some kind of "sickness."

WHAT IS IT?

So, if the problem isn't being sick, then what is it? If the human ability to choose is real, then actions that are "bad" must be deemed some kind of moral failure. And the word best suited for this willful violation of right and wrong is sin. I realize that most people don't regard this as a topic for "polite" conversation, and it is a word that many in our supposedly sophisticated society would like to exclude, but it certainly fits the description. It is clear that something resides in the heart of every human being that impels us to act in ways that are harmful to others in our world, as well as being disappointing or even shame-inducing to ourselves.

Psychologist William Kilpatrick comments on the difference between sin and sickness:

> Sin is often seen as an exciting and pleasurable possibility; sickness is not. Men do not pursue arthritis the way they pursue adultery. In the second place, it is a poor compliment to the species: it robs us of the real dignity we have, which is the freedom of choosing the good. The reverse side of the coin stamped "Smith's sin is only a sickness" is "Smith's virtue is vitamin based." It is a way of reducing human beings to the level of a walking chemistry shop. Often it is a disposition to be generous and kind that makes us excuse other people's faults as sicknesses, but how much of a kindness is it? Is that the way we would like others to think of our own misdeeds? Do we want to be patted on the head like children, while some grownup makes excuses for us: "Poor Billy, he can't help himself," or worse, "Poor Billy, he was born with an endorphin deficiency."[18]

Why is it so hard for people in our modern society to face this reality? There are two major reasons for this. The first is that no one wants to label anyone else a sinner because they recognize that this means that the label can also be applied to them. It's much easier to say someone else is a "sinner," but it's a lot harder to apply that label to ourselves. Despite all the evidence to the contrary, our world now seems to be bent on taking the label of "sinner" off everyone, so no one has to wear it.

Of course, the other reason no one wants to accept the label of "sinner" is because it is a religious term. In a secular society where people choose to live as practical atheists, religion is seen as an ancient relic invented by unsophisticated people.

---

[18] William Kilpatrick, *Psychological Seduction* (Ridgefield, CT: Roger A. McCaffrey Publishing, 1983), 82-83.

If evil is admitted in any form, then that introduces some kind of objective moral law into the discussion. And if moral law comes into the conversation then so does a moral lawgiver. And if the moral lawgiver is seen as God then it is simply more desirable to keep Him out of the discussion and call evil something else.

This approach has huge consequences. Nevertheless, many, such as Richard Dawkins, a long-time atheist professor at Oxford, advocate it. He writes:

> In a universe of blind physical forces and genetic replication, some people are going to get hurt, other people are going to get lucky, and you won't find any rhyme or reason in it, nor any justice. The universe we observe has precisely the properties we should expect if there is, at the bottom, no design, no purpose, no evil, and no other good. Nothing but blind, pitiless indifference. DNA neither knows nor cares. DNA just is. And we dance to its music.[19]

Dawkins' lack of logic is breathtaking. If the universe is "blind" and we "dance to the music" of our DNA, which "neither knows nor cares," then words like "hurt" and "lucky" have absolutely no meaning because, by definition, they express a moral position. In addition, his lack of compassion leaves a gaping hole in his humanity. The universe is blind, so "some people are going to get hurt," and there is nothing but "blind, pitiless indifference" in the end.

So, crime victims like Tom, Holocaust survivors like Yehiel Dinur, the family of murdered Myrna Opsahl, and the Jewish survivors of Jedwabne, should just suck it up because they are not the victims of anything sinful or even "sick." They are simply the unwitting recipients of the blind, pitiless indifference of dancing to the music of our DNA.

---

[19] Richard Dawkins, *Out of Eden* (New York: Basic Books, 1992), 133.

Can we live with that explanation? Is that morally satisfying? Does that even make sense? I think not. The truth is that no one with a conscience can live consistently with such a worldview. If people are merely the accidental result of impersonal random chance, we have no logical reason to object to any action. Yet we intuitively apply moral judgments to the behavior of others multiple times every day. We insist on moral limits that have absolutely no rational foundation in a natural worldview. As the old saying goes, "You may have the freedom to swing your fist in any direction you want, but your freedom ends at the beginning of my nose!"

So, we are back to sin and the moral accountability it implies. Sin is the most accurate description for the moral decisions that cause the hurt and pain and suffering that we see all around us. And we can't ignore it.

Herbert Mowrer, one-time president of the American Psychological Association who taught at both Yale and Harvard said:

> For several decades we psychologists looked upon the whole matter of sin and moral accountability as a great incubus and acclaimed our liberation from it as epoch making. But at length we have discovered that to be free in this sense, that is, to have the excuse of being sick rather than sinful, is to court the danger of also becoming lost. This danger is, I believe, betokened by the widespread interest in existentialism, which we are presently witnessing. In becoming amoral, ethically neutral and free, we have cut the very roots of our being, lost our deepest sense of selfhood and identity, and with neurotics, themselves, we find ourselves asking, "Who am I, what is my deepest destiny, what does living mean?"[20]

---

[20] Ravi Zacharias, *Can Man Live Without God* (Dallas: Word Publishing, 1993), 137-138.

If we are honest, it's easy to see that sin is all around us. G. K. Chesterton, British author and philosopher, said that sin is "the only part of Christian theology which can really be proved."[21] This would surely seem to be true in light of what we have seen so far. It is hard to explain the world we live in without an understanding of sin.

But the problem with sin doesn't end with identifying it. The real question is what to do about it. The answer to that begins with understanding the need to control it. In short, who has jurisdiction over sin?

---

[21] John MacArthur, *The Battle For the Beginning* (Nashville, Tennessee: Thomas Nelson, 2005), 196.

CHAPTER TWO

"If God is dead, somebody is going to have to take his place. It will be megalomania or erotomania, the drive for power or the drive for pleasure, the clenched fist or the phallus, Hitler or Hugh Hefner."[22]
—Malcolm Muggeridge

Who Ya Gonna Call?

Isn't someone going to do something?

If man wants to ascend the throne of his own wisdom, then he must live with the results. But, as we saw in the previous chapter, that doesn't seem plausible, let alone livable. There is something "bad" out there, and the most logical explanation for it is the biblical explanation of sin.

The objective is not only to name it, but also to find out what to do about it. Where can we go to find an answer to our problem? Who has the right and authority to do something about it? That's where we begin this chapter.

JURISDICTION

Every law enforcement agency has a geographical area referred to as jurisdiction. Within each organization are areas of

---

[22] Malcolm Muggeridge. AZQuotes.com, *Wind and Fly LTD*, 2018. http://www.azquotes.com/author/10521-Malcolm_Muggeridge, (accessed March 10, 2018).

responsibility, usually called bureaus, divisions, or precincts. In each area of responsibility, the assignments are further categorized. The purpose of such defined categorization is to specifically identify separation of labor based upon who has legal authority to act as well as who is responsible to take action. For instance, as a narcotic investigator, I fell under the umbrella of the Detective Bureau, which was part of the Fountain Valley Police Department, responsible for police duties within the City of Fountain Valley, in the County of Orange situated in the State of California.

Our police department typically staffed ten detectives—miniscule by some standards and a luxury by others. We did not have contemporary voicemail systems in the early 1990's when I worked as a narcotics detective. If a phone rang, and either the specific detective or division assistant was unable to answer it, our chief expected someone else to pick up the line. Imagine that, a real person answering the phone, a real treat in today's world of voicemail and phone trees.

PICK UP THE PHONE

One day I heard a phone ring. The line belonged to another detective. Her assignment was sex and juvenile related crimes. She was on vacation and the division assistant was out of the office. No one wanted to answer this particular investigator's phone in her absence, as it was rarely a simple message due to the nature of the assignment.

"Hello this is Detective McNeff, can I help you?" The caller wanted to remain anonymous but went on to tell me the perverted tale of a man who collected child pornography. She was concerned that he would begin acting out his fetish desires with boys in the neighborhood.

My mind was in full investigative mode. I tried to determine ways to corroborate her information in order to obtain a search warrant for his home. Finally, she blurted out, "You better hurry!"

"Where?" I replied.

"To his post office box. He is driving there right now. The 'perv' can hardly stand the anticipation. He is picking up his latest order of disgusting magazines."

Making the arrest

I confirmed the location of the mail drop, grabbed one of my partners and flew out of the police department. It wasn't a narcotic investigation, but I was going to gain a great deal of satisfaction if I could catch someone possessing child pornography, since this kind of person is highly likely to engage in lewd conduct with children—many of whom are trusting him as an authority figure in his or her life.

We arrived at the mail drop just in time. We saw the "Cheshire cat" walk out of the business fondling a package in his hands, a goofy smile on his face, and nearly salivating as he visualized the contents that would prove to be nauseating to any decent human being, but not Mr. Lascivious.

I detained the man wearing a purple cardigan sweater with white knuckles gripping his recently ordered smut just as he approached his car.

"Police detective," I said. "What's in the package?"

He quickly developed a speech impediment as well as amnesia. While stuttering, he forgot what he ordered from this particular business in Europe known for producing child pornography and listed on the return address. Fortunately for me, about 70 percent of those involved in crime and caught in the act, actually allow law enforcement authorities consent to search.

"Would you be willing to grant me permission to check the contents of your package?" I asked.

He was not about to demur for fear of appearing guilty.

"Uh, ... uh, well, sure. There is nothing illegal in it," mumbled Lascivious under his breath. When I began opening the package he blurted, "Apparently you don't believe me?"

"I believe everyone until they give me reason to doubt them. Will I trust or doubt you once this package is opened?" My question hung in the air, unanswered. Once I had the package open, I wasn't sure if I wanted to vomit or cry based upon the pictures inside. "I now have reason to doubt anything you say," came my response to a man with a depraved mind.

"But I didn't know that was in there" he pleaded.

"Do you have any more at home?"

"Of course not."

"Would you give me permission to search your house?"

"I think I need an attorney."

"That would be a true statement," I affirmed, as I placed him in handcuffs.

Mentor comes through

The man who encouraged me to pursue my dream of becoming a police officer was the late Ron Godsey. He worked for the Anaheim Police Department (APD). As a teenager participating in youth programs at our church in Anaheim, Ron was a leader that I respected.

One evening while playing volleyball on an outdoor court at church, "Angel" (the designation for the helicopter of APD) flew overhead. I heard Ron's voice call out on the public address system as he hit us with the spotlight out of the sky. How cool, I thought as we all waved at our friend piloting the bird. It was at that point that I wanted to be a "cop."

Although Ron was old enough to be my father, he was still working sex crimes as a detective at APD when this case landed in my lap about eighteen years later. I had experience and expertise writing search warrant affidavits for narcotic cases, but I needed a sex crimes expert to support my opinion in order to obtain the warrant. Ron provided the expertise, and I gained legal authority to search Mr. Lascivious' home.

As expected, we found more child pornography, but not without an exhaustive search. Lascivious' wife thought her husband was being framed until I located a small library of kiddy porn well-hidden on the interior frame of a file cabinet in his office. Once I removed the drawers and discovered the magazines, Mrs. L. turned pale. Suddenly she realized her marriage was in deep trouble.

Even though we were unable to determine if the man had molested any children, the case was satisfying because I believe we prevented future molestations based upon several private conversations I had with others as the case culminated.

Someone needs to do something

Anyone above the age of seven or eight realizes that there are certain situations in life that require someone with authority to act. A seven-year-old intuitively knows that the playground bully who steals your ball at recess needs to be stopped. Likewise, any loving parent who caught Mr. Lascivious trying to peddle his material to their teen-age son would know they needed to do something.

That's why the woman in the preceding story made the anonymous call. Child pornography is wrong, and she knew it. So, she made the call trusting that someone at the police department would pick up the phone and that they would be able to do something about Mr. Lascivious.

Like it or not, we all encounter situations like this constantly in life. And when we do, we know that someone needs to pick up the phone. We often hear, "Someone needs to do something about that," or, "There ought to be a law against that." That's because we inherently know that people who collect (and produce!) child pornography need to be stopped before they act out on their lecherous fantasies.

This leads us to another observation that is the natural extension of the first observation made above. Someone not only needs to pick up the phone to report the crime, but someone who can do something about it needs to answer.

Can you imagine a world in which everyone from Eichmann to Mr. Lascivious was left to pursue his or her desires? What would happen if the anonymous woman had never called the Fountain Valley Police Department that day? And what would happen if there were not a credible person on the line who had the power and authority to do something about Mr. Lascivious? If no one had made the call, and if no one had answered it, Mr. Lascivious would still be out there feeding his warped view of life by targeting young children to molest.

WHO WILL ANSWER?

So, we ask people to make the call but then the next legitimate question is "Who will answer the call?" A poem put to song in 1967 asked this question. Ed Ames recorded the English version of "Who Will Answer?" The first verse asked,

> From the canyons of the mind,
> We wander on and stumble blindly
> Through the often-tangled maze
> Of starless nights and sunless days,
> While asking for some kind of clue
> Or road to lead us to the truth,
> But who will answer?[23]

Ultimately this thing called life is unexplainable without some kind of context. The logical mind rebels against saying that we are all just protoplasm floating through a mindless universe. And when things don't go right, our minds grapple for meaning because we know there just has to be an answer even though we

---

[23] Sheila Davis, Luis Eduardo Aute, "Aleluya No. 1," 1967.

can't find it at the time. The third verse of the song expresses the continual search for answers.

On a strange and distant hill,
A young man's lying very still.
His arms will never hold his child,
Because a bullet running wild
Has struck him down.
And now we cry,
"Dear God, Oh, why, oh, why?"
But who will answer?[24]

Indeed, who will answer when someone raises his or her hand and asks, "Isn't someone going to do something about this guy collecting child pornography?" What would you feel like if someone mugged you and there was no one to call to report the crime? Worse yet, what would happen if there was no law enforcement at all, or the Allies had never entered the war against Hitler?

Do you remember the story of Job in the Old Testament? Job was a righteous man whose ten children were killed in a storm. In addition, he lost his possessions, his business, the respect of his wife, and his physical health. Do you think he was looking for answers?

In essence, one of Job's friends asked the same question we're asking, *"Call now, is there anyone who will answer you? And to which of the holy ones will you turn?"*[25] Job's friend Eliphaz the Temanite was the one who asked this question, but he wasn't much help. He basically tells Job there are no answers and it was his fault in the first place. With friends like this, who needs enemies?

---

[24] Ibid.
[25] Job 5:1

Pretending

So where can we go for answers? Some approach the problem by pretending it doesn't exist. Take war for instance. No one in his or her right mind would ever think that anyone prefers war to peace. That's why those who simply protest war are incredibly naïve. John Lennon fits in this category with his song, "Imagine."

> Imagine there's no countries
> It isn't hard to do
> Nothing to kill or die for
> And no religion too
> Imagine all the people
> Living life in peace...

That's beyond poetic license. Just because a pop star put his thoughts into an iconic tune doesn't mean it's a valid sentiment. In fact, it's almost delusional. Who in their right mind could ever imagine that all of humanity would come to the group realization that there is "nothing to live or die for?" That's not likely to change no matter what we may want to imagine.

Will and Ariel Durant, the venerated and prolific historians, point out that "War is one of the constants of history, and has not diminished with civilization and democracy. In the last 3,421 years of recorded history only 268 years have been without war."[26]

Likewise, anyone who thinks we can solve the crime problem by "loving" each other or sticking a flower in the barrel of every gun in existence is truly misguided. The idea that we could eliminate all murder by eliminating all guns also begs the question. What about knives, bricks, ice picks, axes, explosives, and

---

[26] Will and Ariel Durant, *The Lessons of History* (New York: Simon & Schuster, 1968), 81.

poison, all of which have been used extensively in the murder of our fellow man? Islamic terrorists used planes loaded with fuel to bring down the twin towers of the World Trade Center in New York and kill 3,000 people. Does that mean we should outlaw planes?

My point is that there is always a darkened, sinful heart that pulls the trigger or thrusts the knife into his victim or flies the plane into the building. You can't solve the crime by pretending it doesn't exist.

Sin and social pathology

I took a sociology class once in college. The class had 150 students. The "prof" spent the first three days entertaining answers to the question, "What is the nature of man?" After two and a half days of listening to various people say man is basically "good" (whatever that means), and that our troubles stem from lack of education or poverty, or lack of love from our mothers, I couldn't take it anymore.

Even though I was just beginning my walk with God, I knew the simple answer was "The basic nature of man is that he is a sinner." With more than a little trepidation I raised my hand and the professor called on me. When I gave my answer, you would have thought my fellow open-minded college students wanted me to walk the plank. The hissing and booing was loud and long.

But, to his credit, the professor called off the dogs and asked me to explain. I explained that, even though I had been raised by loving parents who, while not rich, provided me with all of the physical and emotional support any child could have needed, I still ended up on the wrong side of a jail cell by the time I was fourteen. Twice. In a period of two weeks. The class was silent. Finally, the "prof" said, "touché" (whatever that meant) and continued with his journey of trying to define social pathology.

The truth is that sin is at the heart of all social pathology. Well-educated rich people still lie, steal, cheat on their wives, and kill people. Education and economics don't change the heart of man. Neither does having a good family or passing more restrictive laws. If that were the answer we could eventually live in a police state with all kinds of laws to restrict human behavior but it still would not solve the problem that is in the heart of man.

This is not to say that we should do away with all laws and let people do what they want. Rational laws put in place by a civilized society are indeed a deterrent to the dark side of man. If you don't believe that, just imagine a world in which all traffic officers disappear. Every intersection would be a chaotic mess of crumpled metal and broken bodies. Interstate 5 that runs the length of California would become a two-hundred-mile-long raceway!

So—who ya gonna call? If you're on Interstate 5 in California and someone comes roaring past you at 120 miles per hour, the answer is easy. Call the California Highway Patrol. But what about Mr. Lascivious? Obviously, calling the police is a good place to start. But that can only control his outward behavior. Who do you call if you really want to change his heart?

Belief in everything

The answer to that is not as easy as one might think. Our contemporary culture has come to believe in everything and yet believes in nothing. We believe in modern psychology but are unsure if the biological, psychodynamic, behavioral, cognitive, humanistic, or some combination of the dozens of other psychological approaches is correct. We believe in sexual freedom, but when our spouse "cheats" on us, it sure feels wrong. We believe that all religions are basically OK and say the same thing, but fail to realize that Christianity, Judaism, Islam, Buddhism, and Hinduism are all mutually exclusive. You can't believe in heaven and hell and reincarnation at the same time.

My point is if you want to trust your heart and soul with man's answers, pick one and hold on because you will have no idea of where you are going. We started this chapter by saying that every law enforcement agency has a geographical area over which they have jurisdiction. That works well when everyone understands and respects the boundaries.

But the question we've asked in this chapter is "doesn't someone need to do something when the problem we identified in the first chapter pops up?" Who will "answer the phone" to address the problem of sin?

Personal feelings

Apologist Ravi Zacharias writes and speaks extensively about how to address this problem. He speaks about a debate between the philosopher Fredrick Copleston and the atheist Bertrand Russell. Part of the debate went like this:

> Copleston: "Mr. Russell, you do believe in good and bad, don't you?"
> Russell: "Yes, I do."
> Copleston: "How do you differentiate between them?"
> Russell: "The same way I differentiate between yellow and blue."
> Copleston: "But Mr. Russell, you differentiate between yellow and blue by seeing, don't you? How do you differentiate between good and bad?"
> Russell: "On the basis of feeling—what else?"

Zacharias commented that someone with a less gentlemanly demeanor than Copleston might have moved in for the kill by commenting, "Mr. Russell, in some cultures they love their neighbors; in other cultures, they eat them, both on the basis of feeling. Do you have any preference?"[27]

---

[27] Ravi Zacharias, *Can Man Live Without God?* (Dallas, Texas: Word Publishing Group, 1994), 182.

This is a critical question. If sin is man's basic problem, does it make sense to approach it based on personal feeling? One might argue that if man's feelings could be trusted to be completely objective, they would lead him to the correct solution.

But that doesn't seem to be the case. In fact, as we will see in the next chapter, it seems more obvious that man's natural preference is to run from the obvious answer.

CHAPTER THREE

"In a sort of ghastly simplicity, we remove the organ and demand the function. We make men without chests and expect of them virtue and enterprise. We laugh at honour and are shocked to find traitors in our midst. We castrate and bid the geldings be fruitful."[28]
—C.S. Lewis

Black and White Fever

Is our conscience aware of God?

One thing you learn very quickly while riding in a patrol car in California where most police cars are black and white, is the very real existence of what we call "black and white fever." This hypochondriac-like illness strikes when you see a marked police unit in your rear-view mirror. The symptoms are a sudden appearance of sweaty palms and forehead, heart palpitations, and a sudden, jerky movement of the right leg moving from the gas pedal to the brakes. This condition can come on very quickly and resistance is futile, especially if you are speeding. I'm sure you all know what I mean.

---

[28] C. S. Lewis, *The Abolition of Man* (repr., 1944, New York, New York: HarperCollins, 2001), 26.

CULTURE OF MIGHT

Although I became a police officer, resistance and rebellion are traits that come natural to me. Among eleven siblings, I am the youngest of eight boys. I rarely yielded seniority to my older brothers growing up. This led to more brawls than one can imagine. My vice throughout the teen years was not drugs or alcohol but fighting. I wasn't always mad. I simply liked to fight for sport. My desire to mix it up often led to trouble.

When I grew older, I learned to channel the aggression toward productivity. I intuitively knew my ability to engage in hand to hand combat would serve me well in the field of law enforcement. Indeed, this was true when learning arrest and control techniques in the police academy.

Once I hit the streets as a new cop, I rarely needed motivation to workout. Like many gyms and exercise rooms in police departments across the country, ours had a picture of musclebound inmates in the prison yard with a caption that read, "They worked out today. Did you?" Just like I never wanted to be outwitted by a crook, I never wanted a bad guy to have a physical advantage over me. It is essential for cops to possess physical skills and maintain the mindset of a warrior—something I refer to as a culture of might. It is a frame of mind that facilitates our will to survive during deadly encounters, thus keeps us safe and alive. Thank goodness most in law enforcement possess it.

Use of force – Pain compliance

There is no better way to illustrate rebellion and its consequences than sharing stories of cops and the physical conflict they see. One of the basic principles involving the use of force is pain compliance. Depending upon the variables and within lawful boundaries, police officers are justified using techniques that apply pain until an offender physically submits to authority.

Dozens of experiences come to mind that would illustrate my point. They include:

- A narcotics raid when a crook tried to disarm my partner, who was toting a Heckler & Koch MP5 sub-machine gun. The bad guy had "H&K" imprinted on his forehead, as he was butt stroked with the weapon and taken into custody. While this method sounds unnecessarily violent to some, the alternative was firing our weapons at him, most likely taking his life.

- An officer-involved shooting occurred in Fountain Valley when a teenager wanted to play real life *Mortal Kombat* (sic) in a crowded apartment complex. Officers heroically returned fire, wounding the shooter in the process, before he injured or killed someone.

- The first time we deployed our newly acquired *beanbags* several decades ago was comical. The beanbag is launched from a shotgun. A K9 handler from an allied agency was helping us search for the burglary suspect. He turned white as a ghost when our officer deployed beanbags at the non-compliant suspect who had broken into a warehouse. The K9 handler thought we shot the guy with buckshot. He quickly loaded his dog in his police unit to make a quick exit before I told him it was a beanbag, not 00 buck.

Submitting to authority

These situations demonstrate one of the challenges faced by law enforcement officers—to engage in heart-stopping, adrenaline-pumping altercations, and then fall into compliance in what is often times a rigid, paramilitary organizational structure. In other words, a group of Type A controllers submitting their will to the demands of superiors. If the *culture of might* is harnessed correctly, it proves to be a well-oiled machine. If not, it can be destructive in this environment.

My co-author and brother, Jon, can tell a story of its negative affect on me as a new police officer. While off duty, playing in a church softball league, I nearly went to blows with an opponent because of his dissent and arguing with the umpire over a call. My behavior and response was unnecessary, but these values were magnified to unhealthy proportions. As my opponent was tossed from the game and physically confronted the ump, I went after him like a rabid dog looking for someone to bite. Fortunately, my desire to see him arrested was overridden by my realization that I didn't have the authority in that situation to do anything about it.

Because this culture populates police departments nationwide, we often take rebellion to places that are relationally unhealthy—both personally and professionally. This is not unusual. Cops are the law on the street, but just another subordinate employee within the walls of the police building. The skepticism and cynicism are the same, whether you work in a sub-station with three people or the downtown headquarters with thousands.

When people do not fall into place in the professional organization, varying methods are used to gain conformity. When the criminal element offers physical resistance, *pain compliance* is employed to gain physical control. My point is that men and women everywhere, criminal and law abiding, want to go their own way. To one degree or another, we all offer resistance and rebellion.

Why is this so? Why does it seem like some people have an aversion to authority? Or is the situation worse than that? Does everyone have an aversion to authority? Actually, that seems to be more the case.

THE PROBLEM OF AUTHORITY

Inconsistency

A popular bumper sticker seems to verbalize the mantra of our postmodern generation. It says, "Question authority." While the rationale for that is dubious, it describes the mentality of many people today. No one wants a black and white cop car following him because no one wants to submit to authority.

But even a casual analysis reveals we can't live that way. What would happen if we removed the stop signs and red lights on our streets? What about the laws prohibiting rape, theft, and murder? Isn't it obvious that someone who protests authority the loudest would call the police if someone broke into their home and stole all their possessions? Wouldn't these same protestors want someone in authority to do something if their children were raped or murdered?

The problem is evident, but the reason is completely unknown in a world that has ruled God out in favor of evolution. If evolution is true, then it isn't logical to make any moral judgments at all. But if there is no God, why do we look over our shoulder when we do something "wrong?" Where does black and white fever come from?

In a tweet, Richard Dawkins, an avowed atheist and evolutionary biologist and author of *The God Delusion*, wrote, "Date rape is bad. Stranger rape at knifepoint is worse. If you think that's an endorsement of date rape, go away and learn how to think."[29]

It's curious that an atheist who champions evolution would speak like this. The words "bad" and "worse" are moral statements. He also implies some kind of moral standard by telling someone who can't distinguish the difference date rape and rape at knifepoint that they need to "learn how to think."

Philosopher Bertrand Russell espoused the same incoherent view. He believed, "That man is the product of causes that had no prevision of the end they were achieving. That his origin, his

---

[29] Chelsea Schilling, "Dawkins Criticized for 'Disturbing' Rape Tweets", www.wnd.com, (accessed on July 31, 2014).

growth, his hopes and fears, his loves, his beliefs, are but the outcome of accidental collocations of atoms."[30]

That's an incoherent position because it doesn't match up with the realities of life. If we are just accidental protoplasm, then laws and emotions and beauty and creativity and order and morality are all terribly subjective. Where does the development of morality enter into the progression from primordial ooze to knuckle dragging ape to man? If we are just protoplasm or an "accidental collocation of atoms" then what's the big deal about a male protoplasmic entity forcing sex on a female protoplasmic entity? Isn't that OK?

Well no, that's not OK, OK? And everybody knows it. We get black and white fever when we discuss something like rape because our conscience tells us that violent act is just plain wrong. We want to be free, but our conscience tells us people should not be free to rape, pillage, and steal. Any civilization built on the idea that man should be completely free to do whatever he wants is a civilization that is bound to implode under the weight of barbaric actions.

Where's a cop when you need one?

Indeed, if one were to come upon any woman disheveled and beaten, any civilized person would immediately call the police, even if she didn't make a claim to being raped. Everyone wearing a badge has heard someone say, "Where's a cop when you need one?" That's because there is a uniformly recognized need for law enforcement because we all get black and white fever.

Even those who are anti-law enforcement will instinctively call the police when they are robbed or mugged. Why? Because every one of us is born with an innate sense of justice stamped

---

[30] Bertrand Russell, *Mysticism and Logic* (New York: Norton, 1929), 47-48.

on our brain and woven into our hearts. We want someone to do something about the wrong that was done to us.

That's what makes the subject of jurisdiction so difficult. Jurisdiction is the heart and soul of law enforcement. Our police departments exist because we as a society recognize the need to curb the natural tendencies of humanity to speed and beat yellow lights. The popular notion is that police officers deal only with hardened criminals. But they also enforce traffic laws, patrol our neighborhoods, supervise crowd control, and visit classrooms. They exist to catch the brazen serial murderer and the guy who slides through a stop sign.

The same is true in our personal lives. As we said in chapter one, you don't have to be a convicted murderer or war criminal to have a problem with sin. It's in all of us. And God sees every bit of it. That's where it gets tricky. We like God if He stays safely in His place and enforces His laws against everyone else. But we don't want Him messing with our lives. We don't like Him following us.

The problem of submission

Oh, we want Him to follow everyone else. But everyone else feels the same way. What would happen if somehow all moral laws were removed? That would make as much sense as eradicating all police officers. Can you imagine the chaos that would ensue if we did that? Of course, that doesn't make any sense at all even though none of us want to submit to authority.

There are at least three reasons for this. First, we are born as self-centered creatures that carry this desire with us all our lives. One of a baby's first words is "MINE!" But every child must learn that they can't get everything they want when they want it, or they become a juvenile delinquent. At the root of all relational difficulties is this same demand. We all want to have things our own way.

Secondly, we have all seen systems that abuse authority. As Westerners, we look at the chilling abuses of totalitarian leaders like Hitler, Stalin, and Mao with a healthy fear. No one wants to live under that type of authoritarian control. This became even more pronounced in the US after the Watergate scandal of the 1970s. The abuse of power by our president pushed many people to question authority.

A third reason this is difficult is a misconception of the idea of freedom. We perceive freedom to mean that we should be able to do whatever we want. Of course, we don't believe that should be true of everyone else, but we live as if it should be true for us. The problem is that your freedom eventually intersects with my freedom. For example, a person has the freedom to consume alcohol, but they do not have the right to drive while impaired because it could have tragic results for another. And if a person exercises freedom in that way and crashes, someone will call the people in a black and white car.

FACING THE FALL

This presents a huge problem for mankind. We want to do what we want to do, and we don't want to submit to anyone in doing it. But when someone else does something they want to do, and it injures us, our black and white fever kicks in because we know it is wrong.

Where did we catch this fever? The explanations offered by many in our world are numerous and varied. Various sources suggest this comes from our upbringing, our lack of education, the wrong socio-economic class, or our evolutionary background.

These solutions are all unsatisfactory because they ignore a simple universal truth. Everyone has the disease. That was the point of chapter one. But in this chapter, we said that God has the right and authority to answer when man calls with the difficult issues of life.

Yet there are many who don't want to hear that. That's because they ignore (at their peril) the simple evidence the Bible presents about the seeds of rebellion. Failure to understand this will prevent one from ever having any relationship with God.

The seeds of rebellion are seen in the very first book of the Bible. You probably know the story. The fall of Adam and Eve in the Garden of Eden is the origin of man's basic problem of sin. Adam and then Eve were created in a perfect environment. Stunning surroundings, meaningful work, a perfect spouse, and absolutely no sin. Just like your house, right? Probably not.

Satanic deception

But what happened? Into this perfect environment stepped the serpent who embodied the very presence of a beautiful angel of light who had rebelled against God and been thrown to the earth with a third of all the angels. Slithering up to Eve he said, *"Indeed, has God said, 'You shall not eat from any tree of the garden'?"*[31] Now remember, up until this point everything God has said and done for them has been absolutely positive. The only negative thing He said was, "Don't eat of the tree of the knowledge of good and evil."

But Satan twisted God's words to imply something else. In fact, God said, *"From any tree of the garden you may eat freely; but from the tree of the knowledge of good and evil you shall not eat, for in the day that you eat from it you will surely die."*[32] Satan turned God's bountiful provision into a negative prohibition. God said, "Eat anything from the vast storehouse of my creation that you want." Satan distorted that to intimate that God prohibited eating from all of the trees in the garden. How ludicrous.

But it worked. Eve was deceived by Satan's distortion and ate the fruit of the one tree God had prohibited. Now before we take

---

[31] Genesis 3:1
[32] Genesis 2:16,17

Eve totally off the hook by saying she didn't know any better, let's remember that she responded correctly to Satan by accurately repeating God's instructions. Even though the instructions were given to Adam before Eve was created, Eve clearly knew what God had said.

Satanic lies

But then Satan tried another tactic. He told a bold-faced lie. *"You surely will not die."*[33] Was that true? Of course not. Adam and Eve lived a long time, but they eventually died. Satan's lies and tactics continue to lock humanity into both physical and spiritual death. Sin is like that. It has terrible earthly consequences and the worse possible eternal consequences.

Satan's deceit went further. *"For God knows that in the day you eat from it your eyes will be opened, and you will be like God, knowing good and evil."*[34] No one said Satan was stupid. He is an angel of light after all. Most people who read this statement have misunderstood it.

Most people assume that Adam and Eve knew the "bad side of town" and now Satan was telling Eve that she would become wise like God. Indeed, that's what Eve thought. But nothing could have been further from the truth. Up until this point, Adam and Eve had known *only good.* They had seen all of the blessings and beauty that God had to offer. They had the entire garden at their disposal. They had the perfect relationship in that they were *"both naked and were not ashamed."*[35] Physically, emotionally, intellectually, and socially they had everything anyone could want in life.

But Satan's deception and lies made them think they were being cheated. They were led to believe that God was holding out on them, so they ignored God's instructions and crossed the line

---

[33] Genesis 3:4
[34] Genesis 3:5
[35] Genesis 2:25

into a whole new world. *"When the woman saw that the tree was good for food, and that it was a delight to the eyes, and that the tree was desirable to make one wise, she took from its fruit and ate; and she gave also to her husband with her, and he ate."*[36] She thought it was about the fruit. Like so many modern temptations, which promise more than they can deliver, she thought eating the fruit would increase her spiritual and intellectual brainpower.

But God's instructions had exactly the opposite intent. By prohibiting them from eating of the tree of the knowledge of good and evil, God was trying to protect them from evil, not withhold good from them! They already had it as good as it could possibly be. God wanted them to trust Him and benefit from all the good He had provided. But instead, they ignored God's instruction, and despite the warning, they disobeyed Him and went to live on the other side of God's provision.

This is exactly the same thing Satan does to us. Through his deceit and outright lies he makes us think that God has given us a bad deal. So, like Eve, we ignore the black and white car of God's law thinking we can be truly wise by following our own instincts. This is why we rebel and fight against him. But, like her, this is destructive thinking.

Satanic cover-up

Look what this type of thinking does. The Genesis account continues, *"Then the eyes of both of them were opened, and they knew that they were naked; and they sewed fig leaves together and made themselves loin coverings."*[37] As soon as they heard God calling them they got the first case of black and white fever. Look at the first three verbs of the verse. Their eyes were "opened." They now saw what God saw. They had not seen evil before, but now they did.

---

[36] Genesis 3:6
[37] Genesis 3:7

They "*knew they were naked.*" That wasn't anything new. They had been that way their whole created life. But now they wanted to hide—even their bodies. Their nakedness symbolized the shameful symbol of their disobedience.

That's why Adam and Eve "*sewed fig leaves together and made themselves loin coverings.*"[38] What a pitiful attempt to hide from the all-seeing eye of God. Man's attempts to cover his spiritual nakedness before God are just as trite and useless.

RESULTS OF THE FALL

Who told you that you were naked?

The results of this were devastating. Their lack of submission irreparably harmed their relationship with God. When they heard the sound of the Lord walking in the garden they hid themselves. The Lord said, "*Where are you?*" Adam replied, "*I heard the sound of You in the garden, and I was afraid because I was naked; so I hid myself.*"[39] Why was he afraid? Because he had rebelled against God. He ran a red light and he knew it.

Like a skillful prosecuting attorney, God asks Adam, "*Who told you that you were naked? Have you eaten from the tree of which I commanded you not to eat?*"[40] Indeed, who told Adam he was naked? No one. Sin does that to us. Resistance and rebellion against God's laws brings shame. That's just how it is.

Our pesky conscience

This continues to be true for all of us. The Apostle Paul writes that even those who don't have God's written law "*show the work of the Law written in their hearts, their conscience bearing witness and their thoughts alternately accusing or else defending them.*"[41]

---

[38] Ibid.
[39] Genesis 3:9-10
[40] Genesis 3:11
[41] Romans 2:15

Our conscience is what causes us to break out in black and white fever when we do something wrong. We don't need a book on morality to tell us that.

We all want to be shame free. A prominent writer reminds us that we live in an "I'm shame free, but you should be ashamed of yourself" culture.[42] No one wants to be ashamed of anything. I'm not talking about false shame placed on us by false religious teachers. Legitimate shame reminds us that something is wrong.

The prophet Jeremiah was very aware of this. He lived in a time when even the religious leaders led people into the pagan practices of male and female cultic prostitution, incest, animalistic sex, and even offering babies and young children to be burned alive on altars to pagan gods. But, surprisingly, he said, *"They did not even know how to blush."*[43]

We can believe so many of the modern-day religious practitioners or sweep this away in misguided therapy, but then why is there such a joke about a young woman asking, "Will you still respect me in the morning?" It's because she's afraid she will be ashamed of herself for having sex with the guy lying next to her.

It is impossible to underestimate the tragedy of the fall of Adam and Eve. Paul Tripp writes,

> What seemed once unthinkably wrong and out of character for the world that God had made now became a daily experience. Words like falsehood, enemy, danger, sin, destruction, war, murder, sickness, fear, and hatred became regular parts of the fallen-world vocabulary. For the first time, the harmony between people was broken. Shame, fear, guilt, blame, greed, envy, conflict, and hurt made relationships a minefield they were never intended to be. People looked at other people as

---

[42] Albert R. Mohler, Jr., *"Church Discipline: The Missing Mark"* in *The Compromised Church: The Present Evangelical Crisis* (Wheaton, Illinois: Crossway Books, 1998), 174.

[43] Jeremiah 6:15

obstacles to getting what they wanted or as dangers to be avoided. Even families were unable to coexist in any kind of lasting and peaceful union. Violence became a common response to problems that had never before existed. Conflict existed in the human community as an experience more regular than peace. Marriage became a battle for control, and children's rebellion became a more natural response than willing submission. Things became more valuable than people, and they willingly competed with others in order to acquire more. The human community was more divided by love for self than united by love of neighbor. The words of people, meant to express truth and love, became weapons of anger and instruments of deceit. In an instant, the sweet music of human harmony had become the mournful dirge of human war.[44]

Sitcoms make fun of sin, news programming broadcast the painful results of it, and talk around the water cooler has turned decidedly against a biblical worldview. But you can't change the way people feel. Our world continues to try to cover shame up by ignoring it, going to therapy, trying to drink it away, or simply giving in to it. None of that will change the way a young woman, or a young man for that matter, will feel in the morning after they've broken God's moral code.

Guilt and shame

When Adam and Eve sewed leaves together to cover their nakedness they were doing what every person whose conscience has not been "educated" by modern ethicists would do. When God asked, *"Who told you that you were naked?"* He was not imposing a standard on them, He was probing their conscience.

It's important to notice what's going on here. God is not condemning their nakedness. He created them naked and they were

---

[44] Paul David Tripp, *A Quest for More: Living for Something Bigger Than You* (Greensboro, NC: New Growth, 2008), 40.

not ashamed about it. But, when they sinned, their first inclination was to hide and cover themselves. This is what sin does. We don't live openly before God or anyone else because we know that we are spiritually naked.

This is affirmed when God continued, *"Have you eaten from the tree of which I commanded you not to eat?"*[45] Of course God knew the answer. He wasn't asking these questions to fill in His lack of knowledge. Instead, He wanted Adam to verbalize his sin and their pathetic attempt to cover it up.

If we're absolutely honest, we know that we are naked. We know that we are undone in front of the all-seeing, all-knowing eyes of a righteous, holy God. We have a severe case of black and white fever that can't be healed by covering our sin with our pathetic fig leaves.

Spiritual death

But this discussion is deeper than guilt and shame. Let me provide a little fair and balanced reporting at this point. So far, our discussion has centered on Eve. One might rightfully ask, "Where was Adam in all of this?" Good question. The text says, *"she took from its fruit and ate; and she gave also to her husband with her, and he ate."*[46] Why did he do this? He was the one who had received the instruction personally from God. Why didn't he step in and correct this obvious blunder on Eve's part?

My point is that Adam was complicit in this scenario. He may not have thought he was responsible for Eve's actions, but God certainly did. In the New Testament, the apostle Paul, an educated Jewish Pharisee who hated the early Christians until he was miraculously converted on the road to Damascus, tells us that *"through one man sin entered into the world."*[47] This was because

---

[45] Genesis 3:11
[46] Genesis 3:6
[47] Romans 5:12

God created man first.[48] But Adam was AWOL in this passage. He abdicated the role God gave him to protect his wife and was not around when she was tempted by Satan.

So, what's the end of all of this? Paul continues by revealing that death came *"through sin, and so death spread to all men, because all sinned."*[49] That's quite serious, isn't it? Spiritual death in Scripture is explained as eternal separation from God. We die because we sin. And we sin because Adam sinned. This is part of the curse explained later in Genesis 3.

God has written His law in the Bible. But He has also written it in our conscience. When we sin, we violate both. That's what makes our rebellion so hideous. We don't have to read God's law to know we've violated it. When Eve handed Adam the fruit, I believe his palms got sweaty and his mouth got dry. Despite God's specific instructions, as well as his own conscience, he deliberately stepped across the line and ate the fruit.

Why did he do that? He did it because he thought he knew better than God and that he could somehow escape God's punishment. It's the same reason that we speed on the freeway while checking our rearview mirror. We know the speed limit is 55 but we see that "everyone else is doing it" and believe that we can somehow escape the long arm of the law. That is, until a black and white car with red and blue lights on top pulls up behind us.

If we have any doubt that we inherit this rebellious spirit from Adam, listen to David's confession after he was confronted about his adultery by Nathan the prophet. In Psalm 51 he said, *"Behold, I was brought forth in iniquity, and in sin my mother conceived me."* We are born with a rebellious spirit that causes us to ignore God's law as well as our own conscience.

---

[48] 1 Timothy 2:13
[49] Romans 5:12

A two-year-old example

This is easy to observe. Anyone who has kids can see it clearly. When our second child was two, I walked into our bedroom one day to see my wife sewing. Charlie was seated right next to her on the dresser. Just as I walked in I heard my wife say, "Charlie, put the scissors down. You'll hurt yourself." My precious, cute, dimple faced son responded by throwing the scissors at his Mom with the vicious look of a stone-cold killer on his face.

What to do? Every instinct in me told me I couldn't let this pass. He didn't have a sign of black and white fever at the moment! But what would happen if he never caught it? Our conscience can become seared if it is not properly educated when it is violated. Can you imagine what Charlie would have been like as an eighteen-year-old if no one ever stepped in to challenge his lack of submission on an action like this? This was a classic example of a lack of submission (Charlie's) coming in conflict with a case of black and white fever (Mine!). I knew I had to do something. I couldn't let his conscience be distorted by thinking it was OK to throw scissors at his mother.

I told Charlie to tell Mommy he was sorry. Normally, my son would have complied because he saw the error of his ways and recognized the superior insights of his father as well as the potential harm to his mother.

Nope. Not this time. Battle lines were drawn, and reinforcements enlisted. In this corner was the all-knowing, all-loving, all-powerful father with irrefutable logic and a wide array of weapons at his disposal. And in the other corner—the diminutive two-year-old in diapers with his lips pursed and seething fire from his eyes. To my initial, simple request uttered in my most loving fatherly voice, Charlie simply said, "NO!" Mind you, this was not in his cute, giggly little two-year-old voice. This was uttered in the deepest basso profundo his little vocal chords could muster, accompanied by a deep-browed scowl.

The next ten minutes was a battle royal. Rational pleas were met with the same guttural "NO!" Finally, the threat of the "wooden spoon" (the chosen means of ultimate discipline in our house) was brought out and laid on the dresser right beside him.

I pleaded, "Charlie, will you please just tell Mommy you're sorry?"

"NO!"

"Do you want Daddy to use the wooden spoon?"

"NO!"

Yes, I know what some are thinking. Some people slap and beat their kids, calling it discipline. But I'm a firm believer that corporal punishment as a last resort is necessary for some children in certain situations in order to curb their destructive behavior.

Discipline is not punishment. It is necessary to help the child learn and to prevent them from becoming a criminal or self-centered member of society. Proper, physical discipline as a last resort does not beget violence. It prevents it.

So, I exercised proper discipline with my beloved two-year-old. A few simple swats on the back of the legs (beneath the diaper line) were enough to bring the requisite howls and tears. But the battle was not over. He still had not said he was sorry. After hugging him and telling him I loved him and wiping the tears away, I asked him again to tell Mommy he was sorry. Can you believe it? He said, "NO" again, with the same force he had said it the first time.

I've never had to go through this long of a procedure with any of our other kids, but we did this whole thing three times before he finally looked at his mom and muttered, "sorry" through the remainder of his tears.

"Thank you, Charlie, that's all I wanted to hear," I thankfully proclaimed.

We are all Charlie. We are born this way. But parental discipline mirrors the instruction of a loving and kind God who knows everything about us because He created us. Why would you resist that kind of knowledge? Adam and Eve did it to their, and our, own peril. Will you continue to resist the authority and jurisdiction of God?

If you ignore the all-pervasive knowledge of God, you are ignoring the authority of the very One who can answer the most difficult questions of life. To do that is like ignoring the black and white car in your rearview mirror and continuing on your merry way, speeding and running every stop sign you encounter. Does that make sense?

Chapter Four

"When you run away from the Lord you never get to where you are going, and you always pay your own fare. But when you go the Lord's way, you always get to where you are going, and He pays the fare."[50]
—Donald Gray Barnhouse

You Can Run, but You Can't Hide

What is our natural response to God?

While God revealed Himself to me at a young age, and I (Jim) progressed in my spiritual development for years, there was a time that I regretfully admit I ran from God. I willfully chose to lead the life of a spiritual rebel and a moral fool. The following excerpt was taken from my personal testimony in *The Spirit Behind Badge 145*.

When I entered law enforcement, I was committed to my relationship with the Lord. . . . I had a zeal for my faith in Christ that was contagious. I also had a lot of spiritual pride, a fact that escaped my notice. When I graduated the police academy,

---

[50] James Montgomery Boice, *Minor Prophets, And Expositional Commentary: Hosea-Jonah, vol.1*, (Grand Rapids, Michigan: Baker Books, 2002), 268.

I was certain I was called to law enforcement as a ministry, not just a vocation. I believed in spiritual warfare but did not think I was susceptible to the reasons that would make it necessary. It didn't take long to prove differently. Two years to be exact.

. . .

Full of spiritual pride, disconnected from my support network, and with a heart hardened by police work, I became vulnerable to temptations that ordinarily would not have been a problem. But now, they were viable options. . . . Opportunities for an affair were rampant. I made the conscious decision to engage in one.

Once I did, I felt like I had left church and joined the party. On one hand, I felt shame, guilt, and remorse, because I knew it was wrong. I knew it hurt Jamie, and I was aware that I had chosen to be the Prodigal Son (see Luke 15), but I did not care. . . .

I wrote a letter to my family declaring my circumstances. Five of my ten siblings showed up at my doorstep to confront and call me out on my sin . . . I thanked them for their love and concern but really had no use for their wise counsel.

The timing of God's first attempt to get my attention was almost unbelievable. The day following the confrontation with my brothers, I was riding dirt bikes and four wheeling out in the high desert of Southern California. As a result of being reckless, I was involved in an accident. I was intentionally fishtailing (sliding from left to right) when one of my rear tires came off the rim and caused my Jeep to roll three times. I had three passengers in the Jeep who were all wearing seat belts. Fortunately, they walked away from the crash unharmed.

I did not have my seatbelt on, so I was less fortunate. My right leg was wrapped around the roll bar for the first two-barrel rolls; on the third I was ejected. I landed on the parched, hard desert floor and was knocked unconscious. The left front tire of the Jeep followed me to the ground and missed my head

by inches. . . . I was unconscious for more than one hour . . .
That was probably a good thing because among other injuries, I
had three broken ribs and a punctured lung. . . . I was flown via
Life Flight to a nearby hospital. . . .

It took four months, but I finally recovered. You think
the accident would have snapped me out of my rebellion, but
I wasn't ready to listen. . . . Jamie received wonderful counsel
and support from my brother Jon as well as our dear friend,
Kay Rozelle. Although Jamie had biblical grounds for divorce,
she decided to fight for our marriage.

Throughout the next five years, I transitioned from being a patrol officer, to working undercover narcotic enforcement. According to my annual evaluations, I was an all-star.
Unfortunately, my personal life was strictly bush league, defined by a roller coaster pattern of affair, reconciliation, recom-
mitted faith, and then another affair. During this five-year period of time, we had our first two children, Brenna and Brock.
There were times when I did everything imaginable to push
Jamie away, but she always fought for our relationship. She remained in our marriage out of strength, not because she was a
doormat. She developed a sense of confidence in Christ that
was unimaginable given the circumstances.

That relationship with the Lord was the bedrock of her
faith and miraculous strength that allowed her to withstand the
tumult. It was both an attraction and an irritant to me, because,
after all, I just wanted her to leave so I would not have to make
a decision about divorce. . . . On several occasions, I was at the
point of leaving only to change my mind at the last minute. . . .

Nevertheless, in October of 1992 I decided the time had
come to end our marriage of nine years. We had separated for
a short time several years before, but now I was determined
it was over. With the decision made, guilt and shame overwhelmed me. I knew I was messed up and believed Jamie deserved better. Through tears of agony, Jamie told me we were

pregnant with child number three, who would become Jordan. But for the first time she also told me she was done fighting for our marriage. I had done too much damage, and she certainly did not want me to stick around just because she was pregnant. She knew the God she served was more than capable of caring for her.

With news of the pregnancy I began listening to the voice of the Holy Spirit and came to my senses. I began to cut ties, but it was not easy. Affairs are as addicting as narcotics. A short time later, Jamie overheard a telephone conversation. I was making a feeble attempt to end my latest illicit relationship. While this was certainly the right thing to do, I still thought I owed it to Jamie to free her from the person I had become. But with incredible strength of faith, she told me she would stay if I wanted to re-commit to the Lord, to her, and to our family.

By Jamie's courageous love, God finally broke me. I felt trapped in a life of sin that delivered nothing but misery in place of the pleasure and freedom it promised. While my job performance did not suffer (I actually became a workaholic), my personal life was in the gutter. Heartfelt repentance is a humbling experience, but I realized it was the only course of action that would rescue me from the personal and spiritual storm I was in. . . .

Let me assure you, this was not an easy process—not for either of us. But in the end, it was worth every sacrifice. I killed our marriage, but just as Jesus brought Lazarus back to life, our loving Heavenly Father brought our marriage back from the grave as well. While Jamie's forgiveness was imme-diate, rebuilding trust took time. It took a lot of work, daily renewal, and sustained grace. . . .

Regaining Jamie's trust required a series of building blocks. I had demolished the foundation of our relationship, so it needed to be rebuilt one brick at a time. Now, I cannot imag-ine life without Jamie by my side.

Over the years, I have had the good fortune to teach and speak at a few events related to ministry or work, and each time I talk about my family, I get choked up . . . I know that I still get to participate in my family as husband and father because of God's amazing grace and Jamie's desire to fight for our marriage despite the fact she had every biblical justification to give me the boot![51]

TRAFFIC FATALITY

One evening at work, in the midst of my restoration process, I responded to a major auto collision. With my siren blaring and emergency lights flashing, I weaved my way through heavy traffic. My destination was obvious on the horizon—toward a black plume of smoke signifying a petroleum-based fire.

When I arrived, I got out of my police unit and ran toward a small, Triumph convertible, which had overturned and was ablaze. The wheels, inverted and reaching toward the sky, were burning like Roman candles. Engine fluids provided fuel, adding to the enormity of the fire. The heat was so intense that I could not get within five feet of the car before it felt like my uniform would melt to my skin.

"The dude's in there. He's burning alive. You gotta get him out," shouted several witnesses. I had so much adrenaline flowing I felt I could lift the small European sports car off the ground in order to free the trapped driver. I ran around the vehicle looking for a place that was not burning, but there wasn't one.

Then I heard the blood-curdling sounds of a human burning to death, trapped beneath his inverted automobile and the road. His agonizing wail was probably the worst thing I've ever heard from a person, and there are no words that can do justice to the death-yowl that reached my ears.

---

[51] Jim McNeff, *The Spirit Behind Badge 145*, (Nashville, TN: WestBow Press, 2013), 23-29.

I retrieved a blanket and fire extinguisher from the trunk of my police unit desperately hoping to reduce the flames by smothering them. As expected, the fire extinguisher was woefully inadequate, and the medical blanket melted the moment I attempted to use it. It was the most helpless experience I encountered during my career.

The fire department arrived two minutes later, but the driver was clearly deceased by the time the flames were extinguished and the car was turned upright.

Later that evening, I did some self-reflection. *What if something fatal happened to me while I lived a life of rebellion? Is that how I wanted to be remembered?*

I was so thankful that God pursued me, that He simultaneously protected me from my foolish behavior, while still allowing me to suffer the consequences.

And, of course, I'm not the first one who's ever run from God.

Actually, everyone does. That's because everyone is afflicted with black and white fever, the theme of the last chapter. And what happens when we get the fever? We run. I ran from God because I didn't like anyone telling me what to do.

JONAH'S MISSION

Jonah was like that. Despite what most people think, the main theme in his story is not a big fish. The main theme of Jonah is a man running from God. In the process, Jonah finds out that God's jurisdiction includes saving the people he hates more than anything on earth.

As you may remember, the story begins with God's call to Jonah to "*Arise go to Nineveh the great city and cry against it, for their wickedness has come up before Me.*"[52] Notice the clarity of the call. God's command was simple and fully understandable. He

---

[52] Jonah 1:2

said, "*Arise . . . go . . . cry out.*" We don't receive explicit calls like that today, but God is still clear in what He wants from us.

God's instructions were clear. But this was "mission impossible" for Jonah. Nineveh was the capital city of the Assyrian Empire and the Assyrians were the military and racial precursors to ISIS. They were not nice people. Nineveh was located on the east bank of the Tigris River, about 550 miles from Samaria, capital of the Northern Kingdom.

Nineveh was a large impregnable fortress, protected by an outer and inner wall. The inner wall was 100 feet high and 50 feet wide. It was wide enough for four chariots to race side by side. There were 1500 towers on the wall, each 200 feet high. A moat 140 feet wide and 60 feet deep surrounded the city. It was eight miles across the city, which is consistent with Jonah's description of it housing "*120,000 persons who do not know the difference between their right and left hand.*"[53] Most scholars believe that describes the number of young children, which means the population would have been roughly 600,000.

The Assyrians were one of the most sadistic, cruel empires the world has ever seen. One of their kings, a man known as Ashurnasirpal II (883-859 B. C.) bragged about conquering a foreign leader saying, "I flayed [him], his skin I spread upon the wall of the city." He also wrote of mutilating live captives and then stacking their corpses in piles.[54]

Another king named Shalmaneser II (859-824 B. C.) boasted of his cruelties after one of his campaigns: "A pyramid of heads I reared in front of his city. Their youths and their maidens I burnt up in the flames."[55] Sennacherib (705-681 B. C.) wrote of his enemies, "I cut their throats like lambs. I cut off their precious lives

---

[53] Jonah 4:11

[54] John Walvoord, Roy Zuck, *The Bible Knowledge Commentary: An Exposition of the Scriptures* by Dallas Seminary Faculty (Wheaton, Illinois: Victor Books, 1983), 1494.

[55] Ibid.

[as one cuts] a string. Like the many waters of a storm I made [the contents of] their gullets and entrails run down upon the wide earth . . . Their hands I cut off."[56]

Years later a different Ashurbanipal (669-626 B. C.) described his treatment of a captured leader, "I pierced his chin with my keen hand dagger. Through his jaw . . . I passed a rope, put a dog chain upon him and made him occupy . . . a kennel"[57] The prophet Nahum called Nineveh "the bloody city"[58] and a city noted for its continuous evil to others![59] Nice guys! No wonder Jonah didn't want to go there!

JONAH'S MISTAKE

Jonah reacted in a predictable manner. *"But Jonah rose up to flee to Tarshish from the presence of the Lord. So he went down to Joppa, found a ship which was going to Tarshish, paid the fare and went down into it to go with them to Tarshish from the presence of the Lord."*[60] Tarshish is mentioned three times in this verse. It's a city on the western Mediterranean coast of Spain some two thousand miles from Jonah. God asked him to go east to Nineveh and Jonah made plans to go as far west as he could imagine.

And notice his explicit actions. He *"rose up to flee,"* he *"went down to Joppa,"* he *"paid the fare,"* and he *"went down into it."* He was fully bent on his actions, and he never looked back. His intent was to run as far away as he could.

Donald Gray Barnhouse once said, "When you run away from the Lord you never get to where you are going, and you always pay your own fare. But when you go the Lord's way, you always

---

[56] Ibid.
[57] Ibid.
[58] Nahum 3:1
[59] Nahum 3:19
[60] Jonah 1:3

get to where you are going, and He pays the fare."[61] A parallel to this is the old saying, "Sin will take you too far, charge you too much, and keep you too long."

Before we get too critical, we must agree. This is the heart of man. An old hymn says, "Prone to wander Lord I feel it, prone to leave the God I love."[62] Man's natural inclination is to run from God. It started in the Garden of Eden when Adam and Eve sinned. Their sin ruined their fellowship with God, and they ran to the bushes to hide from Him.

So why did Jonah run? Was it because of the danger of traveling 800 miles across the desert sand to confront a group of people who could kill him simply for being a Jew? No. Was it because he had no one to go with him? No. Was it because of the impossibility of the task. After all, 600,000 murderous Assyrians against one Jewish missionary aren't very good odds.

No, Jonah didn't run for any of these reasons. We find the reason for him running in Jonah 4. After God had accomplished His desired task of saving the Assyrians, Jonah expresses his true feelings, *"Please Lord, was not this what I said while I was still in my own country? Therefore in order to forestall this I fled to Tarshish, for I knew that You are a gracious and compassionate God, slow to anger and abundant in lovingkindness, and one who relents concerning calamity. Therefore now, O Lord, please take my life from me, for death is better to me than life."*[63]

This is astounding! This prophet of God ran from God because he knew that God would save the Assyrians. His attitude was literally, "Let 'em go to hell! I don't care." Not only that, he was so miserable over the spiritual outcome for the Assyrians

---

[61] Boice, *Minor Prophets, And Expositional Commentary: Hosea-Jonah, vol.1,* 268.

[62] Robert Robinson, "Come, Thou Fount of Every Blessing," www.lutheranhymnal.com, accessed on March 10, 2018.

[63] Jonah 4:2-3

that he played the ultimate "poor me" game and said he would rather have died than be a party to what God wanted to do.

Don't miss the irony in this. How many times are we asked to rise, but remain seated; to go, but we stay home; to cry out to God, but we never shed a tear about our sin? Jonah's attitude is reflected in so many of us.

Our actions are often just as willful and deliberate as Jonah's. We don't merely play "hide and seek" with God, we play "catch me if you can." We think we are merely living life on our terms, but the reality is that we are running from God. We reject His authority and jurisdiction over our lives because we want to live life according to our rules and do things the way we want.

Francis Thompson was consumed with life on his own terms. Living in England during the time of Queen Victoria, he was raised in a religious setting but resisted God's call on his life. His father wanted him to be a doctor, but he followed his own path to become a poet. Like many young dreamers he soon found out that he couldn't support himself through his chosen profession. Disillusioned, he was soon addicted to opium and lived on the streets to support his drug habit.

Thompson's fortunes changed when a friend, Wilfred Meynell, promised to publish some of his poems. As he later reflected on his ruinous life, he saw Christ's pursuit of him despite his steadfast resistance. As a result, Thompson wrote his famous poem, *The Hound of Heaven*, that revealed his distorted thinking that following Jesus results in a diminished life. The first verse reads:

> I fled Him, down the nights and down the days;
> I fled Him, down the arches of the years;
> I fled Him, down the labyrinthine ways
> Of my own mind; and in the mist of tears
> I hid from Him, and under running laughter.
> Up vistaed hopes I sped;
> And shot, precipitated,

Adown Titantic glooms of chasmed fears,
From those strong Feet that followed, followed after.
But with unhurrying chase,
And unperturbed pace,
Deliberate speed, majestic instancy,
They beat-and a Voice beat
More instant than the Feet-
'All things betray thee, who betrayest Me.'[64]

Why does that strike such a responsive note with most people? Isn't it because that describes our lives? We think we are pursuing things, which will make us happy and fulfilled. After all, don't we have a right to the pursuit of happiness?

Yes, we do, according to the Declaration of Independence. But eventually, we find out that the things we thought would bring happiness really don't. Thus, we continue to run, all the time fleeing the One who alone can bring ultimate happiness, fulfillment, and purpose.

JONAH'S MESS

Jonah made a mess trying to run from God. But in the middle of it all, we know that God was still in control. It was still His world, and He exercised His authority because He had ultimate, sovereign jurisdiction.

Notice God's absolute control throughout the story. *"The Lord hurled a great wind"*[65] that brought the storm that resulted in Jonah being thrown overboard. *"The Lord appointed a great fish to swallow Jonah."*[66] *"Then the Lord commanded the fish, and it vomited Jonah up onto dry land."*[67]

---

[64] Joseph Stowell, M., *Following Christ* (Grand Rapids, MI: Zondervan, 1998), 33-34.
[65] Jonah 1:4
[66] Jonah 1:17
[67] Jonah 2:10

Even after Jonah preached to the Ninevites, we find that *"God appointed a plant"* to grow up over Jonah and provide shade,[68] then He *"appointed a worm"* that attacked the plant, so it withered,[69] and finally He *"appointed a scorching east wind"* to beat down on Jonah and show him that he was nothing without God's provision of such small thing as shade.[70]

The story of the book of Jonah is not the story of a man being swallowed by a fish. It is God's absolute sovereign rule over everything from storms, to fish, to plants, to the sun and wind, to saving a bunch of wicked Assyrians.

And Jonah failed to grasp that. Knowing what God had asked him to do, he went down to the marina, bought his ticket and fled, almost daring God to catch him. But you can't run from God no matter which way you go.

A storm came up. The crew was afraid, and everyone was doing all they could to keep afloat. Not Jonah. He was in his cabin asleep. The captain comes to wake him up and asks, *"'How is it that you are sleeping? Get up, call on your god. Perhaps your god will be concerned about us so that we will not perish."*[71]

How could this be? How could a man of God be so stubborn that he would run from God and then not even be aware of the need around him? It's instructive to examine Jonah's life a little deeper to see what turned him into a runner. The text provides several indicators of how this could happen.

He forgot God

God *"spoke by his servant Jonah"*[72] during a time when the prophets were called the *"sons of the prophets."*[73] They lived and

---

[68] Jonah 4:6
[69] Jonah 4:7
[70] Jonah 4:8
[71] Jonah 1:6
[72] 2 Kings 14:23-27
[73] 2 Kings 2:3-15

studied together and served in various capacities. So, Jonah was part of a select group of men who knew God's Word, fellow-shipped together, and ministered through the proclamation of God's Word.

What happened to *that* Jonah? Very simply, he forgot who he was. He began to view his world through his own eyes, not God's. He allowed his own feelings of anger, bitterness, and fear, domi-nate his mind. That's a horrible place for anyone to be. But it's possible for anyone to ignore their upbringing, their family and friends, and even their own conscience to pursue their own way.

He fled from the presence of the Lord

Jonah 1:3 explains, *"But Jonah rose to flee to Tarshish from the presence of the Lord."* For Jonah that not only meant the direct command that God had given him, it would have included flee-ing the fellowship of his fellow prophets and all those whom he ministered to. This is foolish because no one can ever escape the presence of God, no matter where they run.

In Psalm 139 David said that he could go as high as the sky or as low as hell and not escape God's presence. He could travel faster than the speed of sound (186,000 miles per second!) and not outrun Him. He ended up saying, *"Where can I go from your presence?"*[74] The point is that we can't escape Him no matter where we go.

In Psalm 73 the Psalmist chronicles the folly of doing that. He examines the arrogant people of the world and is jealous. He la-ments that they are prosperous, they have everything they want, they achieve everything they set out to do, all the while mocking the God of heaven. In fact, the writer feels that he has wasted his time by trying to maintain a pure and righteous life.

But Psalm 73:17 hammers home the reality of an arrogant person who seemingly gets along just fine without God. The

---

[74] Psalms 139:7-12

Psalmist writes, "*Until I came into the sanctuary of God; Then I perceived their end.*" The old saying tells us, "Your arms are too short to box with God." We can adjust that and say, "And your legs are too short to run away from God." Sooner or later everyone will return to the sanctuary of God. You might run, but you can't hide.

You might ignore the Bible stories you heard as a kid. You might have fulfilled your vow to leave church when you were old enough and never look back. You might think God is for old women and children. You might even be so arrogant as to shake your fist to the sky and dare God to strike you down for your sin. Or you might simply think that God is irrelevant.

But some day you will come to the sanctuary of God. You'll get fired. Cancer will catch you. Your family will fall apart. You will find yourself alone in your empty house with your big screen TV and 1000 channels. Or you will make it all the way to the end without God—and then you will die—without Him.

When anyone who runs away from whatever form of God's influence that is in their lives, they begin a long path that leads to destruction. Romans tells us that we all "*suppress the truth in unrighteousness*"[75] by denying God's "*invisible attributes*"[76] seen in creation. The next chapter of Romans also tells us that everyone knows of God's laws through "*their conscience bearing witness and their thoughts alternately accusing or else defending them . . .*"[77]

In addition, almost everyone has family members or friends who go to church or talk about God and reflect some kind of religious influence. No one is completely without spiritual light. To walk away from whatever that light is means the person is walking in the wrong direction.

He was a hypocrite

---

[75] Romans 1:18
[76] Romans 1:20
[77] Romans 2:15

Jonah expresses his opinion of himself in Jonah 1:9, "*And he said to them, "I am a Hebrew, and I fear the Lord, the God of heaven, who made the sea and the dry land.*" No, he didn't! Everything about his actions showed that his life and his lips were two different things. He had refused to obey God and go to Nineveh. He didn't have a heart for what God wanted him to do. In fact, as we saw earlier, he was actually angry at God for His redemptive intent toward the Assyrians. Finally, he was willing to sacrifice his family and friends in ministry to flee to get away from what God wanted him to do. "Fear the God of heaven?" Don't think so.

Hypocrisy is a sure sign of someone running away from God. It would have been better for him to keep his mouth shut and leave people wondering about his faith than to open it and remove all doubt. Now they had something to measure him by. Now the sailors knew that his faith was a fake.

In the movie *Tombstone*, Doc Holliday (Val Kilmer) tricks Wyatt Earp (Kurt Russell) into giving him his badge so Doc can go meet Johnny Ringo for their final duel. He rushes to the appointed spot of their duel ahead of Wyatt and guns Johnny Ringo down after flashing the badge in the early evening shadows to trick Johnny into thinking he is fighting Wyatt, not Doc. When Wyatt arrives moments later he sees Doc hovering over the dead body of Johnny Ringo. Knowing that he is not a lawman, Doc removes the badge and throws it on the chest of the dead man, stoically telling Wyatt, "My hypocrisy only goes so far."[78]

Likewise, hypocrites are always exposed. We might say, "I'm a Christian, and I fear the Lord God who made the sea and dry land." But those who know us might reply, "Then why are you running from God?" "Why do you claim something you don't practice?" "Why aren't you committed to a local church, the bride of the one you say you love?" "Why don't your colleagues at work know of your love for Jesus?" "Why do you spend the

---

[78] *Tombstone*, directed by George P. Cosmatos, Hollywood Pictures, 1993.

majority of your time shopping, or working out, or running your kids to soccer practice, and not in studying the Bible or serving at church or writing to missionaries." "Why don't your children ever hear you pray or see you read the Bible?" Could it be that, like Jonah, you're just faking your faith?

But all is not lost, even in this. In a remarkable example of God's providence, the sailors recognize his hypocrisy and yet begin to trust his God. They ask, "*How could you do this?*" They understood his hypocrisy and realized that he was the source of their problems. What an example of the dangers of hypocrisy.

He was a bigot

Jonah responds to the sailors by commanding them to "*Pick me up and throw me into the sea. Then the sea will become calm for you, for I know that on account of me this great storm has come upon you.*"[79] If he knew he was the cause of the storm then why didn't he say, "turn back?" Amazingly, Jonah was willing to sacrifice himself to save the lives of the pagan sailors rather than obey the command of the Lord and go preach to the Ninevites. Why? He hated them! And this was not a passive hatred. He blatantly expressed it to God Himself!

Bigotry is not a "soft crime." It bubbles out in resentment, anger, and hostility. The biblical injunction against bigotry is seen early on in Genesis. Part of the Abrahamic Covenant is that in the Messiah "*all the nations of the earth will be blessed.*"[80] That means that God includes all people groups in His redemptive plan. Jonah was not only rejecting the specific plan of God for the Assyrians, he was rejecting God's general plan for the salvation of the nations. His bigotry would have let them die in their sin with no effort to save them.

He was destined for failure

---

[79] Jonah 1:12
[80] Genesis 18:18

Most of us are aware that, *"Jonah was in the belly of the fish three days and three nights."*[81] This was a Hebrew idiom meaning parts of three days. In the New Testament, Jesus compares Jonah's time in the belly of the fish to the three days and three nights that the Son of Man would be in the grave.

Before we go any further we need to deal with the white elephant in the room. What about the fish? Many would ask, "Do you really expect me to believe that Jonah literally ended up in the stomach of a big fish." That's a very natural question from a human perspective, but we must approach it from God's point of view.

It's important to remember that this isn't the only supernatural event in Jonah's story. We've already seen that God exhibited His control over a storm, a plant, a worm, and a scorching wind, in addition to the great fish. Part of the miraculous nature of the story of the great fish is God causing him to troll the waters in the precise spot where Jonah would be pitched overboard as well as causing him to be swallowed.

Many people have great difficulties accepting the miracles in the Bible, and understandably so. After all, when the Bible talks about miracles, they are presented as improbable events, like the Cubs winning the World Series.

Of course, sports fans know that for years this would have been considered a miracle. But we now know that with the right players and conditions, it's entirely possible to win a World Series as they indeed did in 2016. The point is that, even though it was 108 years between World Series titles for the Cubs, finally winning the Series *was not* a miracle.

The miracles of the Bible suspend natural laws. Palsied legs don't walk, the blind do not see again, the dead are not raised, and fish don't swallow men and spit them out, no matter how big they are.

---

[81] Jonah 1:17

But if we look at this from a different viewpoint, this question takes on a different character. The point here is not to provide an exhaustive defense of the miracles in the Bible. But, if we're talking about God—God with a capital G—the one and only true and living God who is not a man, but the creator of all there is, then why is it so hard to believe that God could perform miracles. Indeed, just the idea of God presumes that He will do miracles. After all, if He doesn't do miracles, then He's not God.

But we don't need physical corroboration to verify a miracle. We will never be able to explain creation, or the virgin birth of Jesus, or His many miracles, or Jonah in the belly of a great fish. But that doesn't mean we should deny them either. Again, miracles are consistent with the idea of an all knowing, all powerful God.

Now back to the purpose of this chapter. Where did Jonah's running from God get him? Did he end up happy? Fulfilled? Content? No, he ended up in the belly of a great fish. In Jonah 2 he likens his dwelling to "Sheol." This is the primary word used 65 times in the Old Testament to describe hell. It refers both to a decaying body and to a lost soul.

This is a symbolic term describing Jonah's surroundings. He was trapped in the stinky, hot, humid, dark belly of a great fish. He had faced the terror of drowning. He had been belittled and disrespected by the crew of the ship. He had left the friendly surroundings of his family, his friends, and his job. He must have thought he was dead since he viewed himself as being in hell. And he was mad at God. Not a nice place to be.

Here's the point. Running from God doesn't pay. You can run, but you can't hide. When we play "catch me if you can" with God, rest assured, God will catch you. But the question is, what are you going to do about it?

CHAPTER FIVE

"I wanna talk about me, wanna talk about I, wanna talk about
number one Oh my me my, what I think, what I like, what I know,
what I want, what I see. I like talking about you, you, you, usually,
but occasionally, I wanna talk about me."[82]
—Toby Keith

The "Selfie" Syndrome

What about free will?

Would you think it odd to discover your local police department watched news coverage of their pursuit in order to stay abreast of the situation? That was the situation I found before me as the patrol division watch commander on a hot summer day in July.

SUICIDAL WOMAN

A citizen told our dispatcher she witnessed a woman sitting in a Chevy Avalanche that was idling in a public parking lot, and a garden hose ran from the tail pipe into the cab while all the windows appeared to be sealed. Those who desire suicide by carbon monoxide poisoning use this technique.

---

[82] Bobby Braddock, "I Wanna Talk About Me," sung by Toby Keith on *Pull My Chain*, 2001.

Officer Oscar Valencia arrived on scene only to find the despondent woman pulling away. Oscar activated his emergency lights, so he could stop and check on her wellbeing. She yielded for a brief moment and then decided to rabbit. Her truck accelerated away and forced Oscar to do the same.

POLICE PURSUIT

As engines revved and tires screeched, the pursuit left city streets and entered the northbound 405 freeway toward Los Angeles. Rolling with lights and siren, Sergeant Steve DeSantis worked his way toward the chase. Simultaneously, as watch commander, I needed to make a decision whether to allow the perilous activity to continue or terminate it.

Dispatchers quickly informed me that the woman previously tried to take her life several months prior at her nearby Fountain Valley apartment.

Conventional wisdom discouraged pursuing such a person in the metropolis of Orange and Los Angeles Counties during heavy traffic in late afternoon. While we certainly would not want our actions to precipitate further danger to uninvolved commuters, in good conscience I could not abdicate our professional obligation to corral a person so desperate as to attempt suicide on multiple occasions.

I requested assistance from HB1, the police helicopter of the Huntington Beach Police Department. They quickly joined our efforts allowing Oscar to back off a bit hoping the woman would avoid driving erratically if she believed our effort had been abandoned. The pursuit left Orange County and traveled north through Long Beach. Since the chase remained on the 405 freeway, I asked the California Highway Patrol (CHP) to take over and HB1 peeled away since the CHP has air support.

Regardless of the reason for the pursuit, it makes sense that, as the initiators, we would see it through despite the assistance received by the CHP or other agencies. While such decisions are fluid and driven by variables, in this case, I directed Oscar and Steve to trail the pursuit, so we could ultimately take custody and seek treatment for the hopeless woman being chased.

LIVE TELEVISION

As I monitored activity in our dispatch center (directly next to the watch commander's office), we discovered the pursuit was being aired on live television in Southern California.

We lost radio communication with Steve and Oscar on our primary city frequency, known as green channel, and since they were no longer the primary units in the pursuit, they were unable to use the emergency frequency, known as red channel—and able to transmit much greater distances. While there were other radio channels available, it became easier to communicate by cell phone.

I periodically made contact with Oscar and told him we were watching the pursuit on live television. This allowed me to provide requisite updated information, as they were unable to hear the CHP calling the pursuit on another radio frequency. Admittedly, it was a unique situation and one in which I had never been in before—watching our own pursuit on live TV.

The distressed woman, who moments earlier was willing to end her life via carbon monoxide poisoning, weaved through traffic in her Chevy Avalanche. Watching a police chase from an aerial view does not provide the genuine sense of danger experienced by units on the ground. The speeds appear much slower than actuality, and collisions appear more sterile.

Nevertheless, the speeds maintained by ground units keeping pace with the desperate woman were about 10-15 mph faster than the flow of traffic. As a result, the risk/reward continued to be acceptable.

Finally, the suicidal woman pulled off the freeway in Culver City, about fifty miles from Fountain Valley. In doing so she caused a minor fender bender but continued on for another block before turning down a dead-end road. In doing so she was trapped by several police units preventing her escape. Realizing she was trapped, she jumped out of the Avalanche and used her hand to simulate a weapon. She apparently hoped officers would open fire, thus ending her life.

When her actions failed to elicit the desired response, she tried to re-enter the SUV. Officers from several police agencies wrangled the violent and hysterical woman flailing her arms and legs into restraints, quite a comical sight as I viewed it from the bird's eye view of the news helicopter.

Oscar and Steve were quickly at the termination point and took custody of the agitated woman armed with nothing more than a simulated finger gun, garden hose, and a bad attitude. In a case like this, there is never argument over who will take custody. As the originators of the pursuit, Culver City Police Department, LAPD, and the CHP were more than happy to let Oscar and Steve have the catch.

WELCOME TO LIFE

Choices

We all make choices. Some are better than others. The woman above made a series of choices that ended up with her in the psych ward in jail. Some would say, "She got what she deserved." Others who know her might say that she was the victim of a variety of negative things that happened to her in her life that drove her to make wrong choices.

In the last two chapters, we pointed out that our natural inclination to catching "black and white fever" is to run from God. In this chapter we will explain that man does this of his own free will. This is a key ingredient in dealing with God's absolute sovereign control of the world. If this seems like a paradox, hold on. We will put this together in the next couple of chapters.

For now, we are simply pointing out that the woman who ran from the police made her own choice to do so, just like we do. Some people think this demonstrates the inability of God to handle life. The writer H.G. Wells once pictured this dilemma in a theoretical stage play that was produced and managed by God. He said,

> As the curtain rises, the set is perfect, a treat to every eye. The characters are resplendent. Everything goes well until the leading man steps on the hem of the leading lady's gown, causing her to trip over a chair, which knocks over a lamp, which pushes a table into the wall, which in turn knocks over the scenery, which brings everything down on the heads of the actors. Meanwhile, behind the scenes God, the Producer, is running around, shouting orders, pulling strings, trying desperately to restore order from chaos. But, alas, he is unable to do so! Poor God! As Wells explains, he is a very little, limited God.[83]

Is that what life is really like? Are we all like billiard balls on a pool table crashing into each other with no purpose or direction? Do our decisions fit into some kind of narrative or are they merely random?

"I gotta be me"

To answer these questions, we must look at the issue of man's will. This is the theme song of modern culture. Years ago, Sammy Davis Jr. sang, "I Gotta Be Me" and the whole world seemed to discover a new theme song. More recently, Toby Keith facetiously sang, "I wanna talk about me, wanna talk about I, wanna talk about number one Oh my me my, what I think, what I like, what I know, what I want, what I see. I like talking about you, you, you, usually, but occasionally, I wanna talk about me."

---

[83] R. Kent Hughes, *Luke: That You May Know the Truth, Preaching the Word* (Wheaton, IL: Crossway Books, 1998), 338–339.

This fascination with self is a manifestation of a culture that sees self as the center of the universe. In his classic book *The Culture of Narcissism* Christopher Lasch argues that selfishness has become the chief component of the American ethos. He concluded that, "[N]ormal people now displayed many of the same personality traits that appeared, in more extreme form, in pathological narcissism."[84]

If Lasch is right, then the will of man is central to everything. Man controls his own spiritual destiny because God is nothing more than a "take it or leave it" proposition. Much like the selfie-stick allows us to place ourselves in the center of every picture we take, so the will of man occupies center stage in determining everything that pertains to life. We have indeed become a "selfie" society.

FREE WILL

But how does this work? It's obvious that man is a player in the ongoing saga of life, but in what way? Is he a free moral agent or a puppet? Is he the art or the artist? Is behavior determined by nature or nurture?

This is often an emotional, visceral struggle for Americans especially who pride themselves on their rights to freedom and liberty. In fact, our recent fascination with taking "selfies" has itself become a picture of our selfie society where personal autonomous freedom has become the greatest value of life. For most people, even suggesting that man is not free in any sense is seen as stripping them of their humanity. The very concept of free will is regarded as self-evident.

But if we are discussing the deepest problems of humanity, we need to discuss free will. At the core of the argument regarding free will is a misunderstanding of what the word "free" means.

---

[84] Christopher Lasch, *The Culture of Narcissism: American Life in an Age of Diminishing Expectations* (New York: Norton, 1991), 230.

When we think of this we assume it means that I am perfectly free to choose between having a banana or an orange for breakfast. I am free to root for the Dodgers or the Giants. I can be a Republican or Democrat, or even Green or Libertarian. Freedom in this sense assumes that there is absolutely nothing coercing or forcing me to make a choice in either direction.

That seems simple enough, but is it true? Or maybe we should ask if it is possible? Is it possible to make any choice completely unfettered by any influence or force? If this is true, then we can visualize this by thinking of all of the choices of life displayed on a buffet with man walking by and picking his own personal preferences to place on his tray. But this buffet leads us to some observations about free will.

Free will must be free of previous influence

The first observation is that to be free in our choices means to be completely free from any previous influence or coercion. That is a basic assumption behind free will. We assume that being free means that man is a blank slate and can therefore objectively make a decision based on complete freedom from any previous influence.

But if we objectively view freedom like this, we come up against a harsh reality. A close, objective examination reveals that no decision is completely without some kind of previous influence or pressure. Think of it like this.

Imagine you have two bowls before you. One is full of your favorite flavor of ice cream ("favorite" is impossible according to free will, but we'll go with it anyway). The other is full of cottage cheese. According to the premise of free will, you must not only be able to choose either, but you must also be able to desire them equally. Of course, this would never happen. This scenario is a logical absurdity. So, is free will in the truest sense of the concept? *You will have a preference. You can't avoid having one. There's no way you could.* Even if you've never tasted either, something will influence your decision. You will prefer one more than the other and choose it based on your preference. In this sense, your will is not absolutely free. Every choice we make is partly determined by something outside of our will. It's the way the universe is designed.[85] (Italics added)

Expanding on this, if my "favorite" ice cream is chocolate it's fair to ask why that is true. Do I have the complete freedom to choose my favorite ice cream or is my choice conditioned by previous influences or conditions? I could have chosen my favorite ice cream because I heard my dad say, "Man, there's nothing better than chocolate ice cream."

But I could just as well have made that "choice" because as a small child my DNA naturally predisposed my taste buds to gravitate toward chocolate every time I experienced ice cream. So, it's probable that my "choice" of ice cream is conditioned by wanting to be like my dad or my taste buds or some other pre-existing condition. Any number of influences can shape my choice.

Free will ignores reality

The reason we can make choices is because man is born with a brain. Though we are born spiritually dead, these faculties still operate in the physical, fleshly realm. One would think that they provide man with the ability to make informed, rational decisions. But in reality, we find that man's will has the ability to ignore the data that our mental faculties provide us.

Because of the brain God has given us, we have the ability to understand certain basic things about God, as well as to deny them. The apostle Paul tells us that we are able to understand that there is a God by looking at the observable universe and

---

[85] Mike Abendroth, Clint Archer, Byron Yawn, *Things That Go Bump in the Church: Explaining the Bible's Most Misunderstood Teachings,* (Eugene, Oregon: Harvest House Publishers, 2014), 43.

God's creation on this earth. Any logical, unbiased person is able to see this *"since the creation of the world His invisible attributes, His eternal power and divine nature, have been clearly seen, being understood through what has been made, so that they are without excuse."*[86]

But despite the brain's ability to perceive this truth, man in his natural state suppresses this knowledge and denies the magnificence of the massive universe around us that screams there is a God.[87] His brain tells him he lives in a wonderful, complex world created by an infinite creator. But his brain also chooses to reject the signs in the heavens and invents his own gods and philosophies about the world. Paul continues,

> For even though they knew God, they did not honor Him as God or give thanks, but they became futile in their speculations, and their foolish heart was darkened. Professing to be wise, they became fools, and exchanged the glory of the incorruptible God for an image in the form of corruptible man and of birds and four-footed animals and crawling creatures.[88]

In addition to rejecting what his brain perceives, man also rejects his own conscience. Paul again explains, that those *"who do not have the Law do instinctively the things of the Law, these, not having the Law, are a law to themselves, in that they show the work of the Law written in their hearts, their conscience bearing witness and their thoughts alternately accusing or else defending them . . ."*[89] The ones without the law refers to all non-Jews since God gave his divine law to the Jewish nation in the Old Testament.

But having the law isn't the issue. The Bible tells us that man has a conscience that tells him what is right and what is wrong.

---

[86] Romans 1:20
[87] Romans 1:18
[88] Romans 1:21-23
[89] Romans 2:14-15

That is, everyone knows it's wrong to lie, cheat, steal and murder. No one has to tell us that. Our conscience can be "educated" by continuously ignoring it and excusing our bad behavior, but deep down we still know when something is wrong.

But the problem isn't having knowledge of creation or a conscience. The problem is in responding in a proper way to this data that God has given us. That's where free will comes in. God has given every person alive the massive evidence of His existence in the universe and the weight of their own conscience to guide their actions. But do we respond by choosing to follow God? No, not necessarily.

Free will follows its nature

That's because free will follows its nature. This is a key factor in understanding the nature of free will. Michael Lawrence observes,

> Some people are fond of debating whether or not we have free will. The Bible's answer is that it depends on what you mean by "free." If by "free" you mean that we do what we want to do, that nothing forces us to believe or to act against our will, then the Bible's answer is "yes." Our will is *always free to act in accord with its nature.* But if by "free" you mean that somehow our will is morally neutral and above the fray, able to choose between good and evil on its own merits, independent of predisposition or motive, then the answer is a clear and unequivocal "no." Our nature is corrupted and, as Paul says, we are sold as slaves to sin. We can no more choose not to be sinners than a fish can choose not to be a swimmer. It's our nature."[90]

The key is understanding the nature of man. Most people assume man is basically good. But "good" is a relative statement.

---

[90] Michael Lawrence, *Biblical Theology in the Life of the Church: A Guide for Ministry* (Wheaton, Illinois: Crossway, 2010), 136.

Good in relation to what? Why, in comparison to everyone else of course. Every mother thinks her son is a "good boy." In fact, it would probably be accurate to say that every person thinks of himself or herself as a "good person."

Over the years, I've had the chance to engage dozens of people in spiritual conversations. One of the questions I've asked is, "If there is a heaven, why do you think God should let you in?" Without question, the answer always boils down to "I'm a good person," no matter how relative that is. One guy told me God should let him in because he kept his Harley Davidson motorcycle cleaner that the guy down the street whose bike was always covered with grease and grime. Now that's creative spiritual analysis!

So, in some sense, we can say that man is good depending on what the measurement is. Some keep their Harleys clean. Others go to church. Almost everyone would say they try to do good and help people. And we have all seen philanthropists contribute to worthy causes and people band together when disaster strikes a community. There are many stories that inspire and motivate all of us to be better people.

But God's assessment of the nature of man is quite different. Looking in Scripture we find these descriptions of the nature of man:

- Man is born spiritually dead.[91]
- No man is righteous—no one seeks God.[92]
- Man doesn't accept the things of God because they are foolish to him, and he can't understand them because they are spiritually appraised.[93]

---

[91] Ephesians 2:1
[92] Romans 3:10-12
[93] 1 Corinthians 2:14

- Man's spiritual vision is blinded by Satan, so he can't see spiritual truth.[94]
- Man loves spiritual darkness because his deeds are evil, and he doesn't want them exposed.[95]
- Man is self-seeking and doesn't obey the truth.[96]
- Man is a slave to sin.[97]
- Nothing good resides in man.[98]
- Man hates God.[99]
- Man is not able to subject himself to the laws of God or to please God.[100]
- Man refuses to love the truth and be saved.[101]

This is not an exhaustive list nor is it new information. Any honest examination of Scripture by an objective person can see these things if they want to. Astute students of the Bible have recognized this for ages. Augustine, the fourth century theologian and philosopher from North Africa whose writings shaped Western Christianity asserted:

> For it was in the evil use of his free will that man destroyed himself and his will at the same time. For as a man who kills himself is still alive when he kills himself but having killed himself is then no longer alive and cannot resuscitate himself after he has destroyed his own life—so also sin which arises from the action of the free will turns out to be victor over the will and

---

[94] 2 Corinthians 4:4
[95] John 3:19-20
[96] Romans 2:8
[97] Romans 6:6
[98] Romans 7:18
[99] Romans 8:7
[100] Romans 8:7-8
[101] 2 Thessalonians 2:10

the free will is destroyed. . . . Free choice alone, if the way of truth is hidden, avails for nothing but sin.[102]

Though the vast majority of people don't like to admit it, this is the nature of man without God. You won't learn this in a university psychology or sociology class. The mantra of the age is that man is basically good. He only does bad things because of his family background, or his environment, or his lack of education. But the clear teaching of Scripture says that man's nature is corrupt from his birth.

THE BONDAGE OF THE WILL

That's not very encouraging. If our very nature is corrupt, then we must rethink the way we look at life. Most people view freewill as a vast array of choices and possibilities that frees them from the restrictions of religion and conventional wisdom. Free will is seen as the ultimate ticket to happiness and self-fulfillment.

But that's not the case. Instead of a ticket to "anything goes," the freewill of natural man means he is confined to his own imagination and desires. But he has no ability to see, understand, or participate in anything from God's perspective.

Scripture is very clear in explaining the restrictive nature of man's choices. Let me elaborate on the list that describes the condition of man given earlier. In his letter to the Roman church Paul said, *"For we know that the Law is spiritual, but I am of flesh, sold into bondage to sin."*[103] Like Paul, we must say, *"I am not practicing what I would like to do, but I am doing the very thing I hate."* Jesus said the same thing, noting, "everyone who commits sin is the slave of sin."[104]

---

[102] Augustine, *The Spirit and the Letter*, 5, in *Augustine: Later Works*, ed. John Burnaby (Philadelphia: Westminster, 1955), 197.

[103] Romans 7:14

[104] John 8:34

This has been clearly taught by prominent Bible scholars for centuries. Once again, Augustine helps us understand that, in his natural state, without any kind of intervention from God, man is a slave to sin in mind, emotion, and will, and can't do anything about it. He said,

> I was bound by the iron chain of my own will. The enemy held fast my will, and had made of it a chain, and had bound me tight with it. For out of the perverse will came lust, and the service of lust ended in habit, and habit, not resisted, became necessity. By these links, as it were, forged together—which is why I called it 'a chain'—a hard bondage held me in slavery.[105]

In short, man in his natural state cannot choose *not* to sin. He is reduced to a spiritual state of total inability, leaving him unable to obey, please, or come to God. He is held in spiritual bondage because he was born spiritually dead[106] and because *"the god of this world has blinded the minds of the unbelieving so that they might not see the light of the gospel of the glory of Christ, who is the image of God."*[107]

William Tyndale, the English Reformer known as "the father of the English Bible" also understood this. He wrote, "The devil is our lord, and our ruler, our head, our governor, our prince, yea, and our god. And our will is locked and knit faster unto the will of the devil, than could a hundred thousand chains bind a man unto a post."[108]

---

[105] Augustine, Confessions, 8.5, cited in Augustine: *Confessions and Enchiridion,* (Philadelphia: Westminster Press, 1955), 164.

[106] Ephesians 2:1

[107] 2 Corinthians 4:4

[108] William Tyndale, *Works of William Tyndale, vol. 1*, ed. Henry Walter (1849 and 1950 repr., Edinburgh: Banner of Truth, 2010), 17.

How bad is it?

This bondage of the will makes the condition of man worse than we think. When a doctor calls someone back in for a "further consultation," the first question is, "How bad is it Doc?" That's the same question we ask about the destiny of our free will. Words like "bondage" and "slave" lead us to correctly think that it's worse than most think. We don't like those words much but it's hard to argue with the truth. All of us understand that at times we find ourselves doing something that we really don't want to do.

We tell our friends that we aced a test when we know we got a C+. We claim deductions on our income tax that we really don't have. We use our company car for personal business. We continue to be drawn back to certain websites when we don't want to go there. And we are powerless to stop. Even for the most self-disciplined who control certain bad behavior by sheer determination or force of their will, there remains any number of behaviors that are unwanted and unconquered.

Paul explains this further a couple of verses later. He comments, *"for the willing is present in me, but the doing of the good is not. For the good that I want, I do not do, but I practice the very evil that I do not want."*[109] In addition to doing the things I don't want to do, I ignore some of the very things that I really would like to do.

We might think that the word "bondage" sounds severe, but it seems to be right on target to anyone who is candid enough to admit it. The alcoholic wants to stop drinking, but she doesn't. The addict wants to stop using, but he doesn't. The businessman wants to stop visiting that website, but he won't.

But let's not get the idea that bondage only refers to those "big" sins. It also refers to the person who wants to stop working so many late hours, but she doesn't. Or another person who

---

[109] Romans 7:18-19

wants to stop speaking harshly to his wife and kids, but he fails. The "smaller" issues like anger, neglect, demeaning speech, perfectionism, and self-centeredness place us in bondage too.

And Paul is also clear in labeling our universal behaviors as sin. The word he uses in the original language is *hamartia*. Originally it meant to "miss the mark." It referred to a mistake out of ignorance, a failure to reach a goal, or an offense against friends or even one's own body.

Thus, it was used to describe an offense against the prevailing order, even though it may have been without evil intent. But it also described deliberate offenses. It came to mean "anything from stupidity to law-breaking, anything that offends against the *orthon*, the right, that does not conform to the dominant ethic, to the respect due to social order and to the polis."[110] Ultimately, it means missing the mark of God's holiness.

THE LIMITATIONS OF FREE WILL

Free will cannot choose God

This leads us to some dramatic conclusions. The first is that man's will is *not free to choose God*. This should be very clear from the list of biblical descriptors of man seen previously. Read the list over carefully and let the impact of how the Bible describes man sink in. It is a devastating list that reveals man has absolutely no ability to respond to God in any way.

This is perhaps the most important observation that can be made about free will, and the one that causes the most anger and confusion among those who don't know God. The one who thinks he is totally free doesn't like to be told that he is not free to do something. But this makes sense if you think about it.

---

[110] W. Günther, "Ἁμαρτία," ed. Lothar Coenen, Erich Beyreuther, and Hans Bietenhard, *New International Dictionary of New Testament Theology* (Grand Rapids, MI: Zondervan Publishing House, 1986), 577.

That's because man's free will puts him in a box. Thinking himself to be totally free, he doesn't realize that his freedom is limited to the box of his own choices. He has all the autonomy he wants to flail around making assertions and denials about everything under the sun. But he doesn't have any ability to choose God on his own because he has suppressed the knowledge of God that would give him the ability to make an informed choice. Thus, he is in a box of his own choices. He can't choose God because he has denied the information that would allow him to do so.

Free will can't control our "dark side"

This also means that the free will of man cannot control our "dark side." This refers to man's natural instincts to lie, cheat, steal, lust, be angry, arrogant, and worse. Everyone does these things. And no one can stop doing them! No matter how strong our will is, these behaviors stay with us all of our life!

This truth is self-evident. Call these tendencies mistakes, or weaknesses, or faults, or whatever you want. As we pointed out in chapter one, the Bible calls them sin. This is why no one is able to even begin living up to his or her own aspirations, let alone what others desire from them.

While each of our lives are certainly filled with "good" things we do, any honest evaluation will also admit that we are all a bundle of less desirable characteristics as well. Everyone lies. Everyone cheats. Everyone steals. Everyone covets or lusts for something that doesn't belong to them. Man cannot choose to stop these ingrained tendencies.

That's not to say that we lie or cheat or steal or lust all the time. But no one can truthfully deny that these impulses are something everyone has. I realize that this implies value and assumes a certain judgment on these activities.

For now, I'm going to assume that we can all agree that lying, cheating, stealing, and coveting are bad. So, if they are bad,

implying that we don't want to do them, but we all do them anyway, what does that say about free will?

It says that our free will is not able to stop doing them. No
matter how hard we try, I think everyone would agree that there
is no one who doesn't do these things. If someone said they *never*
did these things, or they have overcome them by the exercise of
their free will, they are either perfect or they are lying. We know
they are not perfect, so where does that leave us? Doesn't man
have any ability to respond to God?

Free will leaves us helpless and hopeless

The Bible declares *"there is none righteous, not even one."*[111] In
fact, the Bible says man's nature is corrupt from the word "go."
We start out this way from the womb. In a profound statement
regarding the psyche of man, King David said, *"The wicked are
estranged from the womb; These who speak lies go astray from
birth."*[112]

Oh, so that's where it comes from? Can anyone deny this?
Children don't have to be told to rebel. They are born shaking
their fist and demanding their own way. And without proper
civilization by their parents and other positive influences in
life, they will end up as juvenile delinquents or worse, career
criminals.

Most importantly, this is seen in the spiritual realm. Paul asserts that we are born *"dead in [our] trespasses and sins"* because
*"we too all formerly lived in the lusts of our flesh, indulging the de-
sires of the flesh and of the mind, and were by nature children of
wrath, even as the rest."*[113] This describes the nature of man in a
nutshell. Elsewhere, Paul says the *"mind set on the flesh is hostile*

---

[111] Romans 3:10
[112] Psalm 58:3
[113] Ephesians 2:1, 3

toward God; for it does not subject itself to the law of God, for it is not even able to do so."[114]

If we zero in on this, we can see how this relates to man's free will. We are told *"we may know the things freely given to us by God,"*[115] that is, God freely reveals Himself to us, so we can know what He expects of us. But Paul goes on to write *"a natural man does not accept the things of the Spirit of God, for they are foolishness to him; and he cannot understand them, because they are spiritually appraised."*[116] The apostle John tells us *"men loved the darkness rather than the Light, for their deeds were evil. For everyone who does evil hates the Light, and does not come to the Light for fear that his deeds will be exposed."*[117]

This explains something critical about free will. The reason our will cannot overcome sin is because we love our sin. That's why we do it. It's our nature. We may be "good" in relation to other people, but the reason we all have a problem with our "dark side" is because that is our nature.

This is key. Our will simply follows our nature. Yes, we have free will, but the free choices we make are a reflection of who we are. Man has great freedom to choose what he wants to do. The problem is that he can only choose to do things that are consistent with his nature, and his nature is not to seek God or to glorify Him in any way. In this sense, man indeed has free will, but it exists in a state of anarchy against God.

So we say, "I gotta be me!" Congratulations. Where does that get us? With regard to understanding and knowing God, it gets us nowhere. But thankfully, God doesn't leave us there.

---

[114] Romans 8:7
[115] 1 Corinthians 2:12
[116] 1 Corinthians 2:14
[117] John 3:19-20

GOD'S INTENTIONAL RESPONSE

CHAPTER SIX

*"God has never learned from anybody . . . God cannot learn . . .
Because God knows all things perfectly, he knows no thing better
than any other thing, but all things equally well. He never discovers
anything, he is never surprised, never amazed."*[118]
—A. W. Tozer

Godisnowhere

Is there really a God who cares?

As we move into a new section, a little review might be helpful at this point. In the first section of this book we identified the ultimate problem of humanity as sin. But identification doesn't solve any problem. In chapter two we pointed out that man's natural inclination is to find someone to call on to answer that problem. Chapter three suggested that we all get "black and white fever" because we know something is wrong, and chapter four asserted that we all run from God trying to get away from our problem. Finally, in chapter five we said that man's own free will drives his response to his problem.

In the next four chapters we will begin to offer God's response to the ultimate problem of man. The first thing we will do is assert the existence of God. Then we will provide some of the

---

[118] A. W. Tozer, *The Knowledge of the Holy: The Attributes of God, Their Meaning in the Christian Life* (New York, Evanston, and London: Harper & Row, 1961), 1.

evidence for the validity of the Bible in an attempt to build trust in God's response. In chapters eight and nine we will explain God's sovereign decree over all things then finish off the section by showing how God's will interacts with man's will.

SEEKING TRUTH

"You have the right to remain silent," begins the *Miranda* admonition, which became case law in 1966 as the U.S. Supreme Court applied the 5th Amendment of our Constitution to a criminal defendant. "Anything you say can and will be used against you in a court of law. You have the right to an attorney. If you cannot afford an attorney, one will be provided for you."[119]

I have read these rights to criminal defendants thousands of times over the years. Each time, I sought the truth. Yet oftentimes I received a tall tale. But criminal defendants are not the only people twisting facts to either save their hide or manipulate circumstances. To varying degrees, we all do!

There's axiomatic humor that warns, "If you kill a bug, another thousand will come to the funeral." The same could be said for lying—tell one and it will require more to cover your trail.

If I had to select a single virtue that would be the best place to begin curing social ills, it would be honesty. The personal and political agendas of many have led an overwhelming number of people down the road of deceit. Once deception is unleashed, trust will vanish. Most compromised practices that eventually fail are the result of lying. Unfortunately, "spin" is an accepted practice if it helps the individual or organization achieve a goal.

If I had a dollar every time a person willfully lied to me during a criminal investigation, I'd have far more income to tithe! While engaging someone who has blatantly disregarded the truth, law

---

[119] Miranda v. Arizona, http://caselaw.findlaw.com/us-supreme-court/384/436.html, (accessed August 10, 2017)

enforcement officers everywhere have repeated the following dialogue:

> Officer: It's obvious you're lying!
> Crook: How do you know?
> Officer: Your lips are moving.

. While it appears to question the character of a criminal defendant, it's part of reality when dealing with career offenders. There is far more deception coming from their mouths than truth. On the rare occasion when unvarnished truth surfaced from a guilty party, I usually responded with *astonished surprise*.

And contrary to popular opinion, when an innocent person was in our investigative crosshairs, an unfiltered version of the truth helped far more than it hindered their case.

RIGHTS AND RESPONSIBILITIES

A major shortcoming is that people tend to focus on rights while ignoring responsibilities. For example, what happens if a citizen shoots and kills a teen committing a petty theft from a convenience store? Assuming the crime did not involve a violent confrontation, I think we'd all agree it appears to be a *colossal overreaction*. As a result, the citizen would appropriately face criminal charges.

In this scenario the citizen would be afforded his constitutional rights per the *Miranda* decision. In other words, he cannot be compelled to provide an incriminating statement. Those are his rights.

But does the citizen have a responsibility to submit to an interview even if it is condemning? Few people would say yes to this scenario, regardless of guilt. After all, Americans embrace *rights* like Elvis cradled a microphone.

However, let's replace the citizen with a police officer. Did you know that a law enforcement professional has the exact same constitutional rights as a citizen when facing criminal action? So, if the officer exercises his right to remain silent, we get peeved. Why? Because we believe he has a responsibility as a public servant that supersedes his constitutional rights. We want him to take responsibility, not exercise his rights. Yet our criminal laws do not work that way.

As you can see, it can get messy.

Moreover, while our focused *exercise-of-rights* pulls authority from the U.S. Constitution, codified ordinance, case law, and the like, our laws are still imperfect because people are flawed.

There are competing interests when applying human wisdom. So, whether we seek answers to simple or complex legal questions, or finality when it comes to the ever-after, humanity will be off course if we ignore God's counsel.

THINKING ABOUT GOD

This can be illustrated by the riddle someone came up with a number of years ago. The riddle is seen in the word GODISNOWHERE. Close examination reveals you can interpret the word in one of two ways, depending on how you divide it. It either says *God is nowhere,* or *God is now here.* The atheist prefers the first. Our contention is that the last is to be preferred because it comports better with the realities of life.

Obviously, you can't have it both ways. God is either here or He is not. As the Russian writer Dostoevsky said, "If there is no God, all things are permitted."[120] This is a logical statement but those who say they believe it can't live by it. If there is no God, then there is no rational reason for morals or laws of any kind. If we are clumps of protoplasm, there is no reason to infer that what one protoplasmic clump thinks should be preferred over what a different protoplasmic clump thinks. Furthermore, there is no

---

[120] Fyodor Dostoevsky, Constance Garnett, trans., *The Brothers Karamazov* (repr., 1880, Digireads.com Publishing, 2017), 635.

explanation for emotions like love or even hate because they are moral sentiments that have no place in meaningless protoplasm.

The reason that no one can live out Dostoevsky's sentiment is self-evident. If I believe that sentiment, then I believe I can act in any way I want with no moral or legal ramifications. But the person who lives like this screams in fury when another protoplasmic entity dares to respond according to their own whims. In other words, I can steal from you in the name of freedom. But if you retaliate by hitting me on the head with your club I will scream for justice.

A number of years ago a man named Francis Schaeffer wrote a book called *The God Who is There* that explored the reasons for the existence of God. He followed that up with another book called, *He is There, And He is Not Silent*. These are both profound thoughts. God *is* there. Where? Everywhere. He is *not* silent. He *has* spoken. And we can read what He said.

A. W. Tozer was a man who reflected deeply on God and His ways. He wrote, "What comes into our minds when we think about God is the most important thing about us."[121] He explained that God:

[H]as never learned from anyone . . . God cannot learn. Could God at any time or in any manner receive into his mind knowledge that he did not possess and had not possessed from eternity, he would be imperfect and less than himself. To think of a God who must sit at the feet of a teacher, even though that teacher be an archangel or a seraph, is to think of someone other than the Most High God, maker of heaven and earth. . . . God knows instantly and effortlessly all matter and all matters, all mind and every mind, all spirit and all spirits, all being and every being, all creaturehood and all creatures, every plurality and all pluralities, all law and every law, all relations, all causes,

---

[121] Tozer, *The Knowledge of the Holy*, 1.

all thoughts, all mysteries, all enigmas, all feeling, all desires, every unuttered secret, all thrones and dominions, all personalities, all things visible and invisible in heaven and in earth, motion, space, time, life, death, good, evil, heaven, and hell . . . Because God knows all things perfectly, he knows no thing better than any other thing, but all things equally well. He never discovers anything, he is never surprised, never amazed.[122]

This is the God who is there. He is not some kind of doddering old man in heaven scratching His gray beard trying to find someone doing something wrong, so he can squash him like a bug. This isn't the God that is revealed in Scripture at all. His many attributes show He is loving, just, merciful, holy, good, righteous, all-knowing and all-powerful. So, is it reasonable to dismiss Him out of hand when we are discussing the most important issues of life?

THE COSMOS

This chapter is devoted to turn our minds from running from God to having confidence in the existence of God. The best way to do this is to start where He started, with creation. This is the fulcrum that balances everything we know about God. If He is *not there*, then He hasn't created anything. We are just accidental protoplasm floating through space and time.

But ultimately, the vast majority of people are not satisfied with that explanation. So, we are going to begin this assessment by examining the origin of our cosmos and compare what man says about it to what God says.

Now as soon as we say we're going to discuss God and the cosmos there are some people who will say that's not possible. The skeptics say that science and the Bible don't mix. Let's look at one of them.

---

[122] Ibid., 61-62.

Answering Stephen Hawking

Stephen Hawking was one of the most articulate skeptics on the existence of God until he died in 2018. Hawking was one of the world's most renowned experts on what he calls, "the theory of everything." He was a British theoretical physicist, cosmologist, and author, and the Director of Research at the Centre for Theoretical Cosmology within the University of Cambridge. He suffered from ALS (Lou Gehrig's Disease) that impaired his physical abilities, but certainly not his mental capacity.

Over the years Hawking also wrote a number of books postulating his theories about the origin of the cosmos. Possibly the most ambitious was *The Theory of Everything*, popularized in the 2014 movie of the same name.

Hawking claimed the only thing necessary to create the universe is gravity. When asked where gravity came from he replied, "M-theory." It involves supersymmetric gravity that gets very complicated involving things like vibrating strings in eleven dimensions. That's not something the average person can comprehend.

But John Lennox, himself a renowned mathematician, scientist, and professor emeritus of mathematics at Oxford University, points out that many other scientists have significant problems with Hawking's theories. He notes:

> However, Paul Davies... who is not a theist, says of M-theory: "It is not testable, not even in any foreseeable future." Oxford physicist Frank Close goes further: "M-theory is not even defined . . . we are even told 'No one seems to know what the M stands for.' Perhaps it is 'myth'. . ." Jon Butterworth, who works at the Large Hadron Collider in Switzerland, states that "M-theory is highly speculative and certainly not in the zone of science that we have got any evidence for." Butterworth argues, however, that although M-theory could not be tested, it did not require

faith in the religious sense, but was more of a scientific hunch. Half a minute! Don't scientific hunches require faith to pursue the research that may establish them? Doesn't Hawking have faith in M-theory—even if it is faith without much evidence to back it up?[123]

Isn't Lennox right to ask if Hawking has anything more than faith to back up his hunch? Christians are often accused of having blind faith, but it is evident that in this very basic question of the origin of the universe, one of the most esteemed physicists in the world operates on faith too. Lennox further takes Hawking to task, asking,

> Similarly, when Hawking argues in support of his theory of spontaneous creation, that it was only necessary for "the blue touch paper" to be lit to "set the universe going," I am tempted to ask: where did this blue touch paper come from? It is clearly not part of the universe, if it set the universe going. So who lit it, in the sense of ultimate causation, if not God?[124]

Regarding the existence of the universe, we can also look to Dr. Allan Sandage, widely regarded as the father of modern astronomy, discoverer of quasars, and winner of the Craafoord Prize (astronomy's equivalent of the Nobel Prize). Sandage has no doubt about the origin of the universe. He states, "I find it quite improbable that such order came out of chaos. There has to be some organizing principle. God to me is a mystery but is the explanation for the miracle of existence—why there is something rather than nothing."[125]

---

[123] John C. Lennox, *Gunning For God: Why the New Atheists Are Missing the Target* (Oxford, England: Lion Hudson, 2011), 36-37.

[124] John C. Lennox, *God and Stephen Hawking: Whose Design Is It Anyway?* (Oxford England: Lion Hudson, 2011), 44.

[125] John Noble Wilford, "Sizing Up the Cosmos: An Astronomer's Quest," *New York Times*, March 12, 1991, p. 89.

If one of the finest minds around can't come up with anything more than an unverified M-theory, then it makes at least as much sense to look to God as the "organizing principle" of the universe. Obviously, science can't explain how God caused everything to come out of nothing, but the biblical explanation of how this took place deserves our consideration.

A word from God

The evidence that God is there is no more evident than in the physical universe in which we live. The Psalmist tells us, "*The heavens are telling of the glory of God; And their expanse is declaring the work of His hands. Day to day pours forth speech, And night to night reveals knowledge. There is no speech, nor are there words; Their voice is not heard.*"[126]

There isn't any speech because it would be wholly inadequate. Can you explain the beauty of a sunset? Try explaining the grandeur of the whole known universe. Better yet, isn't it better if we just let God talk through His exotic display of colors and lights against a darkened sky that all are perfectly formed and ordered?

But we can also look at God's written explanation in the Bible. When we look at the biblical story of creation, it is clear that it is vastly different from what people like Stephen Hawking have offered. The Bible explains there was no raw material with which to work. God created the universe *ex nihilo*, out of nothing.

We see this in the very first words of the Bible where we find, "*In the beginning God created the heavens and the earth.*"[127] The original Hebrew word for "*create*" is *bara*. It is distinguished from a similar Hebrew word, *yasar*, which emphasizes the shaping of an object while *bara* emphasizes the initiation of the object. The grammatical form of this word is used "only of God's activity and is thus a theological term. This distinctive use of the word

---

[126] Psalm 19:1-3
[127] Genesis 1:1

is especially appropriate to the concept of creation by divine fiat."[128]

If God is not there, then nothing is. But He is there. And a natural place to begin our search for Him is in the cosmos. If we can see His creative power and purpose in the creation of our physical world, then it builds confidence for trusting Him in the events of our lives.

God is there in the creation of the cosmos

The evidence for seeing God's presence in the cosmos is abundant. The psalmist asserts *"He counts the number of the stars; He gives names to all of them."*[129] In addition, there are eighty-eight constellations in our solar system. The Greeks, Babylonians and other civilizations knew about at least forty-eight constellations.

Job even provides the names of three prominent constellations by asking, *"Who makes the Bear, Orion and the Pleiades, and the chambers of the south."*[130] This refers to three constellations visible and known in Job's time. Today *"the Bear"* is known as Arcturus, or Ursa Major, or the Big Dipper. Orion is the constellation that can be seen in the southern sky. Even though it includes the giant stars Betelgeuse and Rigel, most of it is invisible without a telescope. Pleiades is actually a grouping of stars that all travel at the same rate in the same direction and can be seen in the eastern sky.

Job was written around the time of Abraham, which was about 2000 BC. This indicates incredible accuracy in astronomy exhibited in the Bible over 4,000 years ago which is relatively early in recorded history.

---

[128] Thomas E. Mccomiskey, "278 אָרַב," ed. R. Laird Harris, Gleason L. Archer Jr., and Bruce K. Waltke, *Theological Wordbook of the Old Testament* (Chicago: Moody Press, 1999), 127.

[129] Psalms 147:4

[130] Job 9:9

But notice something else interesting from Job. The passage continues by speaking of *"[T]he chambers of the south. . ."* Astronomers today realize that constellations in the southern hemisphere are not visible to those in the northern hemisphere. These were not charted until the 15th century AD. But Job speaks of their existence even though they were not visible to him! Where did he get that knowledge?

First century historian Flavius Josephus provides some clues. Chapter eight of his book *Antiquities of the Jews* contains the following:

> For whereas the Egyptians were formerly addicted to different customs, and despised one another's sacred and accustomed rites, and were very angry one with another on that account, *Abram conferred with each of them*, and, confuting the reasonings they made use of, every one for their own practices, demonstrated that such reasonings were vain and void of truth; . . . He communicated to them arithmetic, and delivered to them the science of astronomy; for, *before Abram came into Egypt, they were unacquainted with those parts of learning; for that science came from the Chaldeans into Egypt, and from thence to the Greeks also* (italics added).[131]

How did Josephus know this? In chapter 1 of *Antiquities of the Jews*, Josephus quotes a Chaldean historian named Berosus:

> Berosus mentions our father Abram without naming him, when he says thus:—*'In the tenth generation after the Flood, there was among the Chaldeans a man righteous and great, and skillful in the celestial science'* And Nicolaus of Damascus, in the fourth book of his history, says thus:—'Abram reigned at Damascus,

---

[131] Flavius Josephus, William Whiston, trans., *The Complete Works of Flavius Josephus*, repr., (Green Forest, AR: New Leaf Publishing Group, 2008), 14.

being a foreigner, who came with an army out of the land above
Babylon, called the land of the Chaldeans [italics added].[132]

Not only does this lend credibility for the historicity of Abram
(biblical Abraham), but these ancient historians also reveal that
Abraham probably knew the astronomical information contained
in Job. This surprises many people.

But amazingly, it's possible that we can date this knowledge
even earlier. Again, we quote Josephus, talking about the children of Seth, the third son of Adam and Eve. He noted,

> Now this Seth, when he was brought up . . . became a virtu-
> ous man . . . so did he leave children behind him who imitated
> his virtues. They also were the inventors of that peculiar sort
> of wisdom, which is concerned with the heavenly bodies, and
> their order. And that their inventions might not be lost before
> they were sufficiently known, upon Adam's prediction that the
> world was to be destroyed at one time by the force of fire, and
> at another time by the violence and quantity of water, they
> made two pillars; the one of brick, the other of stone: they in-
> scribed their discoveries on them both, that in case the pillar
> of brick should be destroyed by the flood, the pillar of stone
> might remain, and exhibit those discoveries to mankind; and
> also inform them that there was another pillar of brick erected
> by them. Now this remains in the land of Siriad [Egypt] to this
> day."[133]

This is astounding! This is not an idle lesson in astronomy.
This is evidence that God's creative powers are historical, accurate, and compelling.

Think of it like this. Imagine a perfectly smooth black sheet of
glass that stretches out for miles in front of you on which the fin-

---

[132] Ibid., 11.
[133] Ibid., 3.

est speck can be seen. Then shrink our sun from 865,000 miles in diameter to a ball two feet in diameter and place it on the black sheet of glass. If you arranged certain items scaled to represent the relative size of the planets on the glass in relation to the sun, and if two feet per step represented the planet's distance from the sun, you would see the items placed as follows:

- 83 steps away – a mustard seed – Mercury
- 60 more steps away – a BB – Venus
- 78 more steps away – a green pea – Earth
- 108 more steps away – a pinhead – Mars
- 788 more steps away – an orange – Jupiter
- 934 more steps away – a golf ball – Saturn
- 2,086 more steps away – a marble – Uranus
- 2,322 more steps away – a cherry – Neptune

By this time, you've walked 2 ½ miles and haven't even reached our smallest planet or the nearest star. Would you like to guess how far the nearest star is from the two-foot ball representing the sun? Another 3,000 steps? 5,000 steps? 10,000 steps? No. It would be 6,720 *miles* to arrive at Proxima Centauri, the third member of the Alpha Centaur system, which is 4.24 light years from the sun. On a photograph it appears as a tiny red dot in the middle of a cluster of stars.[134] And that's just the *nearest* star. Anyone who believes that the magnitude and perfect order of the universe is a result of pure chance operates on more faith than it takes to believe the biblical account.

God is there in the creation of the earth

Just as we can look outward into the cosmos, so we can also look inward to the creation of the earth to see that God is there. The first verse in the Bible is very clear about God's creative

---

[134] Chuck Swindoll, *Day By Day with Chuck Swindoll* (Nashville: Word Publishing, 2000), 156.

work. And He did it in six days. The Hebrew word for day is *yom* and is used twenty times in Genesis 1-3. Some want to distort the meaning of this word to fit better into an evolutionary scheme of things. They say it really doesn't mean a 24-hour day but is used in a euphemistic sense like we would say "back in the day." In this way they can say that *yom* could mean long, long periods of time that would accommodate the scientific *theory* of evolution.

But why shouldn't we accept that it means 24 hours? Granted, it is used metaphorically in Scripture as in describing the com- ing *"day of the Lord"* 28 times. And Peter even says *"[W]ith the Lord one day is like a thousand years . . ."*[135] It is clear that these are figures of speech, which are not to be taken literally in the text.

But that *does not* mean that *yom* means thousands of years in Genesis 1-3. In fact, every place *yom* is used with a number in the Bible it always refers to a 24-hour day! We might also note that the phrase *"And there was evening and there was morning . . ."* is used six times at the conclusion of the account of each day, which also indicates 24-hour days.

Furthermore, Genesis also used the phrase *"after their kind"* eight times.[136] This indicates plants and animals did not go through some long period of changing into another species, or that there was any kind of morphing from one species to anoth- er. This would be necessary in any evolutionary explanation of creation.

Hang on—I realize I might lose you here. We are acclimated to believing it is impossible to live in a scientific age and believe the creation account in the Bible. But consider this. Science is the disciplined pursuit of truth through hypothesis, experimen- tation, observation, and conclusion. That means that science is never finished. It is always questioning and pushing forward to new conclusions.

---

[135] 2 Peter 3:8
[136] Genesis 1:11-25

For example, if the science of astronomy had codified their conclusions in the seventeenth century, we would all believe that there are only roughly 1000 stars. Hipparchus said there were 1,022 stars. But Ptolemy said, "You're wrong. There are 1,056." Then Kepler came along and said, "You're both wrong fellas. There are exactly 1,055."[137] In the days before the telescope, can you picture those guys lying on their backs trying to quadrant off the sky and count the stars?! They could have saved a lot of time by reading Jeremiah's words when he said, "*[T]he host of heaven cannot be counted . . .*"[138]

Despite the fact that science is an ever-changing discipline, our world has fallen under the spell of science as the final arbiter of life. Even many Christians have bought into the allure of science. Some believe that God supervised evolution in order to bring the world into existence. This is known as theistic evolution and it has dramatic implications for trusting the biblical account of creation.

One example of this line of thinking is Frances Collins. Collins, the chief architect of the Human Genome Project and author of *The Language of God*, and his colleagues at the BioLogos Forum, believe that the human genome indicates that Genesis is more of a poem and not a historical account. It is not literal, they say, but *literalistic*. The BioLogos Forum believes that evangelicals should embrace the theory of evolution, and they maintain that doing so should offer no challenges to our Christian faith.

This theory is neither biblical nor scientific. It is not biblical because it boldly asserts a different version of creation than what is presented in Genesis 1-3. Adam is either historic, or he is not. Scripture (including the New Testament where Adam is mentioned nine times) deals with Adam as a historical character.

---

[137] John MacArthur, *Focus on Fact* (Old Tappan, NJ: Fleming H. Revell Co., 1977),

[138] Jeremiah 33:22

Francis Collins and the folks at the BioLogos Forum do not deal with Adam this way. They theorize that Adam may have been a farmer living in Mesopotamia among thousands of other people whom God invested with His presence in a certain way. Their theory completely invalidates the biblical account in Genesis 1-3 as well as the explanation of sin offered in Romans 5 where we find that death entered the world through sin and sin came from Adam. If Adam is not a historical man, and there were thousands of people before him, then Paul's statements on sin and death are wrong. And if this is true, you have destroyed the gospel. You can't have it both ways.

But their theory is also not scientific on several counts. First, it postulates a whole new theory of the origins of man based on incomplete scientific research in that the work of the Human Genome Project is far from conclusive. As any honest scientist will attest, science is an ongoing process of research and recalibration. It is not given to making final pronouncements because they may be proven false later on. If science were a finished product, we would still think the earth was flat or the best thing to do when someone is sick is drain their blood instead of giving them a transfusion.

Secondly, evolution violates the first law of thermodynamics, which states that energy cannot be created or destroyed. But the theory of evolution is predicated on the assumption that energy and matter are repeatedly introduced into a closed system. In reality, the laws of physics and chemistry tells us this is impossible.

This also means that the theory of evolution violates the second law of thermodynamics that states that matter breaks down over time. All physical matter becomes less complex over time, not more complex. But theories of evolution must assume the opposite. For the folks at BioLogos to declare an end of the biblical record of the creation of man is to deny the whole theory of the ongoing process of scientific investigation.

THE KNOWLEDGE OF GOD

He knows me

The crown of God's creative purpose however, is man. Psalm 139 gives us an intimate look at how well God knows us. This is key in developing confidence in trusting God through the toughest events of life. A close examination of this wonderful Psalm shows us that God is certainly not silent about the most important issues of life.

In verse 1 the writer, Israel's King David, says, "*O Lord, You have searched me and known me.*" One of the most difficult issues of life is the feeling of being alone. Many teenagers experience this when they perceive that they don't fit in with a certain crowd. Even adults can end up feeling like they are nobody.

Many years ago, songwriter Neil Diamond commented about this. He wrote, "Well, I'm New York City born and raised, But nowadays, I'm lost between two shores, L.A.'s fine, but it ain't home—New York's home but it ain't mine no more . . . 'I am' . . . I said, to no one there. And no one heard at all, not even the chair." Everyone cries out "I am!" No one wants to be ignored or forgotten.

But God knows everything about you—your birth, your DNA, your parents, your personality, the cleft in your chin . . . everything! You are not ignored or forgotten. Rather than turn us away from God, this builds confidence in calling out to Him in hard times. If God created you and knows everything about you, then it is easier to trust Him when things go bad.

He knows my thoughts

But David goes further. Psalm 139:2 says, "*You know when I sit down and when I rise up; You understand my thought from afar.*" Not only does God know all about us, He knows all about our actions and feelings. Nothing is outside His all-encompassing gaze.

When I was sixteen, my family moved from Kansas to Southern California. The differences in culture were huge, and I didn't handle them well. I ditched much of my junior year in high school and spent a lot of time at the beach. It was the only thing I liked about California at the time. Many times, I would simply wander the sandy seashore by myself wondering if anyone knew I was there. I never thought that much about it at the time, but God knew everything I was going through. He knew the loneliness, the anger, and the teenage angst that were my definition of a crisis at the time. How wonderful it would have been to understand the next verse of David's wisdom.

He knows my path

Psalm 139:3 notes, *"You scrutinize my path and my lying down, And are intimately acquainted with all my ways."* The word for *"scrutinize"* means to *"scatter, cast away."*[139] A derivative of this word is the word "pitchfork." The basic idea is a scattering or spreading effect caused by the stirring up of the air. The second verb in the verse is *"acquainted"* which has the meaning of "be of use," with the primary idea of stewardship.[140]

These concepts almost seem to have opposing meanings, but, seen together, provide a profound teaching of God's care. Taken together, the verse means that God is active in the stewardship of spreading out the effects of all the events of our lives. He is not an absent slumlord. He is not an old gray-bearded man in the sky who strokes his long bristles but is impotent when dealing with man.

Instead, God is such a careful steward over our lives that He is actively involved in shaping all of the varied activities of our lives in ways that accomplish His purposes. Job is even more explicit,

---

[139] R. Laird Harris, Gleason L. Archer, Jr., Bruce K. Waltke, eds., *Theological Wordbook of the Old Testament, vol. 1*, (Chicago: Moody Press, 1980), 251.

[140] Ibid., vol. 2, 625.

"You put my feet in the stocks And watch all my paths; You set a limit for the soles of my feet."[141] God even protects us from going places we shouldn't go and doing things we shouldn't do!

This is also part of God's care for us. Going to the wrong places and doing the "dumb" things in life are part of learning to mature and walk with God. How comforting it is to know that God protects us even when we are resisting Him.

He knows my words

Psalm 139:4 adds another concept to the picture, *"Even before there is a word on my tongue, Behold, O Lord, You know it all."* God not only is a worthy steward of the affairs of life, but He knows all of our silent intentions before we ever verbalize them. No matter what your mouth says, God knows what we mean and what we think! Of course, this includes all the dirt we think about, but it also includes all the unspoken praise, thanks, good intentions, and thoughts that we can't quite form.

This even includes our prayer life. One of the most comforting verses in the Bible says, *"we do not know how to pray as we should, but the Spirit Himself intercedes for us with groanings too deep for words; and He who searches the hearts knows what the mind of the Spirit is, because He intercedes for the saints according to the will of God."*[142] This verse teaches that the Holy Spirit of God knows what we are thinking even when we can't verbalize the words in prayer!

He knows everything about me

No wonder David concludes his thinking in this section by saying, *"You have enclosed me behind and before, And laid Your hand upon me. Such knowledge is too wonderful for me; It is too*

---

[141] Job 13:27
[142] Romans 8:26-27

high, I cannot attain to it."[143] One of the first things doctors do when a baby is born is wrap them in a blanket. Why? Because the baby needs to feel the security of boundaries. Having spent nine months in the friendly confines of the womb, the new "open space" of the hospital room is cold and threatening.

In similar fashion, we need the security that God has surrounded us with when He "encloses" us in the bookends of life, "behind and before," and places His hand on us. This is comforting to the one seeking a God who is willing and able to answer the hard things in life. Nothing escapes His notice. He is capable of handling anything that comes our way.

How does this work in real life? As a teenager, I was all over the map envisioning the things I wanted to be. I went from wanting to be an architect to a racecar driver to a journalist to a lawyer.

But God made me a pastor. And now I can see that all the time I was trying to be something else, God was molding me into what He wanted me to be. This is not to say that God will make you a pastor. God made my brother Jim a police officer. My point is that God can be trusted to be the one you turn to because He created you, He cares about you, and He is certainly capable of handling the issues in your life.

Even now, you might think you've married the wrong person, or that you have the wrong job, or life has handed you something that is simply too big for God to handle. You're wrong on all those points. God has placed you just where He wants you. And there is nothing in your life that has not passed by His all-knowing eyes.

When our oldest daughter was about six years old, she did something that needed parental involvement. Okay, she was in trouble! When I approached her about it I didn't give her all the information I was aware of because I wanted her to come clean

---

[143] Psalms 139:5-6

and tell me the whole story. When I asked her if she had done such and such, she replied, "Do you know?"

God indeed knows. He is aware of everything about you as well as the issues in your life. To some, this may not be welcome news. You might think it infringes on your freedom. But God has revealed His knowledge in written form that tells us all we need to know about who we are and the world we live in. Turn the page.

CHAPTER SEVEN

"The Bible is alive, it speaks to me; it has feet, it runs after me; it has hands, it lays hold on me. The Bible is not antique, or modern. It is eternal."[144]
—Martin Luther

The Breath of God

Has God spoken to us?

Every criminal justice major in college has heard about the Code of Hammurabi. It is one of the oldest forms of codified law dating back to ancient Babylon in 1772 BC. Babylonian King Hammurabi enacted the code. It contained more than 282 laws as standards of conduct. The purpose was to let people know what was expected of them as well as punishment prescribed for each violation.

The code was written with such straightforward simplicity that contemporary lawyers would have a field day with the loopholes. For example, Law #22: "If anyone is committing a robbery and is caught, then he shall be put to death."

Law #21 says, "If any one break(s) a hole into a house (breaks in to steal), he shall be put to death before that hole and be

---

[144] Martin Luther, "Christian History" Issue #34: Martin Luther, *The Early Years,* audiobook.

buried."[145] I guess that is where the term "buried on the spot" originated?

With or without the presence of attorneys, laws were bound to get more complicated as words have varied interpretations by different people. Take the word *robbery* for example. Those outside the legal system often incorrectly equate robbery to simple theft. But those working within the criminal justice system know that robbery requires the presence of *force or fear* to be cast upon another during the commission of a theft.

Codified laws have come a long way since Hammurabi. I worked law enforcement in California—a state that has twenty-nine different statutory codes—not to mention local ordinances from every municipality as well. Whether the violation derived from the Penal Code, Vehicle Code, Health and Safety Code, or one of the other twenty-six codes that contain thousands of laws, there is no shortage of wrongdoing and mandates defined by these statutes. And I will not venture into federal law. It's simply more of the same.

I guess that is why I smirk in exasperation every time we face a crisis, and I hear politicians proclaim we need a new law to handle the most recent problem. More often than not we have adequate laws codified. We simply need people of courage to saddle up, lasso the wayward individuals with existing ordinance, and hold them accountable.

POLICE ACADEMY-101

Recruits in the police academy get drilled in criminal law as part of their training. While standing at attention in column formation, they are required to spew forth the crime, the code section that governs the crime, and the elements required to make

---

[145] "The Code of Hammurabi." *Internet Sacred Text Archive*, Evinity Publishing Inc., 2011, http://sacred-texts.com/ane/ham/ham05.htm, (accessed January 15, 2018).

the act a violation of law. A typical exchange might sound like this:

Drill Instructor: "Recruit McKnight, what is 459 PC?"

Recruit McKnight: "Sir, section 459 of the California Penal Code is burglary."

"What are the elements of burglary Mr. McKnight?" shouts the taskmaster with his face two inches away from the young recruit, his eyes bulging from his head, and the carotid arteries in his neck about to burst.

"Sir, the elements of 459 PC include entering any house, room, apartment, tenement, shop, warehouse, store, mill, barn, stable, outhouse or other building, tent, vessel, floating home, railroad car, locked or sealed cargo container, any house car, inhabited camper, vehicle when the doors are locked, aircraft, or mine or any underground portion thereof, with intent to commit grand or petty theft or any felony," responds the sharp young recruit as he gasps for air at the conclusion of his answer.

Statutory code and case law

If that is not complicated enough, 459 PC refers the reader to section 21 of the Harbors and Navigation Code to define vessel; 18075.55 of the Health and Safety Code to define floating home; 362 and 635 of the Vehicle Code to define various forms of transportation; 243 of the Vehicle Code to define camper, and 21012 of the Public Utilities Code to define aircraft. Then 459 PC does the reader a favor and concludes by defining the word "inhabited" for qualifying purposes, rather than referencing another section.[146]

You would think the statutory codes have things spelled out well enough, but not so. Creative prosecutors and defense

---

[146] California Penal Code 459, http://leginfo.legislature.ca.gov/faces/codes.xhtml, (accessed January 15, 2018).

attorneys alike apply their own definitions to certain words until it requires legal resolution by a competent court of jurisdiction.

For instance, what does it mean to "enter" one of the previously mentioned structures, vehicles, or vessels? Case law has defined "entry" as the slightest encroachment by any body part, tool, or device. That means a perpetrator is not required to get his entire body through the threshold of the victim's home before entry has been made.[147] Once his screwdriver has breached the windowsill as he tries to pry the screen from its position, "entry" is complete and technically there is a violation of burglary.[148]

King Hammurabi knew it was vitally important to have laws in place to help maintain civility and order. We are no different today. But, before Hammurabi's Code, the twenty-nine voluminous codes of California, or the codified statutes in your state, there was another law code that was written down. It has basically served as the standard of law for the western world. I'm referring to the law that was recorded in the Bible.

In chapter six we saw that God is there, and He is not silent. His book, called The Bible, is the way He broke His silence. This written record tells us everything we need to know about God and how to live.

THE ULTIMATE AUTHORITY

No group of people can exist without an agreement on the laws and restrictions that will govern them. The presence of a book of rules and a willingness on the part of the group of people being governed is the basis for any orderly society.

---

[147] People v. Calderone (2007) 158 Cal.App.4th 137, 69 Cal.Rptr.3d 641, review denied, habeas corpus dismissed (holding that kicking in a door constitutes entry).

[148] People v. Davis (1998) 18 Cal.4th 712, 958 P.2d 1083 ("[U]sing a tire iron to pry open a door, using a tool to create a hole in a store wall, or using an auger to bore a hole in a corn crib are sufficient entries to support a conviction of burglary.")

We can even see this in the sports world. All major sports, whether professional or amateur, are governed by an accepted set of rules that are enforced by referees in striped shirts at all officially sanctioned games. Without an expressed willingness to be governed by those rules, as well as the official interpretation of the referees during the game, the games would end in chaos.

It's the same in the spiritual realm. How can anyone think that man can navigate the swirling waters we've talked about up to this point without agreement on a set of rules to live by? If there is no such set of rules, then everyone can do whatever he feels is right in his own eyes. That sounds good, but of course, any thinking person recognizes that this is just not possible in any civilized society.

So, where do we turn? We suggest we look at the Bible. There is no other book that begins to approach the authenticity of the original documents that validates the material it contains. And there is no other book that has the power to change lives. That's because there is no other book that claims to be the Word of God.

The Apostle Paul tells us, *"All Scripture is inspired by God and profitable for teaching, for reproof, for correction, for training in righteousness; so that the man of God may be adequate, equipped for every good work."*[149] The phrase "inspired by God" is only one word in the original language. It is *theopneustos*, which literally means "the breath of God." If that is true, then it's no wonder that it can benefit humanity by teaching us, showing us where we are wrong, telling us how to correct our mistakes, and ensure that we stay on the right path.

There is another verse that goes even deeper into the subject. The writer to the Hebrews tells us that, *"the word of God is living and active and sharper than any two-edged sword, and piercing as far as the division of soul and spirit, of both joints and marrow,*

---

[149] II Timothy 3:16-17

and able to judge the thoughts and intentions of the heart."[150] This speaks to the power of the word of God. The metaphor of bone and marrow graphically depicts how deep the power of Scripture extends. It discerns the issues of the soul and the spirit, that is, that which makes us human and that which forms our spiritual core.

No other book can make these kinds of claims. The Bible is not just a rulebook whereby God "throws the flag" and penalizes us every time we get out of line. The Bible is a book that is meant for our prosperity, to help us learn how to live life. That makes it a worthy book to study and hold on to.

THE CANON OF SCRIPTURE

The word *Bible* originally came from the name of the papyrus or byblos reed that was used extensively for writing in Egypt. Cutting them into one-foot strips, then laying another layer crossways over the top and pressing the water out of them made crude "paper." These were glued together to form a papyrus scroll that would disintegrate fairly quickly necessitating constant copying.[151] By the 2nd century AD, Greek Christians were referring to the collections of sacred scriptures as *ta Biblia*, "the Books." Eventually "biblia" was used by Latin speaking Christians to denote all the books of the Old and New Testaments.[152]

The Bible is comprised of 66 individual books (37 in the Old Testament and 29 in the New Testament). These books were written over a 1500-year period of time in three different languages on three continents by forty authors from every walk of life including kings, poets, scholars, musicians, shepherds, fishermen,

---

[150] Hebrews 4:12

[151] Josh McDowell, *The New Evidence That Demands a Verdict*, rev. ed. (Nashville: Thomas Nelson Publishers, 1999), 17-18.

[152] Merrill Unger, *The Unger's Bible Dictionary*, 3rd ed. (Chicago: Moody Press, 1979), 143.

a farmer, a tax collector, a physician, and a Pharisee.[153] These books were eventually codified into the canon of Scripture. The word *canon* is a Greek word meaning "measuring rod," which references the criterion used to determine which books would be included.

By the end of the first century AD the Jewish Old Testament had been pretty well established, though not formally codified. What we now know as the New Testament books had just been completed around 96 AD, but it became apparent fairly quickly that an official canon of New Testament writings needed to be established.

This was needed because, as the genuine writings of Paul and the apostles were being circulated among the churches, a number of fraudulent documents also appeared. In addition, the persecution of the church forced many Christians to flee their homes in Israel. When Emperor Diocletian issued an edict to burn all sacred Christian books in 303 AD, the church began to take steps to recognize an official canon.[154]

Amazingly, Emperor Constantine came to power in 306 AD and ceased the persecution of Christians. This enabled the Christian community to gather and formally begin the process of canonization. But this doesn't indicate any sort of litmus test that was set up in advance. The following standards were observed more than invented.

Authorship – In the Old Testament, the authorship of Moses, the historical books, the wisdom literature, and the prophets were never questioned. Rejection of any additional books to the Old Testament canon was based on their adherence to the Torah, since "no book that contradicted the Torah would be accepted, because the Torah was believed to be God's Word, and no

---

[153] Josh McDowell, *Evidence for Christianity* (Nashville, TN: Thomas Nelson Publishers, 2006), 30.

[154] Ibid, 171.

subsequent word from God could contradict a previous one."[155] In the New Testament any book not written by an apostle or their associate was rejected.[156]

Agreement – The writings had to be in agreement with other books in the canon. This was an amazing feat that would be impossible in any other collection of writings written over a period of 1500 years. The Bible shows perfect agreement on issues like history, prophecy, salvation, the church, the nature of man, the description of sin, and a host of other issues.

Usage – Possibly the most critical standard was the usage of the book in the life of the church. In 170 AD, Melito, Bishop of Sardis, affirmed the Christian acceptance and usage of the Old Testament canon as accepted by the Jews.[157] In addition, virtually all the New Testament books were "clearly known, reverenced, canonized, and collected well before a hundred years had passed."[158] Brooke Foss Westcott, a noted nineteenth century scholar, did extensive research in the writings of early church fathers Clement, Irenaeus, and Polycarp to ascertain their level of acceptance for the books of the New Testament. Harris summarizes his work, saying, with the exception of 2 Peter, all the books of the New Testament were "universally accepted" by 170 AD.[159] Eventually 2 Peter was settled with the same universal affirmation.[160]

Is it authoritative? – Those examining the books being used also asked if it had authority, having a sense of "Thus saith the Lord?" This might have been a more subjective test, and yet it

---

[155] Norman L. Geisler, William E. Nix, *A General Introduction to the Bible,* rev., (Chicago: Moody Press, 1986), 209.

[156] Ibid., 213.

[157] R. Laird Harris, *Inspiration and Canonicity of the Bible: An Historical and Exegetical Study* (Grand Rapids, Michigan: Zondervan Publishing House, 1971). 188..

[158] Ibid., 202.

[159] Ibid., 217-218.

[160] Ibid., 260.

was clearly seen in the writings of Scriptures such as "*[W]e command you brethren, in the name of our Lord Jesus Christ . . .*" (2 Thessalonians 3:6), or "*[T]he word of the Lord came to Abram . . .*" (Genesis 15:1), where the readers sensed clearly the authority of the Lord was behind the writing.

Is it authentic? – For example, 2 Peter was one of the last books to gain full recognition. But there is no evidence that the book was not written by Peter, and his claim to apostolic authority in 2 Peter 3:2, his bold assertion of the writings of Paul as Scripture in 2 Peter 3:16, and the scope and tenor of the book led to the unquestioned inclusion of the book into the canon. Jude, whose authenticity was never questioned, even quoted from 2 Peter in Jude 4 and 17 forward, cementing the credentials of the book as authentic.[161]

Is it dynamic? – The last issue focused on the inherent spiritual power of the document. The book had to contain a dynamic, life-changing power that only comes from God. This dynamic presence is seen in the prophetic books with the promises of God for the future, the wisdom literature, the historical books that chronicle God's hand on the people of Israel, certainly in the gospels, and in the powerful doctrinal books written by Paul.

THE OLD TESTAMENT CANON

The canonization of the Old Testament was a process that simply recognized what was already in use. The decision to include various documents into the collection was never made by a committee or person. This can be traced in the following manner.

The writings of Moses were the first stage. From the very beginning we know that "*Moses wrote down all the words of the Lord . . .*"[162] and the previous verse indicates the people regarded them as God's words, pledging to obey them. They were stored in the

---

[161] Ibid., 229.
[162] Exodus 24:4

tabernacle beside the Ark of the Covenant, they were read in the hearing of all the people, and future kings used them in making their judgments.[163]

After Moses, an unbroken chain of prophetic writers continued to record God's words. Joshua added his words *"[I]n the book of the law of God . . ."*[164] Samuel *"[T]old the people the ordinances of the kingdom, and wrote them in the book and placed it before the Lord."*[165] These writers were clearly aware of the many prophetic writings covering the entire history of Israel from David to the exile.[166] The acts of David's son Solomon were *"[W]ritten in the records [lit. "writings"] of Nathan the prophet . . ."*[167]

The high respect for the *"law of Moses"* by later writers demonstrated an acceptance of his works as God's words that were non-negotiable.[168] Later prophets continued to receive God's Word. For example, God instructed Isaiah, *"Now go, write it on a tablet before them and inscribe it on a scroll, that it may serve in the time to come as a witness forever."*[169] We find essentially the same instructions to Jeremiah, Ezekiel, Daniel, and Habakkuk.[170] Laird Harris comments:

> The law was accorded the respect of the author, and he was known as God's messenger. Similarly, succeeding prophets were received upon due authentication, and their written works were received with the same respect, being received therefore as the Word of God. As far as the witness contained

---

163 Deuteronomy 31:24-26; 31:11; 17:18
164 Joshua 24:26
165 1 Samuel 10:25
166 1 Chronicles 29:29
167 2 Chronicles 9:29
168 2 Chronicles 30:16; Ezekiel 43:11; Daniel 12:4; Habakkuk 2:2
169 Isaiah 30:8
170 Jeremiah 36:2-4; Ezekiel 43:11; Daniel 12:4; Habakkuk 2:2

in the books themselves is concerned, this reception was immediate.[171]

Acceptance of early writings by those writing later showed they were authoritative. Ezra read from the Pentateuch, regarding it as law.[172] Zechariah recognized *"[T]he law and the words which the Lord of hosts had sent by His Spirit through the former prophets . . . ,"*[173] and Daniel regarded the prophecies of Jeremiah as coming from God.[174]

In addition to the biblical writers, Josephus, the noted Jewish historian (37-101 AD) regarded the canonicity of the Old Testament books that we know as authentic. He stated that although records were kept since the time of Artaxerxes (464-424 BC), they were not on an equal par with earlier holy writings, "[B]ecause the exact succession of the prophets ceased."[175] In his book, *Against Apion* he clearly outlined the Jewish attitude toward the Scriptures, saying,

> For we have not an innumerable multitude of books among us, disagreeing from and contradicting one another (as the Greeks have) but only twenty-two books [due to splitting a number of books like I and II Samuel], which contain the records of all the past times; which are justly believed to be divine.[176]

The Council of Jamnia formally codified the Old Testament canon in 90 AD. The persecution mentioned at the beginning of this chapter pushed remaining Jewish leaders to codify their Scriptures. After the last Jewish holdouts were destroyed on

---

[171] Harris, *Inspiration and Canonicity of the Bible*, 156.
[172] Nehemiah 8:8
[173] Zechariah 7:12
[174] Daniel 9:2
[175] Harris, *Inspiration and Canonicity of the Bible*, 98.
[176] Brian Edwards, *Nothing But the Truth* (Welwyn: Hertfordshire, England, Evangelical Press, 1978), 106.

Masada, this became somewhat of an emergency measure. The primary focus of the council was the right of certain books to remain in the canon, not the acceptance of new books.[177]

The Council did not vote or consider any books. Instead, it considered the decisions of previous rabbis. The tractate *Pirke Aboth* ("Sayings of the Fathers") contains the "chain of tradition" which goes back through the rabbis, through the men of the Great Synagogue, through Ezra and previous rabbis, back through the seventy elders who assisted Moses and to Moses himself.[178]

Though written later, we also find confirmation for the canon of the Old Testament from the Talmud. The Talmud is an ancient "collection of rabbinical laws, decisions and comments on the law of Moses" that were written to preserve the oral traditions of the Jews.[179] The Jerusalem Talmud dated from approximately 350-425 AD. By that time the Talmud spoke of a closed canon where books could not be added or removed. The Talmud said, "After the latter prophets Haggai, Zechariah, and Malachi, the Holy Spirit departed from."[180]

THE NEW TESTAMENT CANON

Much like the Old Testament canon, after the New Testament books were written they were gathered into today's format because of usage among the early churches, not by the decisions of men or councils.

Investigation and writing

After scrutinizing documents of the New Testament to determine authenticity, they were given the full weight of authority.

---

[177] David Ewert, *From Ancient Tablets to Modern Translations: A General Introduction to the Bible* (Grand Rapids: Zondervan, 1983), 71.

[178] Harris, *Inspiration and Canonicity of the Bible*, 156.

[179] McDowell, *The New Evidence That Demands a Verdict*, 28.

[180] Robert Saucy, *The Bible: Breathed From God* (Wheaton: Victor Books, 1978), 97-98.

Luke's testimony puts forth the careful process he went through to accurately determine what had happened and write it down. In Luke 1:1-4 he states,

> Inasmuch as many have undertaken to compile an account of the things accomplished among us, just as they were handed down to us by those who from the beginning were eyewitnesses and servants of the word, it seemed fitting for me as well, having investigated everything carefully from the beginning, to write it out for you in consecutive order, most excellent Theophilus; so that you might know the exact truth about the things you have been taught.[181]

Paul also demonstrated this kind of careful research when he wrote to the new Thessalonian church telling them that he was thankful that *"[W]hen you received the word of God which you heard from us, you accepted it not as the word of men, but for what it really is, the word of God, which also performs its work in you who believe."*[182] This combination of the author knowingly writing God's words and the people knowing that they were reading God's words is a testament to the authenticity of the words of the New Testament.

Usage and acceptance

Once the documents were verified, they were read among the earliest groups that formed as churches. In writing to the Thessalonian church Paul said, *"I adjure you by the Lord to have this letter read to all the brethren."*[183] He gave similar instructions to the Colossian church; *"When this letter is read among you, have*

---

[181] Luke 1:1-3
[182] 1 Thessalonians 2:13
[183] 1 Thessalonians 5:27

it also read in the church of the Laodiceans; and you, for your part read my letter that is coming from Laodicea."[184]

It was evident that Paul's letters carried weight and authority because they were immediately circulated and read among the churches. Both Paul and the people recognized that God was speaking through him. Paul understood that he spoke, "*[N]ot in words taught by human wisdom, but in those, combining spiritual thoughts with spiritual words.*"[185] He even spoke of his words as being "*the Lord's commandment.*"[186] This gave the words their initial authority. They were God's words spoken for the benefit of His people. This is why Paul states the early church was built on the "*[F]oundation of the apostles and prophets . . .*"[187]

New Testament writers equated with Scripture

But the acceptance of authenticity went further. The New Testament writers also equated other New Testament writers on a par with Scripture. Paul recognized Luke's writing carried the same weight as Old Testament Scripture by quoting from both Deuteronomy and Luke when he told Timothy, "*For the Scripture says, 'You shall not muzzle the ox while he is threshing, and 'The laborer is worthy of his wages.*"[188]

Peter does the same thing regarding Paul's writing. The obvious respect and spiritual regard Peter had for Paul is evident when he referred to Paul as "our beloved brother Paul" who wrote to them, "*[A]ccording to the wisdom given him, wrote to you, as also in all his letters, speaking in them of these things, in which are some things hard to understand, which the untaught and unstable distort, as they do also the rest of the Scriptures, to their own destruction.*"[189]

---

[184] Colossians 4:16
[185] 1 Corinthians 2:13
[186] 1 Corinthians 14:37
[187] Ephesians 2:20
[188] 1 Timothy 5:18 – quotes both Deuteronomy 25:4 and Luke 10:7
[189] II Peter 3:15-16

This is all the more remarkable when we understand that Paul had opposed Peter in his letter to the Galatians for temporarily defecting to the Judaizers who wanted to compromise the gospel by a return to Old Testament law. And yet Peter refers to Paul as a *"beloved brother"* who had *"wisdom given to him"* so that *"all his letters"* were regarded as Scripture. This was a mark of great humility and character that allowed Peter to acknowledge Paul's words as Scripture.

The diaspora

The completion of the New Testament documents closed the New Testament era. Upon investigation of these early years it seems evident that almost all the twenty-seven books of the New Testament were known, collected, reverenced, and used by the end of the first century AD. During the first half of the next century, "[G]ood evidence exists that within fifty years of their writing, the Gospels (which make up about a half of the whole) and the major Pauline Epistles were fully accepted as canonical."[190]

But it is also important to remember the persecution we mentioned earlier. As Christians were driven from their homes, they lived under the threat of persecution until the time of Constantine around 320 AD.

This persecution impelled unknowing missionaries who took their newfound faith with them to the known world at the time. It also prevented any kind of collection of documents because pastors and scholars didn't have the luxury of councils and gatherings to discuss issues like the canon. That's why there is no evidence of the process of canonization for a period of time after the first generation of disciples. But that doesn't mean the early documents were lost.

---

[190] Harris, *Inspiration and Canonicity of the Bible*, 202.

Three great bishops of the early church provide a link between the Apostle John and the time of the Apostolic Fathers that was critical in preserving the thread of authenticity. Polycarp (69-155 AD) knew the Apostle John. It is also possible he knew Philip and other apostles as well. Irenaeus, a bishop of Antioch, ordained in 69 AD and martyred some time before 117 AD, is also said to have known some of the apostles. Clement, the bishop of Rome around 95 AD was also contemporaneous with the time of some of the apostles.

All of these men made numerous references to most of the books of the New Testament, alluding to them in their own writings as authoritative, giving reverence to them. These early leaders and martyrs relied heavily on the written words of the New Testament books.[191]

Early documents

There are also a large number of documents that validate the continuous chain of the New Testament documents from the time of the apostles to the earliest copies of the New Testament we have today. *The Code of Hammurabi*, the *Ebla Tablets*, the *Cyrus Cylinder*, the *Rosetta Stone*, and the *Nuzi Tablets* are just a few of the many documents that authenticate the writings of the Old Testament.

In like manner the *John Rylands Fragment* (dating from 117 AD), the *Codex Vaticanus*, the *Codex Sinaiticus*, the *Chester Beatty Papyri*, the *Bodmer Papyrus II*, and the *Muratorian Canon* are listed among the plethora of documents that validate the writing of the New Testament. Anyone who doubts the accuracy and authenticity of both the New Testament and the Old Testament are ignoring the mountain of documentation extant in the libraries of the world today.

The Councils

---

[191] Ibid., 203-207.

When Constantine decriminalized Christianity around 320 AD various leaders began to gather and compare their writings. Eventually they gathered in various church councils to discuss the doctrines taught in these documents. The councils never decided which documents to use. They merely used the documents that had been carried and preserved by itinerant Christians in their churches for the past three hundred years.

One of the first Christian Councils to convene was the Council of Nicea in 325 AD. Although the main issue of the Council was the Christological debate between Arius and Athanasius, it is significant in a discussion of the formation of the canon because the Council spent much time debating specific words and phrases in the Scripture without debating the authority of any of the books discussed. It seems obvious that the books of the New Testament were accepted at the Council as the basis of orthodox faith without debate.[192]

The Council of Laodicea in 363 AD was the first council to affirm the exact canon as we know it today, affirming the reading and usage of the Old Testament and the twenty-seven books of the New Testament. The Council limited future usage of biblical writings to these books only. The Council of Hippo (393 AD) and the Council of Carthage (397 AD) affirmed the same canon.[193]

TWO TESTS

It is also helpful to talk about two tests that can be applied to any writing of antiquity to determine its authenticity. The results of these tests add greatly to our confidence in any ancient document, but especially in reference to the original documents that formed the Bible.

---

[192] John McClintock and James Strong, *Cyclopedia of Biblical, Theological, and Ecclesiastical Literature, vol. 7* (1867-1887, repr., Grand Rapids: Baker Book House, 1867-1887), 44-45.

[193] Paul Enns, Moody *Handbook of Theology* (Chicago: Moody Press, 1989), 172.

Number of documents

All writings of antiquity would have degenerated fairly quickly because the material they were written on decayed rapidly. This made it necessary to consistently make copies of these documents. The number of documents extant in libraries and museums around the world today add credibility to the original document that has long since perished.

There is a treasure trove of documents attesting the Old Testament. Benjamin Kennicott gathered the first collection of Hebrew manuscripts between 1776 and 1780. There were 615 manuscripts, and they were published by Oxford. In the 1890s the most important discovery of Old Testament manuscripts in modern times occurred in Cairo. Two hundred thousand ancient manuscripts were found in a geniza, which is a term used to designate an attic storehouse where old and unused ancient manuscripts were stored until they could be disposed of properly. Some ten thousand of them were biblical in nature.[194]

The British Museum is also a depository of 161 Old Testament manuscripts. And the Bodleian Library at Oxford University lists 146 manuscripts, each containing a large number of fragments. Moshe Goshen-Gosttein estimates that there are tens of thousands of Semitic manuscript fragments, over five thousand of which are biblical, in the United States. That's quite a large number when you consider the delicate nature of preserved manuscripts of antiquity.[195]

Archaeological evidence for the Old Testament documents is also plentiful. Over the years, archaeologists have uncovered a treasure trove of information corroborating the Old Testament. And their witness to the validity of the biblical records is quite

---

[194] Moshe Goshen-Gostein, *Bible Manuscripts in the U. S., Textus 3*, 1962, quoted in Josh McDowell, *The New Evidence That Demands a Verdict*, rev. ed. (Nashville: Thomas Nelson Publishers, 1999), 72.

[195] McDowell, *The New Evidence That Demands a Verdict*, 72.

astounding. The prominent Jewish archaeologist, Nelson Glueck said, "It may be stated categorically that no archaeological discovery has ever controverted a biblical reference."[196] And William Foxwell Albright, the preeminent American archaeologist of his time, affirmed, "There can be no doubt that archaeology has confirmed the substantial historicity of Old Testament tradition."[197]

Examples of these can be seen in the *Ebla Tablets* comprised of 17,000 cuneiform tablets dating from 2300 BC (1000 years before Moses who is regarded by some as living before writing had even been invented), the *Mari Tablets*, the *Cyrus Cylinder* (in the British Museum), and the *Hammurabi Code*, an 8 foot tall black rock column, dating from three centuries before Moses, that contains an etched picture of King Hammurabi receiving a scepter and a ring as well as 282 paragraphs describing the rights and responsibilities of all Babylonians living at the time.[198]

In like manner, the number of New Testament documents available today dwarfs those of any other ancient writing. Of all the ancient documents known to modern scholars, the one with the highest number of extant documents in any library in the world is *The Iliad* by Homer. There are 643 manuscripts of *The Iliad* that still exist.

But that number is not even close to the number of New Testament documents that can be seen in a variety of museums and libraries in the world today. A partial list of the New Testament documents known to exist today in a variety of the languages they were copied into includes:

[196] Nelson Glueck, *Rivers in the Desert: History of Negev* (Philadelphia: Jewish Publications Society of America, 1969), 31.

[197] William Foxwell Albright, *Archaeology and the Religions of Israel* (Baltimore: Johns Hopkins University Press, 1956), 176.

[198] Joseph Free, *Archaeology and Bible History* (Wheaton: Scripture Press, 1950), 121.

- Greek – 5, 686
- The Latin Vulgate – over 10,000
- Ethiopic – 2,000 plus
- Slavic – 4,101
- Armenian – 2,587 plus
- Others – 596
- Total – 24,970[199]

As you can see, the sheer number of documents for the New Testament in comparison to the number of documents for the next highest book of its time is very convincing. The writings of Caesar and Plato are universally accepted and yet some question the credibility of the New Testament. The number of documents for the New Testament argues against that position.

Time span

The other test in lending evidence to the credibility of an ancient text is the time span between the original writing and the earliest copy. The main issue here is the degeneration of ancient writing materials. The issue is simple, the shorter time span between the time of the writing and the earliest copy, the more accurate the copy.

Again, the documentation is overwhelming. Let me illustrate. Everyone accepts the historicity of Caesar and Plato. The following chart,[200] abbreviated from Josh McDowell's *A Ready Defense*, is helpful.

---

[199] McDowell, *The New Evidence That Demands a Verdict*, 34.
[200] Josh McDowell, (Nashville, Tennessee: Thomas Nelson Inc., 1993), 45.

Author	Wrote	Earliest copy	Time span	No. of copies
Julius Caesar	100-44 BC	900 AD	1,000 years	10
Plato	427-347 BC	900 AD	1,200 years	7
Tacitus	100 AD	1100 AD	1,000 years	20
New Testament	40-100 AD	125 AD	25 years	Over 24,000

These are just three of the writers of antiquity that the New Testament documents are compared to. There are many others, but none that exceed the number of documents for the Iliad mentioned above, and none that has less of a time span between the time of the original writing and the earliest copy than the ones listed here. Norm Geisler, a prominent scholar on the New Testament documents notes,

> The average gap between the original composition and the earliest copy is over 1,000 years for other books. The New Testament, however, has a fragment within one generation from its original composition, whole books within about 100 years from the time of the autograph, most of the New Testament in less than 200 years, and the entire New Testament within 250 years of the date of its completion. (3) The degree of accuracy of the copies is greater for the New Testament than for other books that can be compared.[201]

Can the Bible be trusted?

I hope that you can see that the Bible can be trusted. It's disturbing to hear someone dismiss the Bible so easily with excuses like "It's been changed so much over time that it can't be trusted," or "People have interjected their thoughts into it." That's just not

---

[201] Norman Geisler, *Christian Apologetics, 2nd ed.*, (Grand Rapids, MI: Baker Academic, 2013), 345..

true. As we have seen, the biblical record has not been changed and is more trustworthy than any other ancient document.

From this point on, we will rely on the Bible to inform us on the issues at hand. If you do not believe the Bible is God's Word, and that it has been accurately preserved through the years, you will question everything we say from this point forward.

But if the Bible is true, then read on to see the implications.

CHAPTER EIGHT

"There is not a square inch in the entire domain of our human life of which Christ, who is sovereign of all, does not proclaim, 'Mine!'"[202]
—Abraham Kuyper

The Long Arm of the Law

Does God have the final say in all things?

The greatest intelligence resource for an undercover cop is a good informant—someone who has inside information making it easier to target those violating criminal law. While working as the narcotic sergeant, I received information from an informant disclosing criminal activity involving an old nemesis, Taha Mudin.

COOKING METHAMPHETAMINE

In the 1990's, methamphetamine (meth) replaced cocaine as the most popular drug for those abusing central nervous system stimulants in Southern California. Drug dealers no longer had to wait for cocaine to be smuggled into the U.S. from South America. They could produce a replica in their own home or

---

[202] James D. Bratt, ed., *Abraham Kuyper: A Centennial Reader* (Grand Rapids, Michigan: Eerdmans, 1998), 488.

local motel room. Outlaw bikers had been doing it for decades, but it now caught on with others.

The process simply required a combination of chemicals and some knowledge, and suddenly "*cooks*" (those who made *meth*— also known as *speed*, *crank*, and *crystal*) were in business everywhere. It was a high risk, high reward proposition. Because of the risks involved in cooking meth, coupled with the informal and limited education received by most cooks, law enforcement had a new problem on its hands—meth lab explosions. Southern California became the meth capital of the world, and explosions from the makeshift labs became a common news story.

Ephedrine is to methamphetamine what flour is to cake. The California State Legislature responded to the crisis and made ephedrine nearly impossible to obtain. One of the unintended consequences is that asthma sufferers could no longer obtain over-the-counter remedies since ephedrine was the primary ingredient in these medications.

Not to be deterred, the cooks modified their approach. At the time, pseudoephedrine was contained in nearly every cold remedy. As a result, these medications disappeared from shelves and warehouses in record numbers. Pseudoephedrine became like gold to producers of meth, and trafficking it became very profitable. That was one of the business ventures of Mudin.

We arrested him several years prior for possessing a large volume of pseudoephedrine with the intent of producing methamphetamine. Now, he was out of jail, but still on probation when I received the call from my informant.

We performed a probation compliance check at Mudin's home in Fountain Valley shortly after his release. The house was clean, but we knew he would continue his old tricks. Yet he would probably do so from a motel room to avoid detection—a common practice.

At times, *criminal behavior is so predictable, we feel prophetic.* That was the thought that crossed my mind when the informant told me Mudin was trafficking a large volume of pseudoephedrine, 15 miles north, at a motel in Anaheim.

Circumvent the law

Career criminals try to circumvent the law or pretend it isn't there. They ignore it to their peril because in their mind, the risk is worth the reward. And quite frankly, oftentimes it is—especially in California. But simply ignoring the law or shifting your base of operation to another location does not make it go away, as Mudin was about to discover.

My partner and I drove to Anaheim, a city I knew well as it was my childhood home. I remembered the motel as a vacant lot, a simple stone's throw from the streets of my youth. I recalled riding my gold Schwinn Stingray, with a banana seat, on dirt mounds, directly across the street from the military recruiter's office that had been one of my stops on the way to becoming a police officer.

Was the motel being used to facilitate the passage of drugs, or would it become an inferno by a novice trying to make a huge profit on the addiction of others? I was uncertain, but I felt compelled to protect the inhabitants and surrounding neighborhood from their illegal and dangerous activity.

Surveillance

Mudin had checked into the room using an alias. But when I showed the manager his picture, my old nemesis was quickly identified. As a result, we established a stakeout waiting for our "friend" to return.

Stationary surveillance was often measured in accumulated trash, not necessarily time. So, as I gazed at a banana peel, empty sandwich bag, peanut shells, an empty water bottle, and two disposed Styrofoam coffee cups on the passenger side floorboard of my undercover car—a Ford Mustang, I indeed knew I had been there for a significant period of time. Yet after several hours, there was no sight of Mudin.

When analyzing the reliability of information from an informant, motive needs to be considered. In this case, revenge was a possibility. As such, I thought it was likely the informant was involved in a power play and spooked Mudin. Consequently, wanting to avoid an overnight surveillance, we entered his motel room under the authority of a probation search.

Finding precursor drugs

Finding the stash was easy. The room was empty with the exception of a large suitcase loaded with 50 pounds of pseudo-ephedrine tablets. The drugs would be the precursor to produce several pounds of methamphetamine. At the time one ounce of meth would sell for $600, so one pound could produce nearly $10,000 worth of the central nervous system stimulant. Mudin was in serious trouble, since the law was set in stone.

Goon squad

After we had been in the room for a short time some "goons" showed up in lieu of Mudin.

"Narco, get your hands up," I barked while showing them the barrel of my Sig Sauer P220 along with my police badge as they walked into the room with trepidation.

"Whaaaat? Heeey, what's all the fuss about? We're just here looking for a friend," one of the Chicago mobsters replied as cool as you can imagine. Apparently, having police point weapons at them was a routine part of their life.

"And who would that be?" I asked.

"Well, we're not exactly sure of his name. He's just a friend of a friend."

And so, the conversation continued, round and round in circles, neither side wanting to play their hand. Yet when you're the law, you usually have the advantage, which I did in this case.

Under the circumstances, a pat down was warranted. As a result, I found a loaded handgun on one of our visitors.

Although no one admitted it, I am certain they were sent to see if the "coast was clear." Consequently, they quickly discovered it was not, and the guy with the gun went to jail for being a convicted felon in possession of a firearm.

Arrest and extradition

Now Mudin was on the run. Would he be able to overcome his legal dilemma by fleeing to another location or discover the law had authority over him despite his constant disregard for it?

The informant called a few days later to say he left town. Mudin flew to Chicago and planned to stay with friends and wait to see if we issued a warrant for his arrest. I told the informant the warrant was pending, but in the meantime remained quiet. We didn't need Mudin to keep running.

When the informant discovered Mudin was staying with friends in Burbank, Illinois, I called the local police department located across the country and asked if they would serve the arrest warrant.

They were more than willing to oblige their counterparts in California. Hence, local officers in Illinois drove to the house in Burbank and knocked on the front door. Mudin learned that ignoring the law didn't make it less prevalent as he bolted from the rear of the house. After a short foot chase, he found himself face down on the ground wearing a pair of Peerless handcuffs.

Mudin was booked into Cook County Jail while I began paperwork for the extradition process. Once everything was in order, we began the trek that would take us 4,000 miles round trip and return Mudin to face justice in Orange County, California. Mudin later pleaded guilty to the charges and was sent to prison for a second time for the same offense. The long arm of the law was effective once again.

God's method of operation

Most people think that God favors getting guys like Taha Mudin off the streets, but that's about as far as it goes. They haven't really thought much about what He does and doesn't control in this world. Even many Christians view Him as the deists did—a doddering old man who set the world in motion and then retired to His study.

In the previous two chapters we saw that God is there and He has given us a written record that can be trusted. In this chapter we will look deep into the Bible and discover that God has the final say in everything. It may look like the Taha Mudins of this world are out of control and that God has taken a siesta. But we will find out this is not true at all. God is completely in control of all things.

But we can't talk about God's control without talking about what He does and how He does it—God's method of operation. And, contrary to popular belief, He does quite a lot. He has not retired. He doesn't merely show up on Sundays. And He is certainly not incompetent or incapable of handling the affairs of this world. In fact, there is nothing hidden or excluded from His view and His plan.

As Abraham Kuyper, the former Prime Minister of The Netherlands, and founder of the Free University of Amsterdam said, "There is not an inch in the entire domain of our human life of which Christ, who is sovereign of all, does not proclaim, 'Mine!'"[203] This is certainly worth investigating.

THE DECREE OF GOD

Theologians use a phrase the "decree of God" to describe the extent of God's actions. A decree is an edict or an order that causes something to happen. God's decree is "[H]is eternal purpose, according to the counsel of his will, whereby, for his own

---

[203] Bratt, ed., *Abraham Kuyper: A Centennial Reader*, 488.

glory, he hath foreordained whatsoever comes to pass."[204] A little longer definition is voiced by A.A. Hodge who notes that:

> The decree of God therefore is the act of an infinite, absolute, eternal, unchangeable, and sovereign person, comprehending a plan including all his works of all kinds, great and small, from the beginning of creation to an unending eternity. It must therefore be incomprehensible, and it cannot be conditioned by any thing exterior to God himself—since it was matured before any thing exterior to him existed. And hence itself embraces and determines all these supposed exterior things and all the conditions of them forever."[205]

Let me put this into a sports analogy. If you are a sports fan you have no doubt heard about Babe Ruth's "called shot" in the 1932 World Series between the Yankees and Cubs. The score was 4-4 in the fifth inning of game three. The Babe had already hit one home run during the game, so the Cub's bench jockeys were riding him pretty hard. After Charlie Root's first pitch was called a strike, he pointed his bat to the outfield. After strike two he pointed again, this time with more flair.

There has been great debate over the years about what he was pointing at and what he said. But there is distinct video that can even be seen today of him pointing to center field as if to "call" his home run in advance. The rest is history. On the 0-2 count Babe parked the last homer of his postseason career more than 490 feet from home plate. As if to add to the drama of Babe's "called shot," the next batter, Lou Gehrig, homered as well, also his second of the day. The Cubs appeared demoralized. They lost

---

[204] Lewis Sperry Chafer, *Systematic Theology, vol. 7*, (repr., 1948, Grand Rapids, MI: Kregel Publications, 1976), 228.

[205] A. A. Hodge, *Outlines of Theology* (repr., 1860, Edinburgh: Banner of Truth Trust, 1991), 201.

that game 7-5 and went on to lose the next game 13-6 to complete a four-game sweep by the Yankees.

In the same way, God "calls" his shots. Most people are okay with this as long as it only includes the "nice" and "easy" things in life. We believe God is sovereign as long as our team wins the ballgame, or we never get cancer, or a tornado never tears up our city.

But God has jurisdiction over those things as well. God "calls" the most difficult things for people to understand. And He does this in advance, according to His wise, omnipotent decree. This is hard for us to grasp, but let's investigate what the Bible says about this.

THE DESCRIPTION OF GOD'S DECREE

Describing God's decree in fuller detail might be helpful. These characteristics are logical and in keeping with God's character. His decree is:

1. *Self-founded* – Isaiah asked, "*Who has directed the Spirit of the Lord, or as His counselor has informed Him? With whom did He consult and who gave Him understanding?*"[206] God has no tutor, no coach, no mentor, no teacher, no counselor, no peer. He doesn't ask questions or learn from anyone!
2. *Intentional and authoritative* – Again Isaiah notes "*My purpose will be established, and I will accomplish all My good pleasure . . . Truly I have spoken; truly I will bring it to pass. I have planned it, surely I will do it.*"[207] The decree of God is the last word in all things.
3. *Eternal* – The Psalmist proclaims, "*The counsel of the Lord stands forever, the plans of His heart from generation to*

---

[206] Isaiah 40:13-14
[207] Isaiah 46:10-11

generation."[208] God doesn't make His decisions as history unfolds. He doesn't learn. He doesn't grow. His decree is one simultaneous coherent decision.

4. *Effective* – Isaiah helps us again, saying, *"Surely, just as I have intended so it has happened, and just as I have planned so it will stand'... For the Lord of hosts has planned, and who can frustrate it? And as for His stretched-out hand, who can turn it back?"*[209] God is the master of organization. All His plans are fully functional and fulfilled.

5. *Transcendent* – *"...according to His purchase who works all things after the counsel of His will,"* and the *"Lord nullifies the counsel of the nations; He frustrates the plans of the peoples."*[210] God's decree is above man's ability to comprehend. Man relates to the world from the closed system of his own understanding. But God is outside that box.

6. *All-inclusive* – This covers everything that happens in the world at all times. King Solomon wrote, *"He has made everything appropriate in its time. He has also set eternity in their heart, yet so that man will not find out the work which God has done from the beginning even to the end."*[211] What's the alternative? Chance? What person would you want to be in charge?

7. *Fair* – Matthew tells us *"He causes His sun to rise on the evil and the good, and sends rain on the righteous and the unrighteous."*[212]

8. *Immutable* – Perhaps the most powerful example of this is Peter's claim that Jesus was *"delivered over by the predetermined plan and foreknowledge of God, you nailed to a*

---

[208] Psalm 33:11
[209] Isaiah 14:24, 27
[210] Ephesians 1:11; Psalm 33:10
[211] Ecclesiastes 3:11
[212] Matthew 5:45

cross by the hands of godless men and put Him to death." [213]
Jonathan Edwards comments on this passage noting that
this means that "[A]ll the sins of men are foreordained
and ordered by a wise Providence."[214]

9. *For God's glory* – God reveals, *"For My own sake, for My
own sake, I will act; for how can My name be profaned? And
My glory I will not give to another."*[215] This sounds pompous
but it's not. Seeking God's glory simply means that making
God's ways known, and obeying them, is the only way that
accomplishes ultimate good for man and properly reveals
God's perfect provision.

Resisting God doesn't make sense, but we do it anyway. As
songwriter Jim Croce recorded years ago, "You don't tug on
Superman's cape, you don't spit into the wind, you don't pull
the mask off the old Lone Ranger, and you don't mess around
with Jim."[216] The parallel is you don't mess around with God's
unchangeable decree because it's useless and doesn't bring about
anything that is ultimately good for us.

THE APPLICATION OF GOD'S DECREE

Rather than resist it, it is far better to apply it. We make a
grave mistake when we think that God is limited by history or
"nature" or man's activities. Things that look big to us are not
even bumps in the road to God. And it is incredibly naïve for
someone to wave their fist to the sky and dare God to strike them
down for their blasphemy. God is not governed by the pompous
acts of little people who think they have proven there is no God.

---

213 Acts 2:23

214 Jonathan Edwards, *The Works of Jonathan Edwards A. M., Vol. 2,*
(London: William Ball, 34, Paternoster-Row, 1838), 528.

215 Isaiah 48:11

216 Jim Croce, "You Don't Mess Around With Jim," from *You Don't Mess
Around With Jim,* Sony/ATV Music Publishing LLC, Warner/Chappell Music,
Inc., BMG RIGHTS MANAGEMENT US, LLC..

His decree over creation

We gain much in our understanding of His decree by starting in Genesis, the book of beginnings. We find there that "*God created man in His own image, in the image of God He created him; male and female He created them.*"[217] Man was the apex of all that He created. The passage continues, "*God saw all that He had made, and behold, it was very good.*"[218] This is important because this means that God made this pronouncement before we are told that "*[T]he tree of life was also in the midst of the garden, and the tree of the knowledge of good and evil.*"[219]

Given that sequence, the logical question is how could the creation of the "*tree of the knowledge of good and evil*" be "*very good?*" The answer is it was "*very good*" because it provided the soil from which God's plan for the salvation of humanity was born. It's important to remember that God created this tree *before* Adam and Eve sinned. If He had not created things this way we would have ended up as robots.

But God didn't want robots. He can *ordain* evil without *being* evil. He didn't *make* man sin. But, in His sovereign will, He created the space for man's sinful choices so *that* He could exercise his judgment on the sin of man and yet forgive and save him! This is what Paul is talking about when he says, "*For God has shut up all in disobedience so that He may show mercy to all.*"[220] He further tells us that, "*[A]ll have sinned and fall short of the glory of God,*"[221] and, "*He saved us, not on the basis of deeds which we have done in righteousness, but according to His mercy . . .*"[222]

Many artists have depicted the ensuing banishment of Adam and Eve from the Garden of Eden. Masaccio's *Expulsion from*

---

[217] Genesis 1:27
[218] Genesis 1:31
[219] Genesis 2:9
[220] Romans 11:32
[221] Romans 3:23
[222] Titus 3:5

Paradise hangs in the church of Santa Maria del Carmine in Florence, Italy. Masaccio depicts the absolute anguish of Adam and Eve as they are driven away from the garden by an angel who hovers overhead, sword in hand. Adam's head is bowed, and he covers his face with his hands. Eve's head is thrown back and her mouth is open in an anguished cry. The misery of humanity seems to be etched into their whole being as a consequence of their sin.[223]

This wasn't plan B. It was His sovereign plan from before the foundation of the earth. Without sin there would be no salvation. They are both included in His plan.

His decree over time

God's decree also functions in history. The Old Testament prophet Isaiah began his work in 739 BC and provides a picture of this. Isaiah recorded God speaking about a man named Cyrus. God said, "*It is I who says of Cyrus, 'He is My shepherd! And he will perform all My desire.' And he declares of Jerusalem, 'She will be built,' and of the temple, 'Your foundation will be laid.'*"[224]

So, who is Cyrus? Ezra, an Old Testament priest who led the first wave of Jewish captives back to Israel after seventy years of captivity in Babylon, tells us who this is. The very first words of the book of Ezra mention "*[T]he first year of Cyrus king of.*"[225] History tells us that Cyrus, the king of Persia was born in 600 BC, and issued this decree in Isaiah in 538 BC.

Ezra continues, saying the decree was given "*[I]n order to fulfill the word of the Lord by the mouth of Jeremiah . . .*" Jeremiah was a prophet in Israel who prophesied from around 627 BC to 586 BC when the Babylonian King Nebuchadnezzar sacked Israel.

---

[223] James Montgomery Boice, *Genesis: An Expositional Commentary, Volume 1, Genesis 1-11*, rev., (Grand Rapids Michigan: Baker Books, 1998), 242.

[224] Isaiah 44:28

[225] Ezra 1:1

The prophecy of Jeremiah was that *"This whole land will be a desolation and a horror, and these nations will serve the king of Babylon seventy years."*[226]

Now go back to the passage in Ezra to see the content of the decree issued by Cyrus in 538 BC. In order to fulfill the prophesy of Jeremiah, which was that Israel would be in captivity for seventy years, Ezra notes, *"[T]he Lord stirred up the spirit of Cyrus king of Persia, so that he sent a proclamation throughout all his kingdom, and also put it in writing, saying: 'Thus says Cyrus king of Persia, 'The Lord, the God of heaven, has given me all the kingdoms of the earth and He has appointed me to build Him a house in Jerusalem, which is in Judah.'"*[227]

Do the math and you'll discover that Isaiah mentioned Cyrus' name almost 140 years *before* he was even born, and almost 180 years *before* he issued this decree! His decree in Ezra ended the seventy years prophesied by Jeremiah.

There is another wrinkle to this. First century Jewish historian Josephus has an account of Cyrus reading this proclamation by Isaiah. Though Josephus doesn't mention it, it seems very likely that Cyrus was shown the account by Daniel, a Jewish statesman captured as a young man by Nebuchadnezzar who spent almost the entire seventy years of captivity in Babylon.

Daniel tells us that he *"[O]bserved in the books the number of the years which was revealed as the word of the Lord to Jeremiah the prophet for the completion of the desolations of Jerusalem, namely, seventy years."*[228] When Daniel read the prophecies of Jeremiah regarding the seventy years of captivity, we can deduce fairly easily that he would have also read the prophecies of Isaiah. As Josephus notes, when Daniel pointed to Cyrus' name in these Jewish prophets, Cyrus' eyes must have bugged out. It's

---

[226] Jeremiah 25:11
[227] Ezra 1:1-2
[228] Daniel 9:2

quite amazing to think that God "stirred up the heart" of Cyrus through the events of history.

His decree over evil

Now that we know who Cyrus is, let's go back to Isaiah. In the first verse right after the chapter where Cyrus is mentioned we find, "*Thus says the Lord to Cyrus His anointed, whom I have taken by the right hand, to subdue nations before him and to loose the loins of kings.*"[229] A couple of verses later God continues, "*I have also called you by your name; I have given you a title of honor though you have not known Me . . . I will gird you, though you have not known Me; that men may know from the rising to the setting of the sun that there is no one besides Me. I am the Lord, and there is no other.*"[230]

God is explaining Himself to a foreign pagan leader. But that does nothing to curtail the reach of His decree. He is not limited in bringing his people back to their land by time or personalities. Cyrus was simply a pawn in his hands.

Isaiah then makes a startling statement about the decree of God when he describes God as "*The One forming light and creating darkness, causing well-being and creating calamity; I am the Lord who does all these.*"[231] The historical setting of these words provides a potent example of God's decree in real time.

The bottom line is that the years of sin of Israel, the rise of pagan Babylon as a world power, the seventy years of captivity in Babylon, the proclamation of the pagan King Cyrus, and the return of Israel to her own land are all contained in the phrase saying God is "creating calamity." But this calamity is all with a purpose.

Note that God explains to Cyrus that He (God) is "*creating calamity.*" The grammar here indicates this is part of the continuing actions of God. The word "*creating*" is not hard to understand

---

[229] Isaiah 45:1
[230] Isaiah 45:4-6
[231] Isaiah 45:7

in any language. It is the same word we saw in Genesis where we find, "*In the beginning, God created the heavens and the earth.*" The Hebrew word is bara. It has a,

> [P]rofound theological significance, since it has only God as its subject. Only God can "create" in the sense implied by bara. The verb expresses creation out of nothing. The writer uses scientifically precise language to demonstrate that God brought the object or concept into being from previously nonexistent material."[232]

Don't lose the significance of this. God created all of the events that led up to Cyrus' proclamation to rebuild Jerusalem. That's a massive plan that was worked out literally over hundreds of years. This shows us God is surely in control of history and calendars.

We also gain insight by looking at what God's decree creates. The Hebrew word used for "*calamity*" is the noun "*ra*" which means "evil" or "distress." It is used in the Bible to describe physical pain,[233] emotional pain,[234] and the death of a family member,[235] among other things. Isaiah tells us God "*creates*" all of these. They don't just happen. He doesn't merely "allow" them; He "*creates*" them.

This makes most people, even mature Christians, pause a little. How can this be? The question is whether God *allows* evil or *causes* evil. Most people are willing to admit the first answer but not the second. Saying that God *allows* evil seems to be a reasonable way to merge the obvious existence of things that are bad with a loving God.

---

[232] W. E. Vine, Merrill F. Unger, William White, Jr., eds., *Vine's Complete Expository Dictionary of Old and New Testament Words* (repr., 1984, Nashville, Atlanta, London, Vancouver: Thomas Nelson Publishers, 1996), 1:51.

[233] 1 Chronicles 16:22

[234] Genesis 43:6

[235] Ruth 1:21

But is this really true? There is a logical problem with this perception that God *allows* evil because it leads to the logical question, "If God *allows* evil, then why doesn't He *stop it!?*" To be sure, God indeed will stop evil one day and judge it with finality. But what about the time between now and then? This is a serious problem for some.

Charles Templeton was a friend of Billy Graham's in the early 1940's. In fact, many thought that Templeton was destined to be the greatest evangelist since Dwight Moody or Billy Sunday. But his faith began to waiver over a single question. A picture of a North African woman he saw in *Life* magazine prompted the question. He comments,

> They were experiencing a devastating drought. And she was holding her dead baby in her arms and looking up to heaven with the most forlorn expression. I looked at it and I thought, 'Is it possible to believe that there is a loving or caring Creator when all this woman needed was rain?'" Templeton asked, "Who runs the rain? I don't, you don't. He does—or that's what I thought. But when I saw that photograph, I immediately knew it is not possible for this to happen and for there to be a loving God.[236]

Many people stumble over this and end up rejecting God, just like Templeton did. If God only *allows* evil, then we are left to think that either He *can't* stop it, or He *won't* stop it. He is either unable or unwilling. That means He is either unloving or incompetent. Either one is not a very good position for the God of the universe to be in. Neither of these positions is biblical so how can we resolve this?

---

[236] Lee Strobel, *The Case for Faith* (Grand Rapids, Michigan: Zondervan Publishing House, 2000), 14.

RESOLUTION OF HIS DECREE

God cannot do evil

First, we must assert that God cannot do evil. Although he is absolutely sovereign over all things, He neither initiates sin nor is He the author of sin in any way. He doesn't suggest it, encourage it, condone it, approve it, or wink His eye at it. You cannot connect God to the immorality of sin in any manner. Augustine, a leading intellect of the fourth century said, "Since God is the highest good, he would not allow any evil to exist in his works unless his omnipotence and goodness were such as to bring good even out of evil."[237]

We don't merely assume this. The Bible explicitly states this. The apostle John unequivocally states, *"This is the message we have heard from Him and announce to you, that God is Light, and in Him there is no darkness at all."*[238] The writers of the Psalms asserts, *"The Lord is good to all, and His mercies are over all His works."*[239] He also sets the eternal boundaries of His goodness by proclaiming, *"For the Lord is good; His loving kindness is everlasting and His faithfulness to all generations."*[240]

Surely no one could ever objectively assert that God is not good. For those who do, we can only conclude that they have conjured up some kind of being in their mind who doesn't exist. This usually comes from atheists who rail against the concept of God and yet call Him evil and bad.

God punishes evil

Second, we can also assert that God punishes evil. Those who attack God as evil grossly overlook this. Atheist British biology professor Richard Dawkins argues vehemently against God

---

[237] Ibid., 45.
[238] 1 John 1:5
[239] Psalm 145:9
[240] Psalm 100:5

because of his perception of God as "[A]rguably the most unpleasant character in all fiction; jealous and proud of it; a petty, unjust, unforgiving control freak; a vindictive . . . capriciously malevolent bully."[241] His argument for the evil nature of someone who doesn't exist in his mind is incongruous and humorous. This seems to me like the atheist's version of spitting into the wind. If God doesn't exist, why is Dawkins so mad at Him?

But, assuming that God is real, is Dawkins' characterization accurate? The answer to that would be "no." God's *ra* (evil) is never seen as an immoral act when it brings judgment on the wicked. We see this numerous times in the Old Testament, but King Jeroboam is a good example.

An Old Testament man named Jeroboam was promised the kingdom by God after Solomon died with the understanding that he would follow God's commandments. Instead he instituted a whole new system of false worship complete with two new worship centers in Bethel and Dan. He made two golden calves to be worshiped, inserted a whole new set of priests, adopted the pagan sexual practices of the surrounding nations, and even ordered the practice of child sacrifice. He was not a good guy!

But God was repulsed by the new religion Jeroboam "invented" which imitated the pagan golden calf of Moses' time. His response was *"I am bringing calamity (ra) on the house of Jeroboam, and will cut off from Jeroboam every male person, both bond and free in Israel, and I will make a clean sweep of the house of Jeroboam, as one sweeps away dung until it is all gone."*[242]

Is there any doubt that seeing babies sacrificed to some make-believe god would raise an impassioned response from anyone with a sense of morality and compassion? Would anyone in his or her right mind tolerate Hitler or Stalin or the current scourge

---

[241] Richard Dawkins, *The God Delusion* (New York: Houghton Mifflin, 2006), 51.

[242] 1 Kings 14:10

of ISIS for a minute? The normal impulse for most people would be to call for justice to stop the perpetrators of such heinous acts.

God is never depicted as committing an immoral act when He applies *ra* to the wicked. Every person alive should rejoice in this. We are all made to desire justice. All objective human beings rise up and protest when they see injustice done. We all want bad guys to lose and the good guys to win! So does God!

Since we are created in the image of God, a desire for justice is built into each of us. God has a different definition for every single act that looks like evil to us. His actions are holy, just, timely, and perfect, even though we may never see it. We would do well to let God be God instead of trying to superimpose our definitions and purposes on Him.

An additional reason for comfort is the realization that God's judgment is always accompanied by His promise of future blessing. The prophet Zechariah carries both this warning as well as the promise, *"'Just as I purposed to do harm to you when your fathers provoked Me to wrath,' says the Lord of hosts, 'and I have not relented, so I have again purposed in these days to do good to Jerusalem and to the house of Judah. Do not fear!'"*[243]

What a comfort to know that we don't have to fear the exercise of God's judgment. His promise of blessing is always held out to everyone who would follow Him and obey His commands.

God knows the whole picture

Third, we must assert that God knows the whole picture. That's why we can rest with His sovereign oversight concerning the woman holding the thirsty child that Templeton saw. It's tragic and shortsighted when someone rejects God over something they have no control over. Templeton's lack of trust was biblically naïve and presumptive.

---

[243] Zechariah 8:14-15

The Old Testament prophet Jonah is a great picture of this truth. Consider the repeated language that is used to describe God's decree in this story. Notice the underlined words to see God's specific actions – "*God hurled a great wind on the sea and there was a great storm on the sea so that the ship was about to break up.*"[244] – "*And the Lord appointed a great fish to swallow Jonah*"[245] – "*Then the Lord commanded the fish, and it vomited Jonah up onto the dry land.*"[246] – "*then God relented concerning the calamity (ra a) which He had declared He would bring upon them.*"[247] – "*the Lord God appointed a plant and it grew up over Jonah to be a shade over his head*"[248] – "*But God appointed a worm when dawn came the next day and it attacked the plant and it withered.*"[249] – "*God appointed a scorching east wind, and the sun beat down on Jonah's head so that he became faint and begged with all his soul to die*"[250] – "*You had compassion on the plant for which you did not work*"[251] – "*Should I not have compassion on Nineveh, the great city in which there are more than 120,000 persons who do not know the difference between their right and left hand . . .*"[252]

So, think of this. God used a storm, a great fish, and a smelly, reluctant Hebrew prophet to save 120,000 pagan Ninevites! Jonah's attitude was literally, "Let 'em go to hell. They deserve it." And he was right. To avoid God's call, he got on a ship bound for Tarshish, as far away from Nineveh as he could get.

But God had other plans. He not only saved the sailors who eventually threw Jonah overboard when a great storm came up,

---

[244] Jonah 1:14
[245] Jonah 1:17
[246] Jonah 2:10
[247] Jonah 3:10
[248] Jonah 4:6
[249] Jonah 4:7
[250] Jonah 4:8
[251] Jonah 4:10
[252] Jonah 4:11

but He saved the Ninevites as well. That's how God uses bad things to accomplish His will. This is truly amazing.

We see another example in the book of Ruth, which contains the story of a woman named Naomi and her husband, Elimelech, and their two sons. There was a famine in Israel and Naomi and her husband fled to Moab to survive. Moab was a pagan nation next to Israel, which was always antagonistic and combative.

While there, the sons married but then tragedy struck. First Elimelech and then the two sons died. Naomi wanted to return to Israel, but her daughters-in-law begged her to stay and re-marry. In a poignant scene Naomi says, *"[F]or it is harder for me than for you, for the hand of the Lord has gone forth against me."*[253] Remember that phrase.

One daughter-in-law named Orpah stays in Moab. But the other one, Ruth, pleads to return to Israel with her mother-in-law. When they arrive back in Israel, a series of events places Ruth in the path of a man named Boaz. The law of kinsman redeemer was enacted to bring Boaz and Ruth together. This law states that the nearest relative of someone who dies has the obligation to marry the widow of the deceased. In a beautiful picture of Christ's re-demptive love for us, Boaz paid the price of redemption for Ruth and married her.

But this isn't merely an obligation. It's clear Boaz and Ruth fall in love and marry. The providential aspect of this is that the couple become parents of a baby named Obed, who became the grandfather of David, the king of Israel. David, of course, is the progenitor of the promised Messiah. In another astounding twist, the name of Ruth the Moabitess (from a country antagonistic to Israel) appears in the genealogy of the Messiah recorded in the first book of the New Testament.

This is what brings it all together. God's decree is set in the context of His knowledge of the whole picture. It is striking to

---

[253] Ruth 1:13

realize that God used a famine, the deaths of three men, the agony of three widows, *"the hand of the Lord"* against Naomi, and a daughter-in-law from a nation that was antagonistic to Israel, to bring about the birth of Jesus Christ Himself, the Messiah of the Old Testament! God knows the whole picture and controls events to accomplish His divine decree.

When we rest in the knowledge that God is merciful and right in everything He does, we can truly be happy with His decree. That enables us to live openly anticipating what He will do in our lives. That's the subject of the next chapter.

CHAPTER NINE

"Our freedom is always and everywhere limited by God's sovereignty. God is free, and we are free. But God is more free than we are. When our freedom bumps up against God's sovereignty, our freedom must yield."[254]
— R. C. Sproul

God Meant It for Good

How does God's will interact with our free will?

T he use of force is the ultimate tool that law enforcement uses to maintain order in society. The laws are written by our state and federal legislators and implemented by law enforcement officers. Without the ability to use force to bring about compliance to these laws we would live in chaos.

CAUSATION

It's helpful at this point to interject the concept of causation into the conversation. Legal scholars distinguish between proximate and ultimate cause when evaluating responsibility for crime. Yet far too few words are uttered regarding *causation*.

Proximate cause is the immediate reason something happens. A person runs a red light thus causing an accident. That is the *proximate*, or most immediate reason for the collision. But it is

---

[254] R.C. Sproul, *Grace Unknown*, (Grand Rapids, Baker Books, 1997), 27.

later found that *Dan the driver* had been carjacked by *Bob the bandit*. As a result, Dan was forced to drive at an excessive rate of speed to affect Bob's getaway. So, the actions of Bob the bandit are determined to be the *ultimate* cause of Dan's accident.

It is highly likely that everyone operating an automobile has at some point in his or her driving career, run a red light!

Everyone!

Law abiding people, law violating people, and in-between people!

We are not robots. People err. But how many of us have robbed a bank, kidnapped and carjacked someone, and forced them to run a red light that caused a collision? Voila! Not too many! The numbers just decreased by millions.

But today there is an alarming increase in the number of people who deny that they are the *ultimate cause* of their own destructive behavior. Instead of accepting responsibility for their actions, many strong voices in our society have shifted the blame for the *ultimate cause* of the activity to cops. This has resulted in many law enforcement agencies retreating from conflict. Consequently, offenders have been encouraged to violently challenge authority.

Ferguson, Missouri

A classic example of this was found in Ferguson, Missouri on August 9, 2014 when Officer Darren Wilson of the Ferguson Police Department confronted 18-year-old Michael Brown.[255] Brown was a much larger man than Wilson. He had previously been involved in a strong-armed robbery of a convenience store nearby and was walking in the middle of the street when confronted by Wilson who was driving his patrol vehicle.

---

[255] Jim McNeff, "Turmoil in Ferguson," *Law Enforcement Today*, https://www.lawenforcementtoday.com/turmoil-in-ferguson/ (accessed July 15, 2017).

Brown refused to comply with Wilson's directives. Moreover, he violently attacked Wilson who was in a vulnerable position seated in his police unit. As Brown wrestled with Wilson for his gun, it went off and Brown turned to get away. When Wilson made overtures toward Brown, the much larger Brown spun and charged Wilson, prompting him to use deadly force to spare his own life.[256]

Consequently, we all know riots erupted. This incident became a hinge point for policing in America. It spurred many reforms and eventually the use of body worn cameras by any police agency that could figure out a way to pay for the technology.

Subsequent multi-layered criminal and civil rights investigations exonerated Wilson. He was cleared of wrongdoing, yet his life was devastated, and Michael Brown was dead.[257]

So, while Darren Wilson was the *proximate cause* of Michael Brown's death, Brown's criminal behavior was the *ultimate reason* for his demise.[258] If Wilson had not asserted his will against Brown when he saw him walking down the middle of the street, it's reasonable to assume that Brown's criminal lifestyle would have continued unchallenged. Furthermore, if Wilson had not been authorized to use lethal force during the violent, potentially disarming attack by Brown, the officer could have suffered grave consequences, including the loss of his own life.

This was affirmed by the grand jury that refused to bring charges against Officer Darren Wilson after he used deadly force

---

[256] Corky Siemaszko, "Ferguson cop Darren Wilson tells his side of Michael Brown shooting to ABC news, says he feared for his life," *New York Daily News*, http://www.nydailynews.com/news/national/ferguson-darren-wilson-sends-letter-thanks-article-1.2023191 (accessed March 3, 2018).

[257] Jim McNeff, "Al Sharpton – When Looney Tunes Came to Town," *Law Enforcement Today*, https://www.lawenforcementtoday.com/al-sharpten-when-looney-tunes-came-to-town/ (accessed July 15, 2017).

[258] James P. Gafney, "Ferguson Grand Jury – Point/Counter Point," *Law Enforcement Today*, https://www.lawenforcementtoday.com/ferguson-grand-jury-pointcounter-point/ (accessed July 15, 2017).

and killed Michael Brown. The issue of causation is not always what it seems to be at first glance.

THE PROVIDENCE OF GOD

God operates the same way. He has the right to use lethal force. He has the right to exercise His will when it conflicts with ours. Our behavior may be the proximate cause of an act, but the ultimate cause of all behavior is God's sovereign will.

The problem

This presents a problem in discussing the free will of man and the decree of God. In chapter five, under the section on man's problem, we discussed the limitations of man's will. We might call this the proximate cause of man's actions. In chapter eight, in the section on God's response, the decree of God was presented as the ultimate cause of the actions of man.

The free will of man and the decree of God seem like opposing views that can't be reconciled. If God is the all-powerful creator of everything there is, then it is reasonable to conclude that He also preserves and governs His creation as well. But it seems as if man is also a player on this stage. If so, how does that work? The way that these two seemingly opposing doctrines come together is called the providence of God.

An accurate understanding of providence avoids several common errors. First, providence is not *deism*, which teaches that God created the world and then abandoned it. Second, providence is not *pantheism*, which teaches that, in reality, God is the sum of the component parts of the physical universe. Third, providence denies that the events of life are mere chance, where everything we confront is pure randomness. Lastly, providence is not fate, the illogical belief that some kind of force out there causes certain things to happen for some kind of unspecified reason.

What does it mean?

In the interest of clarification, let's start by defining our term. Millard Erickson describes providence as "continuing action of God by which he preserves in existence the creation which he has brought into being and guides it to his intended purposes for it."[259] Wayne Grudem provides a longer definition:

> God is continually involved with all created things in such a way that he (1) keeps them existing and maintaining the properties with which he created them; (2) cooperates with created things in every action, directing their distinctive properties to cause them to act as they do; and (3) directs them to fulfill his purposes.[260]

Most people don't understand God's providence because they've never thought too much about it. One might be aware of the word, but not understand its meaning or implications. But it's also possible that we don't know about providence because it challenges our perception of our own self-control.

Providence doesn't say you're not in control, just that you're not in total control. For example, if you're on a plane going to New York, you can read, work on your computer, have a Diet Coke or an orange juice, chat with the person in the seat next to you or do any number of other things. These are all your choices. But the plane is going to New York, no matter what you choose to do inside the plane.

---

[259] Erickson, *Christian Theology* (Grand Rapids, MI: Baker Book House, 1992), 1:387.

[260] Wayne A. Grudem, *Systematic Theology: An Introduction to Biblical Doctrine* (Leicester, England; Grand Rapids, MI: Inter-Varsity Press; Zondervan Pub. House, 2004), 315.

Compatibilism

In trying to explain how man's will fits together with God's will some have used the word *compatibilism*. This carries the providence of God a step further by showing that man's free will operates in a way that is compatible with God's decree. This simply means that man's actions have a dual explanation, one observable, and one not observable. It means that man is morally accountable for his actions, and *free* in that sense, and yet his choices never overrule God's decree. How is it possible for both of these assertions to be true? Aren't they incompatible?

If we look closely at Scripture we will find that the answer to this question is no. The problem comes when we look at them as being mutually exclusive. We tend to think in black and white. It's either God's will *or* it's man's will. But closer examination reveals this isn't true.

Millard Erickson helps us bring the two together by noting "The plan of God does not force men to act in particular ways but renders it certain that they will freely act in those ways."[261] A.A. Hodge describes the relation of the decree of God to human choice. He writes,

> The decree itself provides in every case that the event shall be effected by causes acting in a manner perfectly consistent with the nature of the event in question. Thus in the case of every free act of a moral agent the decree provides at the same time
> a. That the agent shall be a free agent.
> b. That his antecedents and all the antecedents of the act in question shall be what they are.
> c. That all the present conditions of the act shall be what they are.
> d. That the act shall be perfectly spontaneous and free on the part of the agent.

---

[261] Erickson, *Christian Theology*, 353.

e. That it shall be certainly future.[262]

These observations help us to affirm that God's sovereign will doesn't deny man's free will. This is the other side of the paradox. Both work together but in a way where we must say that God sovereignly wills free will to man. Man exercises his free will in setting his own agenda. But behind the scenes God is at work, accomplishing exactly what He set out to accomplish. Man makes his decisions to accomplish his agenda. And God uses those decisions to accomplish His.

If . . .

This may tax our brains a little bit to get our minds around these dueling concepts, but reality tells us they are both true. In a million scenarios during the course of life, man can never know what would have happened if he had made a different decision.

When I was in high school an acquaintance of mine heard that a mutual friend had been in an accident. Rushing to the scene, which turned out to be a minor collision, my friend ran into the street without looking in an effort to get to his friend on the other side. In a tragic turn of events, he was killed by an oncoming car. *If* he had arrived just a few seconds later, the traffic would have been clear, and he would not have been killed.

We can also see this in the book, *Five Days in November*, written by former Secret Service agent Clint Hill. Hill was the agent who crawled onto the trunk of the presidential limousine trying to reach Jacqueline Kennedy on that fateful day in Dallas on November 22, 1963. For the past fifty-six plus years Hill has agonized over what would have happened *if* he had only jumped onto the trunk a second sooner. Perhaps he could have saved President Kennedy from the second round fired by Lee Harvey Oswald.

---

[262] A.A. Hodge, *Outlines of Theology*, (1860; reprint, Grand Rapids: Zondervan Publishing House, 1972), 203.

How often we do the same thing. *If* I had listened to my parents I would have finished college and gotten a better job. *If* I had bought that stock I would be rich today. *If* I had married Joe instead of Tim I would have had a happy life. *If . . . if . . . if.*

Non-choices

And how about the other side of the *if* game? What about our non-choices that saved us from tragedy? When I was in seminary, I was driving home one day when I stopped at a red light with no one else around. Deep in thought, I didn't notice when the light turned green, so I sat there for a couple of seconds before I took my foot off the brake. Just then, a car came screaming from my left straight through the intersection at a high rate of speed. *If* I had reacted normally I would have been directly in his path and no doubt been killed.

Of course, obsessing about the things that might or might not have happened if we had made different choices can make us lose our grip on reality. In the movie *Back to the Future*, Doc warned Marty that he could not go back in history and alter the decisions made there because that would alter the time-space continuum. *If* we could go back in time, that might prove to be true. But we can't, so there is no use obsessing about it.

Everything is beautiful

Rather than worrying, we must learn to trust that God perfectly balances His control of the events of our lives even though we will never know the outcome of different decisions we might have made. God's omniscience touches on His providence at this point.

Jesus was once denouncing cities where He had met with rejection despite the miracles that He had performed among them. Showing that His omniscience extended even to events that never happened, He said, "*Woe to you, Chorazin! Woe to you, Bethsaida! For if the miracles had occurred in Tyre and Sidon which occurred in you, they would have repented long ago in sackcloth and ashes.*"[263] Jesus knew what would have happened if He had performed His miracles in other cities that He never visited.

But we're not Jesus. Nevertheless, we can rest in knowing that our free will doesn't override His sovereign will. In fact, we will never know all of the ins and outs of what might have happened if we had made different decisions.

Solomon exposed this dilemma when he observed "*There is an appointed time for everything. And there is a time for every event under heaven—*"[264] And then he painted contrasts between a time for birth and death, tearing down and building up, weeping and laughing, mourning and dancing, loving and hating, war and peace, etc.

He capped off his discussion with a profound statement. He said God, "*has made everything appropriate in its time. He has also set eternity in their heart, yet so that man will not find out the work which God has done from the beginning even to the end.*"[265] The word for "*appropriate*" is the Hebrew word *yapeh*, which means "fair, beautiful, excellent."[266] It's used to describe beautiful women, handsome men, the beauty of a perfect olive tree, and any number of items and people who are delightful and perfect in form and function.[267]

It's easy to see how birth, building up, laughing, dancing, loving, and peace are "beautiful." But how about the other side? How do we fit death, tearing down, weeping, mourning, hating, and war under the umbrella of "beautiful?" That can only make sense when we see that God is the one who brings these things

---

263 Matthew 11:21

264 Ecclesiastes 3:1

265 Ecclesiastes 3:11

266 Paul R. Gilchrist, "890 הָפָי," ed. R. Laird Harris, Gleason L. Archer Jr., and Bruce K. Waltke, *Theological Wordbook of the Old Testament* (Chicago: Moody Press, 1999), 391.

267 1 Kings 1:3; 1 Samuel 17:42; Jeremiah 11:16; Isaiah 33:17; Zechariah 9:16

together, calling each of them "beautiful" in their own time. The reason these things are "beautiful" is because God has perfectly positioned each event under heaven to be carried out in His perfect time.

IMPLICATIONS OF PROVIDENCE

It overrides the evil intent of man

We can see the beauty of God's providence a number of places in Scripture. One of these is in the story of Joseph in the Old Testament. You may recall that Joseph's brothers were jealous of him and sold him into slavery in Egypt, telling their father that he had been killed. Their actions were hateful and murderous.

But other factors were at work. Years later, when the brothers were forced to go to Egypt to get grain because of a famine in Israel, they were confronted by their long-lost brother Joseph, whom God had now elevated to be second in command of all Egypt.

After first revealing himself to his brothers, Joseph said, *"God sent me before you to preserve for you a remnant in the earth, and to keep you alive by a great deliverance."*[268] Then in one of the most powerful statements in the Bible Joseph said, *"As for you, you meant evil against me, but God meant it for good."*[269]

Joseph's brothers surely meant for evil to come to Joseph. And on a human scale it did. Years of separation from his family and the knowledge that his brothers hated him must have been a terrible burden for young Joseph to bear.

But God *also meant* for something to happen. Actually, we know of two things He meant to happen. The first is that He meant to save Joseph's family from the famine in Israel. After the way they treated Joseph, they may not have deserved it, but this was part of God's plan.

---

[268] Genesis 45:7
[269] Genesis 50:20

It accomplishes God's purposes

The second thing God intended to do had far greater reach. When Joseph said *"God sent me before you to preserve for you a remnant in the earth . . ."* there was much more to this than meets the eye. In order to understand the full effect of what God was doing we need to go back to Genesis and understand the Abrahamic covenant. This was a series of promises God made to Abraham. These are basically contained in two verses where God promises, *"And I will make you a great nation, and I will bless you, and make your name great; and so you shall be a blessing; and I will bless those who bless you, and the one who curses you I will curse. And in you all the families of the earth will be blessed."*[270]

When God promised to make a great nation from Abraham, that obviously involved people. But by the time his great grandson Joseph was born, that only involved Abraham's great grandchildren. That's not a nation. But God was busy building one.

Neither Joseph nor his brothers could possibly have known of God's plan to elevate Joseph to second in command in Egypt, bring a famine to Israel that would force his brothers to travel to Egypt to get food, have the brothers reunited with their long lost brother, bring the rest of the family to Egypt, keep them there for the next 400 years while they grew into a nation of at least two million people, and then miraculously deliver them from slavery and return them to their homeland in Israel, all for the purpose of preserving a people from whom He would bring a promised Messiah to the earth over 1500 years later through whom He would bring salvation to all the people of the earth.

That's just too big, too vast, too far-reaching for anyone to plan or manipulate. But that was God's plan and purpose. When Joseph said, *"God meant it for good,"* he literally meant that God intended to preserve the *"remnant"* family that would form the

---

[270] Genesis 12:2-3

nation God promised to Abraham. And He did it on the back of the murderous intentions of Joseph's brothers.

An even more profound example of this truth is seen in the crucifixion of Jesus. Preaching to the very people who had screamed for Jesus to be crucified a few weeks earlier, Peter said, *"[T]his Man, delivered over by the predetermined plan and fore-knowledge of God, you nailed to a cross by the hands of godless men and put Him to death."*[271]

Jesus died at the intersection of man's murderous intentions and God's predetermined plan. God used the sinful, murderous desires of dozens of people to bring about His ultimate plan to bring salvation to humanity through the sacrifice of His Son on the cross. The Jewish leaders, Pilate, and the crowd all acted on their free will to kill Jesus. Yet God also exercised His absolute decretive will by using the venomous actions of the crowd to accomplish His eternal will. D. A. Carson is helpful here. He notes,

> Herod and Pontius Pilate and the rest conspired together; they did what they wanted to do, even though they did what God's power and will had determined beforehand should be done. That is why many theologians have refused to tie "freedom" to absolute power to act contrary to God's will. They tie it, rather, to desire, to what human beings voluntarily choose. Joseph's brothers did what they wanted to do; Herod and Pilate and the rulers of the Jews did what they wanted to do; the Assyrians did what they wanted to do. In each case, God's sovereignty was operating behind the scenes: the human participants, to use the language of the early Christians, did what God's power and will had decided beforehand should happen. But that did not excuse them. They did what they wanted to do.[272]

---

[271] Acts 2:23

[272] D. A. Carson, *A Call to Spiritual Reformation*, (Grand Rapids, Michigan: Baker Academic, 1992), 157.

It governs kings and earthly authorities

But there's more to God's providence. We also see it in His rule over kings and earthly authorities. The prophet Isaiah tells of God using wicked Assyria as His "rod of anger" to punish His people.[273] The Assyrians were some of the most cruel, barbaric people who ever lived. They ran spears from the anus out the mouths of conquered subjects. They skinned people alive. They put hooks in the mouths of deposed kings and led them around like dogs. All of these acts are memorialized on bronze reliefs in the British museum in London.

Yet God used them to punish the wickedness of His own people when they fell into cultic prostitution, incest, and child sacrifice. But then He turns His wrath on Assyrians themselves because of their arrogant and barbaric acts. Isaiah reminds us of God's perspective, *"By the power of my hand and by my wisdom I did this, For I have understanding; and I removed the boundaries of the peoples, and plundered their treasures, and like a mighty man I brought down their inhabitants . . . Is the axe to boast itself over the one who chops with it? Is the saw to exalt itself over the one who wields it?"*[274]

There is not a ruler on earth who is not under the complete power of God's jurisdiction. We can be thankful that, *"The king's heart is like channels of water in the hand of the Lord; He turns it wherever He wishes."*[275]

It governs the creation of life

We also see God's providence over individual lives. Sarah is an example of this. God made the promise of making a great nation from Abraham, but he and Sarah had no children. That's a problem if you're trying to build a nation. Sarah and Abraham

---

[273] Isaiah 10:5-19
[274] Isaiah 10:13,15
[275] Proverbs 21:1

recognized this and were understandably frustrated. When she was seventy-five they decided that maybe God wanted to give them a child through her servant girl Hagar. So, Abraham had sex with her, and Ishmael was born.

But that wasn't God's plan. Sarah was barren because God wanted to increase Abraham's faith. Finally, when she was ninety-years-old, Isaac was born. Talk about relief! In the New Testament, Paul tells us something of Abraham's state of mind as well as Sarah's physical condition. He says, *"Without becoming weak in faith he contemplated his own body, now as good as dead since he was about a hundred years old, and the deadness of Sarah's womb; yet, with respect to the promise of God, he did not waver in unbelief but grew strong in faith, giving glory to God . . ."*[276] Obviously, God was not deterred by the "dead" reproductive organs of both Abraham and Sarah in making a baby.

I recall the time when one of my younger brothers and his wife invited themselves over for dinner. They didn't live close, so this was a little unexpected. I had performed their wedding some ten years previous to this, and we knew that they had been trying for years to get pregnant with no results. We had barely sat down at the table when my sister-in-law began tearing up and through a smile of jubilation blurted out, "I'm pregnant!" This was the first of two children for them, proving again that God is sovereign over the womb.

It governs random affairs of life

Next, we learn that God's providence even extends to various random affairs of life. The story of the exodus from captivity in Egypt offers a stark example of this. Exodus records, *"Now the sons of Israel had done according to the word of Moses, for they had requested from the Egyptians articles of silver and articles of gold, and clothing; and the Lord had given the people favor in*

---

[276] Romans 4:19-20

the sight of the Egyptians, so that they let them have their request. Thus they plundered the Egyptians."[277] Imagine slaves walking out with the gold and silver of their captors—without a fight! Surely the Egyptians knew better. In fact, after they thought about it, they pursued the children of Israel in a gigantic case of seller's remorse.

We find another rather humorous example in 1 Samuel. In the ongoing cat and mouse game that David played with King Saul, who was trying to kill him, we come across an account of David retreating into a cave. Shortly after, Saul also enters the same cave—to relieve himself. After secretly cutting off a piece of Saul's robe while he was in the cave, David called out to Saul after he left, letting him know that he had also been in the cave. Understanding David's benevolence, Saul acknowledged, *"You have declared today that you have done good to me, that the Lord delivered me into your hand and yet you did not kill me. May the Lord therefore reward you with good in return for what you have done to me this day."*[278] I guess! God's providence extended to the timing of Saul's natural body functions!

Free will and man's responsibility

So, what do we do about this little problem we all have? It should be obvious we can't ignore it. Actually, that's what most people do. But that's really a form of rebellion against God's sovereignty because we are born wanting to retain control of our life. In fact, we are born demanding to do what we want. And we continue that way throughout our lives without some kind of intervention.

The free will of man, who follows his natural instincts, is the reason God is justified in holding man responsible for his actions. Man sins against God because he wants to.

---

[277] Exodus 12:35-36
[278] 1 Samuel 24:18-19

John Piper helps us understand the implications of this by noting, "Our will is free if our preferences and our choices are really our own in such a way that we can justly be held responsible for whether they are good or bad."[279] If a person really wants to hold on to his free will, it's logical that he must accept the consequences.

Again, this doesn't seem radical for most people. To have free will means we must be willing to live with the consequences of our choices. But this isn't just a "little problem" as I stated above. If the problem in our nature is sinful as described in chapter one, then there must be consequences. Spiritual consequences.

Running out of time

And there will be consequences. The Bible is clear that God holds people responsible for their actions. The writer of the letter to the Hebrews said, *"[I]t is appointed for men to die once and after this comes judgment . . ."*[280]

One would think this would make any clear-thinking individual at least a little nervous. Anyone who accurately perceives the spiritual box they are in because of the limitations of their own decision-making apparatus, will seek a way out. But that's only if they understand that sooner or later they will run out of time.

In his book *Christless Christianity*, Michael Horton includes a story taken from NBC's medical drama ER that illustrates this point. Let's pick up the scene here.

> Lying in his hospital bed while he is dying from cancer, a retired police officer confesses to a chaplain his long-held guilt over allowing an innocent man to be framed and executed. He asks, "How can I even hope for forgiveness?" and the chaplain replies, "I think sometimes it's easier to feel guilty than forgiven."

---

[279] John Piper, "A Beginner's Guide to Free Will," www.desiringgod.org. (accessed July 30, 2016)
[280] Hebrews 9:27

"Which means *what*?"

"That maybe your guilt over his death has become your reason for living. Maybe you need a new reason to go on."

"I don't want to 'go on,'" says the dying man. "Can't you see that I'm dying? The only thing that is holding me back is that I'm afraid—I'm afraid of what comes next."

"What do you think that is?" the chaplain gently inquires. Growing impatient, the man answers, "*You tell me.* Is atonement possible? What does God want from me?"

After the chaplain replies, "I think it's up to each one of us to interpret for ourselves what God wants," the man stares at her in bewilderment. "So people can do anything? They can rape, they can murder, they can steal—all in the name of God and it's OK?"

Growing intense, the dialogue draws to its climax. "No, that's not what I'm saying," the chaplain responds.

"Then what *are* you saying? Because all I'm hearing is some New Age, God-is-Love, have-it-your-way crap! . . . No, I don't have time for this now."

"You don't understand," the chaplain counters.

"No, *you* don't understand! . . . I want a *real* chaplain who believes in a *real* God and a *real* hell!"

Missing the point of this Man's struggle, the chaplain collects herself and says in the familiar tone of condescension disguised as understanding, "I hear that you're frustrated, but you need to ask yourself—"

"No," the man interrupts, "I don't need to ask myself anything, I need *answers* and all of your questions and all of your uncertainty are only making things worse."

With no more to evaluate than his tone, she encourages calm. "I know you're upset," she begins, provoking his final outburst of frustration: "God, I need someone who will look me in the eye and tell me how to find forgiveness, because I am running out of time."[281]

The clock is ticking on all of us. What happens when time runs out? There are only two possible destinations for those who die. The next chapter introduces the default destination for those who do not submit their will to God.

---

[281] Michael Horton, *Christless Christianity: The Alternative Gospel of the American Church* (Grand Rapids, Michigan: Baker Books, 2008), 37.

THE ULTIMATE REALITY

"There is no doctrine which I would more willingly remove from Christianity than this, if it lay in my power. But it has the full support of Scripture and, specially, of our Lord's own words; it has always been held by Christendom; and it has the support of reason."[282]

– C. S. Lewis

One Second After You Die

What is the result of rejecting God?

I n the first section of this book, we examined the nature of man's problem, and then in section two, we followed that up with a discussion on man's response to his problem. This section deals with the ultimate reality of God's response to man's problem. The short answer to this ultimate reality is that either man will trust in his own solution to his problem or he will trust in God's solution to his problem. You can't have it both ways.

Of necessity, this means that we must deal with the concept of death. After all, this is the ultimate reality. We all live—then we die. But what happens then? We ended the last section with the man demanding an answer to his problem because he was

---

[282] C. S. Lewis, *The Problem of Pain* (repr., 1940, New York, NY: HarperOne, 2001), 121.

"running out of time." We begin this section dealing with this hard subject.

THE DRAG RACE

They drove north on Brookhurst Street coming to a fresh red light at Warner Avenue. Although this is a heavily traveled intersection, it was late at night and traffic was light. The street contained three and four lanes in each direction. There was plenty of room for side-by-side competition. What better time and place for an illegal drag race?

The competing vehicles were a bit eclectic. They included a small, foreign sports car, an American muscle car, and a full size "dually" pick-up truck. As they waited for the green light signaling the beginning of their street race, there was probably some non-verbal communication that occurred from one challenger to another. Whether it included revving engines, a nod of the head, or simple eye contact with raised eyebrows, we don't know.

Yet witnesses were clear about one thing. This was a drag race pure and simple.

The illegal competition occurred during a light drizzle. Therefore, intermittent windshield wipers were necessary to maintain a clear field of vision.

When light rainfall occurs, motor oils previously dripped on asphalt rise to the surface. As a result, streets become far more dangerous than normal driving conditions. Between water moisture and motor fluids, the roadway literally develops oil slicks. Consequently, cars easily hydroplane, and drivers lose control in these circumstances.

As the traffic light phased green two cars and a truck hit the gas to see who was driving the fastest automobile. Wheels spun on the wet slurry, but each driver maintained control for a few hundred yards as they quickly accelerated to unsafe speeds.

Suddenly, the white one-ton, full-sized GMC dual wheeled pick-up lost control and went into a spin toward the center median.

The "dually," occupied by the driver and two passengers, spun like a top as the physical barrier between north and southbound traffic was about to be breached. The truck, with four rear tires, hit the center curb line and launched into the air. This large, 7,000-pound, out-of-control "dually" flew like a Frisbee from northbound into oncoming southbound traffic while the competitors sped away, never to be seen or heard from again.

As the truck mimicked an aircraft touching down on a runway, it violently collided head-on with a Toyota Tundra pick-up truck driving in the opposite direction.

BOOM!

The sound of two vehicles coming together in this manner was similar to an explosion. Moreover, it looked like one as well.

The engine compartment of the Toyota compressed like an accordion into the firewall. The airbags deployed and cushioned the driver in the interest of saving his life. Amazingly, he received serious injuries, but none that were life-threatening.

The occupants of the GMC pick-up were not as fortunate. The right front passenger door came completely unhinged in the massive collision and launched like a missile flying more than a hundred feet from the point of impact. The rest of the truck became a giant ball of muddled wreckage.

Sometime during the flight and collision, all three passengers were ejected. They were not thrown far, but the truck burst into flames and they were in the fire zone. Initial responding officers referred to it as an "inferno." No one could get close to the blaze as it crackled and popped from various items incinerating in the heat. And there was no sign of a driver or passengers making it to safety.

The fire department rushed to the scene, yet their heroic efforts to preserve life fell short. Furthermore, due to the nature of the blaze, they used foam to extinguish the out-of-control flames that began spreading to trees above.

As firefighters worked to douse the fire, they eventually located three bodies lying nearby, lost in a sea of suds. There was no life in any of them. . . . Each individual was literally burnt to a crisp.

Although I responded from home as the Traffic Bureau commander, the remaining blackened foam at the scene looked like the residual effect of a giant bubble bath that met a campfire. Hence, it was a nasty, grimy mess to trudge through.

Once it was safe to get close to the charred wreckage, I walked up to the deceased people, one of whom drove the other two to their demise.

When encountering dead bodies, there is no mistaking the presence of death. The absence of the soul-generating life in a person is unmistakable. Yet in this case, the three people who were burnt beyond recognition didn't even come close to resembling human beings, let alone being able to identify gender. They all had the appearance of melted-mannequins that were coated with charcoal paste. Beyond their morbid appearance, rigor mortis had set in by the time I was able to cast my eyes on their condition.

When this occurs, the muscles stiffen in place. Consequently, each decedent appeared in a position of anguish, either reaching for help or curled in the fetal position as death arrived. Witnessing the scene made it necessary for everyone to check their emotions while performing various tasks.

It was the first major field work for one of our young, civilian crime scene investigators. I had to ensure she was able to finish her job as she looked like she'd seen a ghost. While this wasn't true, there was no mistaking she had seen ghastly death in ghoulish form.

UNSATISFYING ANSWERS

Unfortunately, a story like this serves as a tragic reminder of the end of life. Death is typically unintended. Generally, people do not want to die. That's because death is the ultimate reality. No one escapes. Eventually everyone runs out of time.

But what happens one second after you die? Few people seem to really contemplate this question. If they do, the answer is usually a flippant "I guess I'll find out then." Or they might simply believe that there is nothing after death. No afterlife, no heaven, no hell.

Years ago, the group B*lood, Sweat, and Tears* sang, "I swear there ain't no heaven, and I pray there ain't no hell"[283] which has become the unofficial mantra for many people. But does that make sense? What gives anyone the confidence to say that heaven and hell aren't real. Even praying "there ain't no hell" depicts a certain misgiving about life after death.

As mentioned previously, John Lennon penned a similar thought when he sang, "Imagine there's no heaven, it's easy if you try, no hell below us, above us only sky."[284] It's nice to imagine that. But is it true? The Bible asserts that the answer to that question is a clear "no."

These responses are unsatisfactory because they provide no reason for living. If there is nothing after we die, then love and hate and morals and virtue and pain and suffering have no meaning if we live and die with no concluding act. They also don't address the clinging to life and fear of death that is built into each of us.

---

[283] Laura Nyro, "And When I Die," on *Blood, Sweat & Tears*, Celestial Music, Inc/Cherry River Music, Inc BMI, 1967

[284] John Lennon, Yoko Ono, "Imagine," on *Imagine*, Downtown Music Publishing, 1971.

WHERE TO BEGIN?

We will begin our conversation with the most awful discussion of the reality of hell because that is the default position of every person ever born into this world. Unless God intervenes, hell is the destiny of all who want to pursue their own free will in life. If the man mentioned in the last chapter runs out of time before he responds to God's call on his life, he will end up in hell.

Jesus taught *"the gate is wide and the way is broad that leads to destruction, and there are many who enter through it."*[285] But, in addition to this being the default position of every person ever born, this is also the path most people will choose. In the end, God will give them exactly what they want. If one wants a life without God, that is exactly what they will get.

The enormity of the topic is probably why so many people have tried to avoid the issue. A good portion of this lack of belief is due to some erroneous discussions on hell that have found their way into the culture, many by false religious leaders.

One of the most recent people to do this in modern culture was Robert Schuller, the founding pastor of the *Crystal Cathedral* in Garden Grove, California, that eventually went bankrupt and was sold to the Catholic Church. He built an empire on self-help and positive thinking. Is it any wonder that his theology had a distorted view of sin and hell? He said, "Sin is any act or thought that robs myself or another human being of his or her self-esteem . . . And what is 'hell'? It is the loss of pride that naturally follows separation from God—the ultimate and unfailing source of our soul's sense of self-respect."[286]

In a more recent development Rob Bell, then the pastor of *Mars Hill Bible Church* in Grandville, Michigan wrote a book called *Love Wins* in 2011 that pretty much dismissed the hell

---

[285] Matthew 7:13
[286] Robert Schuller, *Self Esteem: The New Reformation* (Waco, TX: Word Books, 1982), 14, 68.

of the Bible. For him, hell is the worst of things that happen on earth. It's molestations, rapes, genocide in Rwanda, poverty, violence, and so forth.[287] He reasoned that,

> [I]f something is wrong with your God, if your God is loving one second and cruel the next, if your God will punish people for all of eternity for sins committed in a few short years, no amount of clever marketing or compelling language or good music or great coffee will be able to disguise that one, true, glaring, untenable, unacceptable, awful reality.[288]

It's no wonder that today Bell lives the life of a California surfer dude who hangs out with Oprah. Scriptural truth has become irrelevant to him in his pursuit of self. If you pick and choose which doctrines of the Bible you want to believe, pretty soon you jettison the whole thing.

Another sign of cultural gullibility was voiced in a recent book written by real estate broker Bill Wiese. In *23 Minutes in Hell*, Wiese claimed to have visited hell through out of body experiences and visions. He fails to explain why everyone there was dead but him. He describes being confined to a 15' by 10' cell where two foul smelling beasts threw him against a stone wall, broke his bones, and then ripped open his flesh. Despite the superhuman strength of the creatures, he managed to crawl out of the cell where he heard the agonizing cries of the billions of people held captive in hell before Jesus rescued him and told him to go back to earth and tell people that hell was real.[289]

Why do people believe this stuff? It certainly isn't biblical. Writers like this want us to believe them, but that puts each one

---

[287] Rob Bell, *Love Wins: A Book About Heaven, Hell, and the Fate of Every Person Who Ever Lived* (San Francisco, CA: HarperOne, 2011), 71-73.

[288] Ibid., 175.

[289] Bill Wiese, *23 Minutes in Hell: One Man's Story About What He Saw, Heard, and Felt in that Place of Torment* (Lake Mary, Florida: Charisma House, 2006), 26.

on a par with writers of the New Testament. That's why they are to be completely rejected. Scripture indicates we should never listen to these kinds of people.

So how do we begin talking about hell? Should we make fun of it and use it as an expletive? Why is the word *hell* used in conversation in such diverse ways? One might say, "That was a hell of a game," meaning it was a great game. But the same person might also say, "That was a hell of a thing to do to them," meaning that something terrible had been done. Why do they say, "Hell no!" and not "Heaven no?"

Worst of all, we often hear people say, "Go to hell!" This is either a way to trivialize the word by using it in a casual way as if it didn't exist, or it's a way of pronouncing the absolute very worst condition on someone we can imagine. So, it's either a form of escape or our most severe condemnation.

C.S. Lewis acknowledges the enormity of this problem in *The Problem of Pain*. We can all agree with him when he writes,

> There is no doctrine, which I would more willingly remove from Christianity than this, if it lay in my power. But it has the full support of Scripture and, specially, of our Lord's own words; it has always been held by Christendom; and it has the support of reason.[290]

RICH MAN – POOR MAN

One of the most instructive stories in the Bible about heaven and hell is the story of the rich man and the poor man that Jesus told in Luke 16:19-31. This story makes the biblical teaching on hell extremely personal because it actually opens the curtain for us a bit and lets us follow the journey of two men from their earthly lives to their lives after death. It's the only story like this in the Bible.

---

[290] Lewis, *The Problem of Pain*, 118.

Let me be clear at this point. This story teaches that one second after you die, there are only two possible destinies—heaven or hell. And the people who end up in heaven will no doubt surprise a lot of people. But the same is true of those who will end up in hell.

This was the case of the rich man. *"He habitually dressed in purple and fine linen, joyously living in splendor every day."*[291] The purple garments were probably Phoenician wool dyed purple that came from murex, a rare and expensive sea mussel. His inner garments were *"fine linen,"* a fabric known as "byssus" from Egypt. It usually sold for twice its weight in gold.[292]

He was a *"lover of money,"* just like the Pharisees, who was "joyously living in splendor" in a palatial estate.[293] We know this because the word used to describe the "gate" of his house is "pylon." This designated an ornamental gate at the entrance to a palace.

We're also told that the man was a Hebrew because, when he was in distress in hell, he called out to *"Father Abraham."* So, he wasn't a pagan or an atheist. He was a devout Jew and an upstanding member of the community. But good people, even "religious" ones are often far from God. The devout Jews listening to Jesus tell this story certainly believed that the rich man would end up in heaven. After all, he was a Jew and, no doubt, a "good man."

This brings up an important point. People often ask, "What about all the good people in the world who die without ever knowing anything about Jesus? Is it fair that they are condemned to hell without knowing Christ?"

There are two problems with this question. The first is that the Bible says there is no such thing as a "good" person. The Bible

---

[291] Luke 16:19

[292] J. J. Van Oosterzee, *The Gospel According to Luke: An Exegetical and Doctrinal Commentary*, trans. John Peter Lange and Charles C. Starbuck, (1874, repr., Eugene, Oregon: Wipf and Stock Publishers, 2007), 253.

[293] Luke 16:19

says, "*There is none righteous, not even one; there is none who understands, there is none who seeks for God; all have turned aside, together they have become useless; there is none who does good, there is not even one.*"[294] That's a universal standard.

The other problem is a misunderstanding of why people are condemned to hell in the first place. They are not condemned because they don't know Jesus. The Bible indicates they are condemned because they suppress the truth that God provided them in creation and their own conscience,[295] they love the darkness of their unbelief because their deeds are evil,[296] they harden their hearts against God,[297] and they choose to obey unrighteousness, wrath and indignation.[298] Thus, they deserve God's judgment because of their choice to continue in sin.[299] Man is condemned to hell by his own works, not because he hasn't heard of Jesus.

Before we go accusing God of anything let's remind ourselves that arriving at the doors of hell is ultimately by man's choice. J.I. Packer reflects this when he writes,

> God's wrath in the Bible is something that men choose for themselves. Before hell is an experience inflicted by God, it is a state for which man himself opts, by retreating from the light which God shines in his heart to lead him to Himself. . . . In the last analysis, all that God does subsequently in judicial action towards the unbeliever, whether in this life or beyond it, is to show him, and lead him into the full implications of the choice he has made.[300]

---

[294] Romans 3:10-12
[295] Romans 1:18-20; 2:14,15
[296] John 3:19
[297] Hebrews 4:7
[298] Romans 2:8
[299] Romans 6:23; Galatians 6:7-8
[300] J. I. Packer, *Knowing God* (Downers Grove, Ill.: Inter-Varsity, 1973), 138.

Torment and agony

The story in Luke tells us that, *"the rich man also died and was buried. In Hades he lifted up his eyes, being in torment, and saw Abraham far away and Lazarus in his bosom."*[301] This was totally unexpected by the Jews listening to the story. That's because they not only had the idea that all Jews would go to heaven because they were God's favored ones, but rich people would get in because riches were a special sign of God's blessing.

But here the rich man dies and goes to hell! Talk about an uncomfortable subject! God is no respecter of persons. He doesn't play favorites nor does He pick on any group of people. He is completely impartial. That means that there will be many rich men like this man in Luke who will be very surprised when they die.

One second after he died, the rich man was *"In Hades he lifted up his eyes, being in torment, and saw Abraham far away and Lazarus in his bosom. And he cried out and said, 'Father Abraham, have mercy on me, and send Lazarus so that he may dip the tip of his finger in water and cool off my tongue, for I am in agony in this flame."*[302]

Notice there are two different words to describe the torment of hell. First, we find the rich man was *"in torment."* This word could be translated as "torture." It is used to describe the torture of physical disease,[303] the destruction of a storm,[304] the sting of a poisonous scorpion,[305] and the eternal torture of fire and brimstone.[306]

The second word is seen at the end of the passage when he says, *"I am in agony in this flame."* The word for *agony* here can

---

[301] Luke 16:22-23
[302] Luke 16:23-24
[303] Matthew 4:24
[304] Matthew 14:24
[305] Revelation 9:5
[306] Revelation 20:10

refer either to physical or mental pain. Since it is used with *torment* in the same passage it would seem that *agony* stresses mental pain. In the Old Testament, it was used to describe lost opportunity[307] and bitterness of the soul.[308] In the New Testament Paul uses it to describe the agony of the loss of friends who will not be saved,[309] and the grief of parting with dear friends who you will never see again.[310]

It's obvious that this *agony* is mental and emotional which makes it unbearable. The rich man's experience in hell was dramatically different from anything he had experienced on earth. He was in a place of mental *"agony"* because he knew where he was and why he was there.

Weeping and gnashing of teeth

Matthew further explains this agony by noting hell will be a place of *"weeping and gnashing of teeth."*[311] The word for weeping is onomatopoetic. That's a fancy word that simply means the word itself sounds like what it describes. The Greek word is *klaio*. You can almost hear the sound as you say the word. It means, "to cry aloud, weep; bewail." In secular Greek it "doesn't merely express remorse or sorrow, but physical or mental pain which is outwardly visible."[312]

The phrase *"gnashing of teeth,"* is used seven times in the gospels to describe hell. The picture is of one who clenches their jaw and grinds their teeth in anger. The noun form of this word is used in Acts 7:54 to describe the rage of those listening to the

---

[307] Zechariah 12:10

[308] Isaiah 38:15

[309] Romans 9:2

[310] Acts 20:38

[311] Matthew 8:12

[312] H. Haarbeck, "Lament, Sorrow, Weep, Groan," ed. Lothar Coenen, Erich Beyreuther, and Hans Bietenhard, *New International Dictionary of New Testament Theology* (Grand Rapids, MI: Zondervan Publishing House, 1986), 416.

sermon of Stephen. They were *"cut to the quick and they began gnashing their teeth at him."* In fact, they were so furious they killed him. This is anger that borders on rage. It describes the perpetual outlook of the person in hell. They will not be repentant. They will be furious with God for sending them there!

The fire of judgment

The last descriptor we see in Luke refers to flames. Fire is a predominant picture of hell in the New Testament. The word for hell used in the original language of the New Testament is *Gehenna*. The word referred to a literal valley that skirted the southern side of the city of Jerusalem. You can still make out the contours of this valley today if you visit the city.

Gehenna, or "Valley of Hinnom," was a place of extreme carnage. It was the place where the Valley of Hinnom met the Kidron Valley in an area called Hakeldama (field of blood) where Judas hung himself. In Jesus' time it was the city dump where all the garbage and human refuse of the city was discarded.

In ancient times it had been the site of some of the most horrific practices that Jews adopted from pagan cultures. The prophet Jeremiah called it *Topheth*, which referred to the practice of child sacrifice that had been adopted by Israel through religious syncretism with pagan cultures.[313]

One possible root of *Topheth* is *tōp*, or drum, referring to the drums used to drown the cries of children who were sacrificed alive to Molech the pagan god. Others regard the root of *Topheth* to mean "the place of burning" dead bodies.[314] This practice even

---

[313] Jeremiah 7:32

[314] Merrill Frederick Unger et al., *Unger's Bible Dictionary* (repr., 1957, Chicago, Illinois: Moody Press, 1979), 1109.

reached the palace when both the wicked kings Ahaz[315] and Manasseh[316] sacrificed their own sons in this horrific manner.[317]

It's hard to imagine a place more associated with vile, repulsive practices. The picture of innocent babies being burned alive, the overflow burial ground for Jews killed when they lost their land to the Babylonians, and the garbage dump for human waste and trash where fires burned continuously became a picture of Jesus' depiction of hell. What a terrible place.

That's one of the reasons why fire is a fitting picture of hell. Fire is used many times in the Bible to picture God's judgment. But it doesn't necessarily mean literal flames. When Jesus used the term *"unquenchable fire"* He was not necessarily referring to literal fire. In the previous verse, He promised that He would baptize His disciples *"with the Holy Spirit and fire."*[318] This refers to *"tongues of fire"*[319] that appeared in the book of Acts as supernatural manifestations of the coming of the Holy Spirit. But they weren't literal flames.

We also note Malachi says the coming Messiah will be *"like a refiner's fire and fuller's soap,"*[320] obviously referring to His judgment and cleansing activities, not literal fire and soap. Likewise, Jesus came to *"cast fire upon the earth"*[321] but in that context it seems pretty clear that Luke is talking about judgment, not literal fire. Jesus' eyes are described as a *"flame of fire"*[322] but that doesn't mean they look like a blowtorch. Instead, this is in the context of Jesus judging the seven churches of Asia Minor.

---

[315] 2 Chronicles 28:3

[316] 2 Kings 21:6

[317] R. Laird Harris, Gleason L. Archer Jr., and Bruce K. Waltke, eds., *Theological Wordbook of the Old Testament* (Chicago: Moody Press, 1999), 979.

[318] Matthew 3:11

[319] Acts 2:3

[320] Malachi 3:2

[321] Luke 12:49

[322] Revelation 1:14

This leads us to believe that when fire is used to describe hell, it's used to describe the all-consuming nature of God's judgment, not literal flames. But that doesn't diminish the nature of God's judgment.

When mass murderers and ethnic cleansers and racist bigots and sexual perverts and all sorts of criminals, rapists, pedophiles, crooked politicians, military tyrants, thieves, market manipulators, genocidal killers, jihadists, and liars do their thing, people scream, "Why doesn't God do something?!" When they see six million Jews exterminated in the ovens of Germany in WWII they cry out "Where is God?"

In the end, God will finally say, "Here I am!" He will answer the cumulative millennia of sin by condemning all those who don't find refuge in Him to an eternity apart from Him. His final action of justice will shut the mouths of all who have questioned His very existence, His power, His love, and His justice forever. The final judgment of God in condemning all who reject Him to hell will show that His jurisdiction encompasses the final pit of darkness prepared for all who will not bow to Him.

Isolation

It's hard to believe that people make jokes about hell. Many seem to think that hell will be like hanging out in their favorite haunt with all their friends. Country singer Toby Keith sings about his favorite bar where "we got winners, we got losers, chain smokers and boozers. An' we got yuppies, we got bikers, An' we got thirsty hitchhikers."[323] He sings that he loves the bar because it's his kind of place. Some think that's what hell is like. "As long as I'm with my buddies I'll be all right." Is that the way it will be? Why not ask the rich man in Luke's story?

---

[323] Scott Emerick, Toby Keith, "I Love This Bar" lyrics © Tokeco Tunes, Sony/ATV Music Publishing LLC, Round Hill Music Big Loud Songs

The rich man had knowledge of both Lazarus and of Abraham. In fact, he not only knew Lazarus, but he still regarded him as an inferior. Upon arriving in his new destination *"he cried out and said, 'Father Abraham, have mercy on me, and send Lazarus so that he may dip the tip of his finger in water and cool off my tongue, for I am in agony in this flame.'"*[324] He still thought he could boss Lazarus around. He also expressed an awareness of earthly family relationships when he later asked Abraham to send someone to warn his brothers not to come to his place of torment.

This is part of the torment of hell. The rich man's personality, memory, and consciousness were all intact. All his mental faculties were working. Being confined there didn't remove the agony of lost relationships and the panic that his loved ones might also end up in that awful place.

But notice that he is alone. There is no mention of his buddies. I'm sure he must have had some in his wealthy earthly days. And he must have been preceded in death by some relatives. Where are they now? One of the most haunting aspects about hell is that it is spent alone. There is no hint of human companionship or commiseration there.

We also see this in Jesus' statement that those condemned to hell will be thrown *"into outer darkness."*[325] It's not too hard to understand darkness, is it? Darkness is the absence of light. There will be no gathering around the campfire with your buddies to sing "Kumbaya" in hell. And the "outer darkness" seems to emphasize removal from all sources of light. The old saying that "one is a lonely number" will be exacerbated in the dark, lonely confines of hell.

God's authority

---

[324] Luke 16:24
[325] Matthew 22:13; 25:30

There is no doubt this is a hard, hard teaching in the Bible. But we must see this in terms of God's final jurisdiction over all things. One of the final pictures of hell in the Bible tells us that those condemned *"will be tormented with fire and brimstone in the presence of the holy angels and in the presence of the Lamb."*[326] This isn't petty or smug. It's the vindication of God's holiness and justice against those who flaunted their wickedness as if God didn't exist.

We also find that God will not be a casual observer of those who end up in hell. He is to be feared because He *"has authority to cast into hell; yes, I tell you, fear Him!"*[327] The word for "cast" is the same word used numerous times in the gospels when Jesus casts demons out. It is the simple word "to throw." Other places indicate He will *"throw out the worthless slave into outer darkness,"* [328] *"bind him hand and foot, and throw him into the outer darkness,"*[329] and *"throw them into the furnace of fire."*[330] These passages indicate a forceful, decisive action of God in consigning sinners to hell.

Throwing someone into the furnace of fire doesn't sound very empathetic. But that's only if we don't want to see the heinous acts of the one being thrown. In the book of Revelation God describes them as *"the cowardly and unbelieving and abominable and murderers and immoral persons and sorcerers and idolaters and all liars, their part will be in the lake that burns with fire and brimstone, which is the second death."*[331]

My point is that the justice and holiness of God demands that He throws all vestiges of rebellion and sin into hell. If He didn't we wouldn't be happy, and He wouldn't be God.

---

[326] Revelation 14:10
[327] Luke 12:5
[328] Matthew 25:30
[329] Matthew 22:13
[330] Matthew 13:42, 50
[331] Revelation 21:8

Forever and ever

As if that weren't bad enough, Scripture describes hell as never ending. That only adds to the misery of those in hell. In Luke's account of the rich man's torment, the grammar of the verb *"being in torment"* in the original language, points to a continuous state of being. Elsewhere in Scripture, we find hell described as *"eternal punishment,"*[332] a place where *"the worm does not die and the fire is not quenched,"*[333] a place of *"everlasting destruction,"*[334] where *"the smoke of their torment ascends forever and ever; they have no rest day and night."*[335]

There is no annihilation, no second chance, no reprieve, no comfort, no hope, and no end in sight. Those in hell are subject to the fury and wrath of God forever and ever! The phrase *forever and ever* is used twelve other times in Revelation to describe both the eternal nature of the reign of Jesus Christ, as well as the ongoing nature of hell.

Many people have struggles with the fact that hell is eternal. D. A. Carson responds,

> Hell is not a place where people are consigned because they were pretty good blokes, but they just didn't believe the right stuff. They're consigned there, first and foremost, because they defy their maker and want to be at the center of the universe. Hell is not filled with people who have already repented, only God isn't gentle enough or good enough to let them out. It's filled with people who, for all eternity, still want to be the center of the universe and who persist in their God-defying rebellion.[336]

---

[332] Matthew 25:46

[333] Mark 9:44

[334] 2 Thessalonians 1:9

[335] Revelation 14:11

[336] Lee Strobel, *The Case For Christ: A Journalist's Personal Investigation of the Evidence for Jesus* (Grand Rapids, Michigan: Zondervan, 1998), 165.

So, what is God supposed to do? Imagine what would happen if we had no laws. What would happen if no one were punished for running stop signs, or stealing cars, or raping our daughters? Why did the world demand the Nuremburg Trials at the end of World War II for "crimes against humanity?" At the time, Hitler was just the latest in a long, long line of kings, potentates, and dictators who have ruled and abused their people with a murderous iron fist.

And of course, the cry for justice goes beyond national leaders. It extends to every criminal, burglar, thief, murderer, pimp, rapist, tax cheat, Wall Street manipulator, sex-trafficker, pornographer, corrupt politician, crooked judge, drug dealer, liar, adulterer, child molester, gay activist, mafia boss, jihadist, and false teacher who has ever walked the face of the earth. And, as we saw in chapter one, the call for justice extends to each one of us because we are all sinful whether we recognize it or not.

So, it makes no sense to be upset with God and call Him cruel when He exercises His divine righteousness and divine justice on those who deserve it. Everyone who ends up in hell has a long rap sheet of charges without ever serving time. Whenever justice is corrupted or not executed people cry out, "Why doesn't someone do something about this?" God will. He will bring deserving people who have not come to Him with a contrite and repentant heart to ultimate justice and condemn them to an eternity in hell for their crimes.

There is another reason, and possibly the strongest, that can be advanced for the eternal nature of hell. If God is eternal (as He is), and His offer of salvation brings eternal life with Him (which it does), then the logical result of rejecting the offer of eternal salvation from the eternal God makes this a question of infinite value. David Clotfelter in his book *Sinners in the Hands of a Good God* writes that this:

[E]xplanation of hell's eternity is one first used by the medieval theologian Anselm of Canterbury and most clearly expressed by Jonathan Edwards. This is the argument that because God is a Being of infinite worth, to whom we owe an infinite obligation, sin against God is an infinite evil requiring an infinite punishment. And since the punishments of hell cannot be infinite in intensity, as that would violate the principle that the lost are punished according to their deeds, it must be the case that hell is infinite in duration.[337]

It's no wonder the writer to the Hebrews reminds us, *"For if the word spoken through angels proved unalterable, and every transgression and disobedience received a just penalty, how will we escape if we neglect so great a salvation?"*[338] How can that be compared to anything we can understand? It would be like receiving an offer of all the riches in all the banks, real estate, oil fields, mines, and stock markets in the world along with a commitment of new medical technology that would keep you young, alive, and vibrant forever, coupled with a genie who would guarantee that your heart would always be filled with love, virtue, and integrity—and you turned it all down! Why would anyone do that?

Plea for mercy not answered

That doesn't mean there won't be a plea for mercy for those entering hell. The account about the rich man and Lazarus contains the rich man's tragic plea for mercy. *"Father Abraham, have mercy on me, and send Lazarus so that he may dip the tip of his finger in water and cool off my tongue, for I am in agony in this flame."*[339] The plea is tragic because it shows the agony of awareness and because it isn't answered. There is nothing worse than

---

[337] David Clotfelter, *Sinners in the Hands of a Good God: Reconciling Divine Justice and Mercy* (Chicago: Moody Publishers, 2004), 91-92.
[338] Hebrews 2:2-3
[339] Luke 16:24

parched thirst under a blazing sun. But this mental and spiritual thirst is not quenched.

Abraham responds by saying, *"Child, remember that during your life you received your good things, and likewise Lazarus bad things; but now he is being comforted here, and you are in agony."*[340] The final verdict for the rich man is that *"during your life you received your good things . . ."*[341] That is, he lived the life he wanted. And he got what he wanted out of life—money, prestige, possessions, and a life without God.

This is the tragic mistake most people make. We work for what we want in this life. Some even get it. But few ever stop to consider what comes after this life. Most people work hard just to survive. If we're fortunate to live in a developed country, we have the chance to achieve a life of relative ease. Some even have the fortune to accomplish great things and pile up a lot of stuff.

But one second after you die, when it matters most, all who reject God will come up short. Each person will get what they wanted in life—time spent doing what they wanted, and a life without God. And now in death, they will also get what they wanted all along—a life without God. When we turn a deaf ear to God in life, He will turn a deaf ear to us in the afterlife. What a tragedy.

Many people think that the ultimate value in life is to be free to do whatever they want to do. People treasure the freedom to say what they want, go where they want, and decide whatever they want about the ultimate issues of life, God, and the afterlife. What they don't realize is that human freedom ultimately exists in a box. As we saw in the last chapter, this box is the limitations of their worldview. When they die, they will find out that they have no freedom to escape the confines of their box. They will be limited to what they chose with their own free will.

---

[340] Luke 16:25
[341] Ibid

A great chasm

The parable of the rich man and Lazarus adds another monumental truth about hell in Luke 16:26. *"And besides all this, between us and you there is a great chasm fixed, so that those who wish to come over from here to you will not be able, and that none may cross over from there to us."* The word for *"chasm"* pictures a yawning gap that's impossible to cross. There's no helicopter. There's not even a rickety old rope bridge. There's no invisible force to hold you up like Indiana Jones. There's only a vision of a far, far, cliff on the other side that you will never reach. Never.

This is worse than *Hotel California* where you can "check out any time you want, but you can never leave."[342] This is no mythical hotel. It's hell. In hell there is no exit door, no "get out of hell free" card, no purgatory just in case you missed it on earth, no soul sleep. This is not a dream. It's a nightmare. There is only one way in and it's our own will that gets us there. We can't get out, and no one will come in from the outside to help. There is no fence to sit on, no demilitarized zone. There is only a wide, yawning chasm that can never be crossed.

Johnny Cash knew this. Cash was an American singer/songwriter whose influence spanned the last half of the twentieth century. He wrote, "I wear the black for those who've never read or listened to the words that Jesus said." He continued, "How well I have learned that there is no fence to sit on between heaven and hell. There is a deep, wide gulf, a chasm, and in that chasm is no place for any man."[343]

---

[342] Don Felder, Don Henley, Glen Frey, "Hotel California," on Hotel California, Asylum Records, 1977.

[343] Ray Comfort, *What Hollywood Believes: An Intimate Look at the Faith of the Famous* (Bartlesville, OK: Genesis Publishing Group, 2004), 122.

What about my brothers?

The parable of the rich man and Lazarus ends with an agonizing plea by the rich man to cross this chasm. He pleads with Abraham to send someone to tell his brothers, believing that *"if someone goes to them from the dead, they will repent."*[344]

Maybe this is the most severe part of hell. In hell there will be a conscious awareness of loved ones and their eternal destiny. They will do anything to warn their loved ones about this awful place. Can you imagine what it would be like to round a corner on a highway and unexpectedly run into the flaming wreckage of a tanker truck loaded with gas, knowing that your family is in a speeding car right behind you? You would do everything you could to warn them!

Abraham's answer is startling in its severe truth. He responds, *"If they do not listen to Moses and the Prophets, they will not be persuaded if someone rises from the dead."*[345] In other words, "No, they won't repent!" In essence Abraham says that "even if you could return from hell with your clothes smoking and your hair on fire, your loved ones wouldn't repent. Why? Because they have the same warnings you had Mr. Rich Man. You didn't read the Bible. You didn't listen to your conscience. You were too busy to consider spiritual things. And it's the same with your loved ones. Unless they repent, one second after they die they will understand the cost of their rebellion." What a terrible price to pay for rejecting God.

---

[344] Luke 16:30
[345] Luke 16:31

"Many are willing to give up everything for Christ's sake, excepting one darling sin, and for the sake of that sin are lost for evermore."[346]
—J. C. Ryle

It's Impossible

What can I do to inherit eternal life?

On April 27, 1990, the headline of *The New York Times* read, "'I'm Sorry,' Says a Killer of 4 Just Before He's Put to Death."[347] The convicted murderer was not your typical death row inmate. So, who was the condemned killer, and why is his story unique?

HEINOUS CRIMES

Ronald "Rusty" Woomer's path to death row began on February 21, 1979. He and Eugene Skaar left West Virginia with a plan to steal rare coins from a collector, 67-year-old John Turner, of Cottageville, South Carolina. When the pair reached Turner's

---

[346] J. C. Ryle – *Expository Thoughts on the Gospels: Luke, vol. 2*, (1858; repr., Cambridge: James Clarke, 1976), 272.

[347] Associated Press news, *New York Times*, "'I'm Sorry,' Says Killer of 4 Just Before He's Put to Death," http://www.nytimes.com/1990/04/28/us/i-m-sorry-says-a-killer-of-4-just-before-he-s-put-to-death.html, (accessed July 17, 2017).

home on February 22, they took the coins and fatally shot Turner in the head.

From there, Woomer and Skaar drove to a neighboring community. They forced their way into the home of Arnie Richardson, looking for money and guns. Woomer shot Richardson, 27, in the head, killing him. Then, in a further barbaric act, killed Richardson's 35-year-old, mentally handicapped sister-in-law, Earldean Wright, to silence her screams. They also wounded Richardson's daughter.

Later that day, the ruthless duo of Woomer and Skaar kidnapped Della Sellers, 34, and Wanda Summers, 24, from a convenience store on Pawleys Island, where the women worked. They took the ladies to a remote wooded area and brutally raped them. Woomer then shot each one. Sellers died, yet Summers survived, losing half her face to the shotgun blast.

As police closed in on the pair while they were holed up in a Myrtle Beach motel, Skaar committed suicide to avoid capture. The drugged-out Woomer surrendered peacefully. The next day, shaking and still high, he confessed to the murders.

Making the self-righteous uncomfortable

This part of the story gets *uncomfortable* for the self-righteous. We are all right with God's grace extending to those that are *marginally* sinful, but condemned murderers? Really? Can they get "in" too?

About this same time, the Lord was leading a newly converted businessman, Bob McAlister, into prison ministry through the influence of a few friends.[348] His first contact with prisoners was when he went to see a man in the old Central Correctional Institution in downtown Columbia, South Carolina. This led to further opportunities.

---

[348] Bill Stringfellow, "The Rusty Woomer Story," republished in its' entirety by Revelation Messengers, http://www.revelationmessengers.com/rustywoomer.html, (accessed July 17, 2017).

McAlister had previously worked as a reporter, so he was familiar with the corrections commissioner. This relationship allowed him access to death row inmates that may have been unlikely otherwise. Before long, he was there every Friday night.

One night in October of 1985, after McAlister had visited a few of his "regulars" on death row, he was getting ready to leave the prison. Yet before he left, he was drawn to stop at one more cell. By now, he was accustomed to some terrible sights, but he had never seen anything like this.

In "The Rusty Woomer Story," Bill Stringfellow described the scene this way:

> The inmate was sitting on the floor of his cell, looking like a pale, dirty shrimp. The concrete floor was strewn with papers, half-eaten sandwiches, toilet paper, old copies of Playboy and Penthouse magazines. The cell stank. The man stank, too. His long, dirty blond hair and beard matted and greasy. His face was chalk-colored, like a rubber mask, like a dead person. And all over the cell, and all over the man, crawled dozens of cockroaches. He didn't even move as they swarmed over his shoulders, his hair and his legs. Bob had met this inmate before and had exchanged a few words with him. His name was Rusty Woomer.[349]

As a new Christian convert himself, McAlister didn't think in terms of demonic possession or even the physical presence of evil. But that night he had the bone-chilling reality of what he was facing. There was little doubt the presence of the Holy Spirit directed his thoughts and actions. He knew that Satan had a hold on Woomer. So, he called on the name of Jesus to cast out the devil and death in that cell.

Then he said, "Rusty, just say the name 'Jesus.' Call on Jesus." Nothing happened for several moments. Then the man's lips

---

[349] Ibid

moved slowly. "Jesus," he whispered, "Jesus. Jesus." Stringfellow continues:

> Bob gripped the bars of the cell so hard his hand hurt. "Rusty," he called out again, "look around you, son. Look at what you are living in." To his amazement the man slowly sat up straighter, his eyes actually focusing on the floor and walls of his cell. They widened as he saw the roaches. "Your cell is filthy, and so are you," Bob said gently. "The roaches have taken over, and you're spiritually a dead man. Son, Jesus can give you something better. Don't you want to pray to give your life to Him instead?"
>
> Rusty nodded, his eyes glistening, then streaming with tears—the first tears he had wept in 15 years—as his heart cracked open. He bowed his head like he remembered doing in his childhood. Then the amazing thing happened.
>
> "Jesus," Rusty prayed, "I've hurt a lot of people. Ain't no way that I deserve You to hear me. But I'm tired and I'm sick and I'm lonely. Please forgive me, Jesus, for everything I've done. I don't know much about You, but I'm willing to learn, and I thank You for listenin' to me."[350]

So, the man who kidnapped, raped, maimed, and murdered in 1979 became a Christian in 1985. But that didn't change the fact that he was a convicted inmate on death row.

Over the course of the next five years, there was plenty of evidence to "convict" Woomer for being a genuine follower of Jesus. His lifestyle demonstrated that Jesus Christ was the Lord of his life. Redemption in Christ brings transformation in life that cannot be duplicated any other way.

McAlister spent hours upon end with Woomer leading up to his execution in 1990. "Rusty, what will be your thoughts when they strap you in that chair?" he asked. "The human side of me is scared to sit down and be electrocuted," Woomer replied.

---

[350] Ibid.

But I'm gonna be holdin' Jesus' hand. Long as He's my partner, what can I say? After all, there's no way I'm gonna lose. If they execute me, the next thing I'll know is that I'll be resurrected and taken to heaven. If they don't, I'll be the same. He's made it impossible for me not to praise and love Him and tell people about what He's done.[351]

Rusty Woomer's story has a lot of critics. We are rightfully skeptical of "jailhouse conversions." There has been more than one inmate who had a *come-to-Jesus* moment in an attempt to get a "get out of jail free" card.

So, some may doubt that Woomer's experience was anything more than emotional hype. Or they may think that, since he committed such heinous crimes, he is disqualified from any kind of beneficial religious experience. Many people would prefer that he rot in hell if there is such a place.

That's precisely why the subject matter of this chapter is so important. The question boils down to whether Rusty Woomer should indeed rot in hell or is there any way that someone as undeserving as he is can get into heaven.

The Bible uses the word *saved* to describe this process. Though many people mock this word it is a wonderful biblical word that explains what it means to literally be saved from the fires of torment and judgment described in the last chapter.

But how does this happen? What did Woomer do to *get saved*? If he was indeed saved from the fires of eternal torment, how did that happen? Furthermore, is it possible for anyone to do anything that contributes to his or her spiritual salvation?

The biblical answer to that question is "no." But there have been many attempts to conceal the biblical response and cloak it in false religion or human wisdom. We will examine some of the prominent false attempts to answer this question, and then we will see what the Bible says about the issue.

---

[351] Ibid.

FALSE ATTEMPTS

Roman Catholicism

Possibly one of the most prominent purveyors of a false answer to this question is the Roman Catholic Church. In western culture, the Reformation of the 16th century signaled a massive break with the thousand-year domination of the Roman Catholic Church in Europe over the issue of salvation. But many Catholics and Protestants today can't tell the difference between the two groups, despite significant theological differences.

The key issue of the Reformation is: How is a man saved from the eternal fire of hell? Despite the fact that the Bible says, *"For we maintain that a man is justified by faith apart from works of the Law,"*[352] Catholic dogma insists otherwise. The Catholic reaction to the Reformation was the Council of Trent, a group of Catholic theologians who met from 1545 to 1563. This produced a massive amount of material denouncing the Reformers biblical teaching on salvation by grace alone through faith alone in Christ alone. Two statements (among hundreds made) show the false teaching of the Catholic Church regarding salvation:

> *If anyone says that *by faith alone* the sinner is justified, so as to mean that nothing else is required to cooperate in order to obtain the grace of justification . . . let him be anathema (*Council of Trent*, Sixth Session, Canon 9).[353]
>
> *If anyone says that the guilt is remitted to every penitent sinner after the grace of justification has been received, and that the debt of eternal punishment is so blotted out that there remains no debt of temporal punishment to be discharged either in this world or in the next in Purgatory, before the entrance

---

[352] Romans 3:28

[353] H. R. Schroeder, trans., *The Canons and Decrees of the Gospel of Trent* (Rockford, Illinois: Tan Books and Publishers, Inc., 1978), 43.

to the kingdom of heaven can be opened-let him be anathema (*Council of Trent*, Sixth Session, Canon 30).[354]

These statements categorically deny what the Bible says about salvation and have never been disavowed or changed by the Catholic Church in any way. They continue to be a stumbling block to millions who need to know what the Bible says about being right with God.

Liberal theology

Liberal theologians are still trying to conjure up new ways to be right with God outside the demands of the Bible. Leander S. Harding, Episcopal Theologian, rector of St. John's Episcopal Church in Stamford Connecticut said, "When the self-determining self finds 'the real me' salvation is achieved and the ultimate self has achieved contact with ultimate reality."[355]

Rob Bell has a radical view on being saved. He solves the problem by stating, "The love of God will melt every hard heart, and even the most 'depraved sinners' will eventually give up their resistance and turn to God."[356] In short, Bell solves the problem simply by saying, "What Jesus does is declare that he, and he alone, is saving everybody."[357]

The health and wealth gospel

A huge distortion of biblical faith is seen in what some call the modern "health and wealth" movement. Simply put, God wants His people to be free from sickness, worry, and poverty—especially poverty. And each of us has the key to unlocking these things, if we will just act on our God-given rights to them.

---

[354] Ibid., 46.

[355] "No Fault Division" in *Christianity Today*, July 1, 2004.

[356] Rob Bell, *Love Wins: A Book About Heaven, Hell, and the Fate of Every Person Who Ever Lived* (New York, NY: Harper One, 2011), 107.

[357] Ibid., 155.

One of the most popular purveyors of the pious platitudes promising prosperity is Joel Osteen. Thousands of people flock into his "church" each week to hear how they can have faith in themselves. Osteen, the son of a Baptist pastor turned prosperity gospel proponent, doesn't come across as a sleazy, sweating TV evangelist. His boyish looks and folksy charm leads people into his smiling presence by telling them what they want to hear.

But his teaching isn't about God, or even God's Word. He continuously presents a self-centered gospel with a phrase or misquoted Scripture to give his thoughts a ring of authenticity. He is a false teacher selling fake faith. He declares,

> That's why it is so important that we get in a habit of declaring good things over our lives every day. When you get up in the morning, instead of looking at that mirror and saying, "Oh, I can't believe I look like this. I'm getting so old, so wrinkled," you need to smile and say, "Good morning, you good-looking thing!" No matter how you feel, look at yourself in that mirror, and say, "I am strong, I am healthy. God is renewing my strength like the eagles. And I am excited about this day." In other words, don't talk about the way you are; talk about the way you want to be. That's what faith is all about. In the physical realm, you have to see it to believe it, but God says you have to believe it, and then you'll see it.[358]

If the problem of man is sin, then this is nothing more than the proverbial lipstick on a pig. Positive self-talk won't do anything to eradicate wrinkles or sin.

The signs and wonders movement

Another monstrous distortion of conversion is seen in what is popularly called the "Signs and Wonders" movement. The most

---

[358] Joel Osteen, *Become a Better You: 7 Keys to Improve Your Life Every Day* (New Yori, NY: Howard Books, 2009), 111-112.

recent manifestation of this bizarre teaching is Bill Johnson. Johnson is pastor of Bethel Church in Redding, California where glory clouds and gold dust and feathers emanating from the AC vents are claimed to be the presence of God. Johnson also fostered the Jesus Culture music enterprise that features concert extravaganzas led by people who have ostensibly spoken with Jesus. "Fire tunnels" that feature shaking, jerking, falling down, laughing uncontrollably, and receiving the "fire" of the Holy Spirit are also part of the show.

Or, if you want a real impartation of the Holy Spirit, you can engage in "grave sucking" by prostrating oneself on the grave of a dead saint to receive the power of the Holy Spirit given to them. It's hard to believe that thousands of people continue to be duped by this latest example of emotional extravaganza where heretical teaching and bizarre behavior is the standard.

Pop theology

Of course, there are always different forms of pop theology that distort the truth of the Bible and offer various forms of aberrant teaching. One of the most popular forms recently released is *The Shack* written by William Paul Young in 2007 and then followed up by the movie version in 2017.

If one finds it hard to discern the spiritual values in the book or the movie, all questions are removed in Young's recent book *Lies We Believe About God*. He addresses his version of the gospel clearly saying,

> The Good News is *not* that Jesus has opened up the possibility of salvation and you have been invited to receive Jesus into your life. The Gospel is that Jesus has already included you into His life, into His relationship with God the Father, and into His anointing in the Holy Spirit . . . God has acted decisively and universally for all humankind . . .

Are you suggesting that everyone is saved? That you believe in universal salvation?

That is exactly what I am saying.

This is real good news! Here's the truth: every person
who has ever been conceived was included in the death, burial,
resurrection, and ascension of Jesus.[359]

In case you can't tell, his universalist stance contradicts the
biblical doctrines of sin, man, salvation, the atonement, Jesus'
work on the cross, hell, etc., etc., etc. Other than that, *The Shack*
is a pretty good book. But it's not for people looking for ultimate
truth.

Gospel "light"

If we're honest, we must also look at the mistaken theological
beliefs of many evangelicals regarding salvation. The accepted
mantra by many evangelicals is to tell people "God loves you and
has a wonderful plan for your life," and then get them to fill out
a card, raise their hand, or walk the aisle. Many well-meaning
people think it's as simple as praying a magical prayer "inviting
Jesus into your heart," and voila—you're in! But those same people might be surprised to find out that "the sinner's prayer" is not
in the Bible.

One of the most prominent church growth pastors in
America has reduced the gospel to, "First, believe. Believe God
loves you and made you for his purposes. Believe you're not an
accident. . . . Second, receive. Receive Jesus into your life as your
Lord and Savior. Receive his forgiveness for your sins."[360] A simple invitation follows:

---

[359] William Paul Young, *Lies We Believe About God* (New York, NY: Atria
Books, 2017), 117-119.
[360] Rick Warren, *Purpose Driven Life: What on Earth Am I Here For?*
(Grand Rapids, Michigan: Zondervan, 2002), 58-59.

Wherever you are reading this, I invite you to bow your head and quietly whisper the prayer that will change your eternity. "Jesus, I believe in you and I receive you." Go ahead. If you sincerely meant that prayer, congratulations! Welcome to the family of God! You are now ready to discover and start living God's purpose for your life.[361]

Wow! Is that all there is to it? The problem with this, and all these approaches is none of them are in the Bible. It seems today that the chief aim of many pastors is to get the "unchurched" into church by any means necessary. And many have become very good at it by appealing to the felt-needs of non-Christians. But a crowd is not a church and, unfortunately, Jesus did not teach trying to appeal to the crowd.

The effect of false teaching

The cumulative effect of this combination of blatant false teaching and the misguided focus of well-intentioned evangelicals is that scores of people have been drawn into some kind of spiritual experience, many thinking they are saved when they are not. The hallmarks of biblical conversion are simply missing.

This is nothing new. A.W. Tozer pointed out the problems with this kind of theological sleight of hand years ago. He noted:

It is now common practice in most evangelical churches to offer the people, especially the young people, a maximum of entertainment and a minimum of serious instruction. It is scarcely possible in most places to get anyone to attend meeting where the only attraction is God. One can only conclude that God's professed children are bored with Him, for they must be wooed to meeting with a stick of striped candy in the form of religious movies, games and refreshments.

---

[361] Ibid.

So we have the strange anomaly of orthodoxy in creed and heterodoxy in practice. The striped-candy technique has been so fully integrated into our present religious thinking that it is simply taken for granted. Its victims never dream that it is not a part of the teachings of Christ and His apostles.

Any objection to the carryings-on of our present golden calf Christianity is met with the triumphant reply, "But we are winning them!" And winning them to what? To true disciple-ship? To cross-carrying? To self-denial? To separation from the world? To crucifixion of the flesh? To holy living? To nobility of character? To a despising of the world's treasures? To hard self-discipline? To love for God? To total committal to Christ? Of course, the answer to all these questions in "no."[362]

This begs the question, "Well, if you can't get saved through any of those ways, then exactly how do you get saved?" Good question. Let's attempt to answer it by seeing what Jesus says about it.

HOW HARD CAN IT BE?

It's impossible with man

Jesus actually answered this very question in His discussion with a young man in Luke 18:18-30. He didn't have a title, but Luke called him a "ruler," probably indicating he was some kind of businessman. Luke also says he was "very rich" and the paral-lel passage in Matthew says he was "young." So, this rich young ruler seemingly had a lot going for him.

Notice some other things about the young man. Mark's gos-pel says he "*ran up to Him . . .*"[363] Respectable men in that cul-ture didn't run. Running meant you had to hike up your robe and

---

[362] A. W. Tozer, *Man: The Dwelling Place of God* (Harrisburg, PA: Christian Publications, 1966), 136.

[363] Mark 10:17

expose your ankles. That wasn't considered dignified. He also "*knelt before Him*."[364] This was a posture that showed respect and honor. Finally, he called Jesus "*Good Teacher*."[365] This man was anxious and respectful, and we can assume that he was honestly looking for an answer to his question.

He asked, "*Good Teacher, what must I do to inherit eternal life?*"[366] What a set-up! Any Christian wanting to share their faith would love a softball question like this. Yet, as we are about to see, Jesus' response was much different than we might expect. This man seemed ripe for the gospel. And he was rich, which would make him a great candidate to attract others.

The wrong track

But something went wrong. If this was anyone else, one could certainly conclude that he blew this evangelistic opportunity. But this is Jesus. And what did He say? As we see this story unfold, it becomes evident that it obliterates two core beliefs of many people today.

First, this story challenges the assumption that man can choose of his own accord to be saved. Notice he asked, "*What shall I do?*"[367] (underline added). This presumes that God's plan rewards the right questions or human effort. The man may as well have said, "Listen Jesus, I know how these things work. I want to go to heaven so let's cut to the chase. Just tell me what I have to do, and I'll do it." This man seemed to demonstrate spiritual interest. But his choice to seek Jesus out and get some questions answered didn't get him saved.

The second erroneous assumption is people will get saved if we don't do anything to "offend" them. Many Christians today are deathly afraid of saying the "wrong thing" in presenting the

---

364 Ibid.
365 Ibid.
366 Luke 18:18
367 Mark 10:17

gospel or thinking that they will say something that will "offend" the person they are talking to.

Not Jesus. He wasn't being harsh, but His immediate response was to rebuke the young man. He responded, *"Why do you call Me good? No one is good except God alone."*[368] Jesus was a good teacher, but that's not the point of His life and ministry. There is not one example in the Talmud of a rabbi being addressed as "good." So, this man was well intentioned but naïve. Jesus' response must have been completely unexpected and biting. "Wait a minute young man. You must know that no one is good but God, so why are you calling me good unless you recognize that I am God?" But clearly the young man didn't understand that.

Keep the Law

Notice that Jesus doesn't say anything about faith; He doesn't give him the "four spiritual laws" or explain the "plan of salvation." He doesn't even give Him the facts of the gospel. Instead, He went right to the heart. Perceiving that he was an obedient Jew, He exposed his false sense of morality. Jesus said, *"You know the commandments. 'Do not commit adultery, Do not murder, Do not steal, Do not bear false witness, Honor your father and mother.'"*[369] Jesus continued, *"If you wish to enter into life, keep the commandments."* [370]

What is Jesus doing here? Rather than trying to elicit a quick acquiescence to certain spiritual truths, Jesus went right at the man's heart. While it is true that one must believe certain foundational truths to be right with God, it is also true that a person must see their sin before they will ever be moved to truly believe. That's what Jesus is doing here.

But the young man doesn't get it. Not realizing he was exposing the pride of his heart, he replied, *"All these things I have kept*

---

[368] Luke 18:19
[369] Luke 18:20
[370] Matthew 19:17

from my youth."[371] He seems to be saying, "Is that all there is to this?" Check. Done. Wow! Really?

J.C. Ryle wrote, "An answer more full of darkness and self-ignorance it is impossible to conceive! He who made it could have known nothing rightly, either about himself, or God, or God's law."[372] Had he never lied? Had he never stolen anything? Had he never dishonored his parents? From this time on, Jesus knew he was seeking to justify his self-righteous actions.

Many make this mistake. Many think their *relative* righteousness is a substitute for God's *absolute* righteousness. But God demands perfection. No doubt he thought, *I've never committed adultery. I've never murdered anyone. What a good boy am I!*

It's a heart problem

In essence, the rich young ruler was practically saying that he was perfect. He said he kept all five points of the law that Jesus quoted. Now frankly, I doubt if that was true. And so did Jesus. So rather than let him off the hook, Jesus pressed him further. *"One thing you still lack; sell all that you possess and distribute it to the poor, and you shall have treasure in heaven; and come, follow me."*[373]

This is not an instruction for everyone to sell everything they own. It is a specific instruction given to this man because his riches were the very things that prevented achieving his goal of eternal life. His ticket to heaven was keeping the commandments, but he was not willing to give up his money, which showed where his heart really was. It wasn't set on heaven; it was on his money. Jesus clarified this principle when He said, *"[F]or where*

---

[371] Luke 18:21
[372] J. C. Ryle, *Expository Thoughts on the Gospels: Luke, vol. 2*, (1858; repr., Cambridge: James Clarke, 1976), 271.
[373] Luke 18:22

your treasure is, there your heart will be also."[374] The man wanted eternal life in heaven—but not enough to give up his money.

John Wesley met a rich plantation owner while visiting America. He toured the man's vast estate on horseback for hours. At the end of the day they sat down to dinner. "Well, Mr. Wesley, what do you think?" Wesley replied, "I think you're going to have a hard time leaving all this."[375] That was the rich man's dilemma.

The truth is, you can't have the kingdom of God and your kingdom too! J. C. Ryle said, "Many are willing to give up everything for Christ's sake, excepting one darling sin, and for the sake of that sin are lost for evermore."[376] It may be different with different people, but "one darling sin," one thing, one possession, one attitude that counters total surrender can prevent one from obtaining eternal life.

The rich young man's response revealed his heart. Luke records, "*But when he had heard these things, he became very sad, for he was extremely rich.*"[377] The parallel passage in Mark tells us he "*went away grieving, for he was one who owned much property.*"[378] He came to Jesus asking about receiving eternal life. He left without receiving it because his heart could not give up its hold on his money.

It's impossible

When Jesus saw the man's response He said, "*How hard it is for those who are wealthy to enter the kingdom of God!*"[379] Entering the kingdom of God isn't difficult. It's impossible! Jesus explained

---

[374] Matthew 6:21
[375] Randy Alcorn, *Money, Possessions, and Eternity* (Wheaton: Tyndale House, 2003), 159.
[376] Ryle, *Expository Thoughts on the Gospels: Luke*, vol. 2, 272.
[377] Luke 18:23
[378] Mark 10:22
[379] Luke 18:24

further, *"For it is easier for a camel to go through the eye of a needle than for a rich man to enter the kingdom of God."*[380]

There are some who say this refers to a gate in Jerusalem called "The Needle Gate" that was too small for camels to get through. It is said that camels would need to have their packs removed, and then they would have to crawl through on their knees for security purposes. The interpretation of this passage is that, while it is hard for a camel to get through the "eye of the needle," it's not impossible. Thus, the application is that, while it's hard for a person to be saved of his or her own accord, it's not impossible.

But that's not what Jesus is saying. First of all, no such gate ever existed in first century Palestine. Second, it seems best to observe the natural reading of the text that indicates the camel fitting through the eye of a needle is simply an extreme hyperbole. It's absolutely impossible for a camel to fit through the eye of a needle.

And it's absolutely impossible for anyone seeking to earn his or her way into heaven to get there. He wants a cross to hang around his neck as a piece of "Jesus jewelry," but He doesn't want Jesus. Thomas Watson said, "Morality can drown a man as fast as vice. A vessel may sink with gold or with dung."[381] The rich young man discovered that neither morality nor riches could gain him eternal life. What a tragedy for many today who think they are either good enough to get in by their works or their money or their position.

Then who can be saved?

The disciples who were listening to Jesus at this point had a rather obvious question. *"Those who heard it said, 'Then who can*

---

[380] Luke 18:25
[381] Thomas Watson, *The Beatitudes* (Edinburgh: Banner of Truth, 1975), 175.

be saved?"[382] If a righteous Jew who kept the law (or so he said) and was also very rich couldn't get in, then who could?

Jesus agrees with this assessment. He replied, *"The things that are impossible with people are possible with God."*[383] This is the beginning of true conversion. It starts with God, not man. God is God, and we are not. When man approaches God with something in his hands, he can't receive what God has to offer. But when we approach God empty handed, ready to receive, then all things are possible with Him.

Peter showed signs of beginning to understand this. He said, *"Behold, we have left our homes and followed you."*[384] Peter is trying to contrast the disciples' actions with the rich young ruler. "Listen Jesus. He wasn't willing to leave his riches, but look, we've left everything to follow you." That's quite a statement. And it was true. The disciples had left their homes, their families, their businesses, the possessions, their reputations, everything they had, to follow Jesus.

Jesus replied, *"And He said to them, 'Truly I say to you, there is no one who has left house or wife or brothers or parents or children, for the sake of the kingdom of God, who will not receive many times as much at this time and in the age to come, eternal life.'"*[385] Jesus was saying, "I know you have Peter. And you need to know that you will be rewarded with eternal life."

Most people never make this connection. For a variety of reasons they ignore the summons to leave everything and follow Jesus as Peter did. As a result, they never take care of eternal business.

---

[382] Luke 18:26
[383] Luke 18:27
[384] Luke 18: 28
[385] Luke 18:29-30

The book of life

In the last book of the Bible the apostle John reveals Jesus Christ sitting on a great white throne to judge the living and the dead. Since all believers have already been removed from this earth, the accused gathered in this court are the total number of unbelievers in all of recorded history. John says,

> And I saw the dead, the great and the small, standing before the throne, and books were opened; and another book was opened, which is the book of life; and the dead were judged from the things which were written in the books, according to their deeds. And the sea gave up the dead which were in it, and death and Hades gave up the dead which were in them; and they were judged, every one of them according to their deeds.[386]

I think this is perhaps the most sobering passage in the entire Bible because it is final. This is it. The finality of it all is seen in very stark terms. There is no hope and no excuse for them. There will be no debate, no plea bargain, no second chance. There will be no public defender, only the prosecuting attorney, God Himself. And when the sentence is pronounced, there will be no appeal to a higher court, no parole, and no chance of escape.

How do they get there? The Bible says the unsaved *"suppress the truth in unrighteousness"*[387] in rejecting the enormous sign of His creative powers in the universe *"so that they are without excuse."*[388] Furthermore, *"they show the work of the Law written in their hearts, their conscience bearing witness and their thoughts alternately accusing or else defending them."*[389] John clearly explains that *"the Light has come into the world, and men loved the darkness*

---

[386] Revelation 20:12-13
[387] Romans 1:18
[388] Romans 1:20
[389] Romans 2:15

234 • JON MCNEFF / JIM MCNEFF

rather than the Light, for their deeds were evil."[390] Jesus also said,
"*[Y]ou are unwilling to come to Me so that you may have life.*"[391]

People will have no excuse when they stand at the Great White
Throne Judgment. God's jurisdiction will be very clear. He will
judge everyone who has rejected Him by giving them what they
want. John Phillips describes them:

> There is a terrible fellowship there. . . . The dead, small and
> great, stand before God. Dead souls are united to dead bod-
> ies in a fellowship of horror and despair. Little men and paltry
> women whose lives were filled with pettiness, selfishness, and
> nasty little sins will be there. Those whose lives amounted to
> nothing will be there, whose very sins were drab and dowdy,
> mean, spiteful, peevish, groveling, vulgar, common, and cheap.
> The great will be there, men who sinned with a high hand, with
> dash, and courage and flair. Men like Alexander and Napoleon,
> Hitler and Stalin will be present, men who went in for wicked-
> ness on a grand scale with the world for their stage and who
> died unrepentant at last. Now one and all are arraigned and on
> their way to be damned: a horrible fellowship congregated to-
> gether for the first and last time.[392]

After God's final destruction of death, John pronounces the
final judgment: "*And if anyone's name was not found written in
the book of life, he was thrown into the lake of fire.*"[393] All because
their names were not found in the book of life. There is no more
important book in the history of the world.

I'm sorry

---

[390] John 3:19
[391] John 5:40
[392] John Phillips, *Exploring Revelation* (Chicago: Moody, 1987), 242-243.
[393] Revelation 20:15

Randy Alcorn in his book called *Heaven*, tells an account that illustrates the importance of your name being written in the book of life.

Ruthanna Metzgar, a professional singer, tells a story that illustrates the importance of having our names written in the book. Several years ago, she was asked to sing at the wedding of a very wealthy man. According to the invitation the reception would be held on the top two floors of Seattle's Columbia Tower, the Northwest's tallest skyscraper. She and her husband, Roy, were excited about attending.

At the reception, waiters in tuxedos offered luscious hors d'oeuvres and exotic beverages. The bride and groom approached a beautiful glass and brass staircase that led to the top floor. Someone ceremoniously cut a satin ribbon draped across the bottom of the stairs. They announced the wedding feast was about to begin. Bride and groom ascended the stairs, followed by their guests.

At the top of the stairs, a maitre d' with a bound book greeted the guests outside the doors.

"May I have your name please?"

"I am Ruthanna Metzgar and this is my husband, Roy."

He searched the M's. "I'm not finding it. Would you spell it please?"

Ruthanna spelled her name slowly. After searching the book, the maitre d' looked up and said, "I'm sorry, but your name isn't here."

"There must be some mistake," Ruthanna replied. "I'm the singer. I sang for this wedding!"

The gentleman answered, "It doesn't matter who you are or what you did. Without your name in the book you cannot attend the banquet."

He motioned to a waiter and said, "Show these people to the service elevator, please."

The Metzgars followed the waiter past beautifully decorated tables laden with shrimp, whole smoked salmon, and magnificent carved ice sculptures. Adjacent to the banquet area, an orchestra was preparing to perform, the musicians all dressed in dazzling white tuxedos.

The waiter led Ruthanna and Roy to the service elevator, ushered them in, and pushed G for the parking garage.

After locating their car and driving several miles in silence, Roy reached over and put his hand on Ruthanna's arm. "Sweetheart, what happened?"

"When the invitation arrived, I was busy," Ruthanna replied. "I never bothered to RSVP. Besides, I was the singer. Surely I could go to the reception without returning the RSVP!"[394]

Saying "I'm sorry. I forgot to respond to God's RSVP" will not be an option on judgment day. Saying "I'm sorry" was not enough for Rusty Woomer. Saying "I'm sorry" is not good enough for anyone. So, if this is impossible with man, what is the answer?

---

[394] Randy Alcorn, *Heaven* (Carol Stream, Illinois: Tyndale House Publishers, Inc., 2004), 31-32.

CHAPTER TWELVE

"There is nothing that keeps wicked men at any one moment out of hell, but the mere pleasure of God."[395]
—Jonathan Edwards

The Good Bishop

How does God bring us eternal life?

The clear answer to "What must I do to be saved?" is not what most people think. As we saw in the last chapter, the Bible's answer to this question has nothing to do with human effort. Man can't do anything on his own to be saved. But God can. This can be explained in one word—grace. Grace accomplishes what law and sheer effort promise but can never deliver. A changed heart that results in salvation comes only by God's grace.

One of the most powerful literary examples of grace comes from Victor Hugo's *Les Miserables*. In the story, we meet a common thief, Jean Valjean, who is befriended by an elderly and kind bishop. Valjean responds to the kindness of this bishop by stealing expensive silverware and running away. Once he is apprehended, the police drag him back to the bishop. Then the bishop does the unthinkable:

---

[395] Jonathan Edwards, *Sinners in the Hands of an Angry God* (Alachua Florida: Bridge-Logos, 2003), 38.

"Ah, there you are!" he cried, looking straight at Jean Valjean. "Am I glad to see you! But, heavens! I gave you the candlesticks too, you know; they are made of silver like the rest and you can get two hundred francs for them, easily. Why didn't you take them with the cutlery?"

Jean Valjean's eyes nearly popped out of his head; he looked at the venerable bishop with an expression no human tongue could convey.

"Monsignor," said the sergeant, "is what this man said true, then? We saw him hotfooting it out of town. He looked like he was on the run. So we arrested him to be on the safe side. He had all this silver—"

"And he told you," the bishop broke in with a smile, "that it had been given to him by some old codger of a priest whose place he'd spent the night in? I can see how it looks. So you've brought him back here? There has been a misunderstanding. . . ."

"My dear friend," said the bishop [to Jean Valjean], "before you go, here are your candlesticks. Take them." He went to the mantelpiece, swept up the two candlesticks, and handed them over to Jean Valjean. . . . The body of the would-be-thief was shaking. He took the two candlesticks automatically and with a stricken look on his face. "Now," said the bishop, "go in peace."

Jean Valjean leaves the bishop's house, stunned by the grace being shown to him. He did not recognize himself. He could not make sense of what was happening to him. He steeled himself against the old man's angelic act and against his gentle words. . . . He defended himself against such heavenly forgiveness by means of pride, which is like a stronghold of evil inside us.[396]

---

[396] Victor Hugo, *Les Miserables: A New Translation* by Julie Rose (New York: Random House, 2008), 96-97.

Grace is like that. It is underserved and unexpected. But ultimately, it is the power of grace that breaks through the hardest of hearts. Trevin Wax describes the power of grace in the life of the thief:

> Grace is offensive. It chipped away at this old thief's heart. Not long after being forgiven by the bishop, Valjean robs a young child. Now that Valjean has been the recipient of undeserved favor, his sin propels him into a moment of crisis. He sees himself for who he is in light of the grace that has been shown to him. At once, his heart and mind are forever changed, conquered by grace.[397]

Victor Hugo continues by describing the moment grace broke through for the hardened thief:

> Jean Valjean cried for a long time. He shed hot tears, he sobbed, more helpless and fragile than any woman, more terrified than any child. While he was crying, day dawned brighter and brighter in his spirit, and it was an extraordinary light, a light at once ravishing and terrible.[398]

Each one of us is Jean Valjean. But the thing that's missing in our lives is a kind, gracious bishop. Where is he? And can he offer grace for more than single sins? All of us have done much more than steal a couple of candlesticks. How can we find the grace of the bishop that will cover our sin?

Everything we've said up to this point cries out for this kind of resolution. Humanity has a problem called sin. There is no earthly person to step in with a solution. But God is there and provides His answer in the Bible. People feel the presence of God but try

---

[397] Trevin Wax, *Counterfeit Gospels: Rediscovering the Good News in a World of False Hope*, (Chicago, IL: Moody Publishers, 2011), 127.

[398] Hugo, *Les Miserables*, 96-97.

to run from Him. Despite the fact that God rules this universe with absolute control, He allows us to exercise our free will. But people are unable to choose to follow God on their own because that is not our nature. So, we are in a spiritual quandary. We are sinful, guilty before a holy God, destined for a physical, literal hell, and unable to do anything about it on our own. Something, or someone must step in to help if we are to be saved.

And that's exactly what happened. The Bible is clear that it is only by God's grace that people can be saved. But what does that mean? Someone once said that the word grace is written on every page of the Bible, so where do we begin?

David was an adulterer and a murderer. Isaiah said he was a *"man of unclean lips."*[399] Rahab and Mary were both prostitutes. Peter *"fell down at Jesus' feet, saying, 'Go away from me Lord, for I am a sinful man!'"*[400] Matthew was a hated tax collector. Paul was busy killing Christians when Jesus confronted him on the road to Damascus and drastically changed his heart and the course of his life.

And yet all of these people are counted as saved in Scripture. In the last chapter, we asserted that it is impossible for anyone to get saved by their own merit. So how did these people get saved? What happened to them? Furthermore, how does that happen today? This all begins with God. If God did not change the heart of the sinner, he would not be saved. So, let's look at God's part in salvation before we examine man's part.

GRACE

God's part in salvation can be summed up in one word—grace. This is where we get back to Jean Valjean. He had the gracious act of the bishop to cover his sin. Without that, the police would

---

[399] Isaiah 6:5
[400] Luke 5:8

have incarcerated him. But what does this mean for us? Where do we get such grace?

If we look at salvation as two sides of a ledger, man's side has the words *repent* and *believe* on it. But if we look at God's side it has only one word—*grace*. The word means "gift" and is an apt picture of God's action in salvation.

We've seen before that God is absolutely sovereign and that man can't choose God on His own. That's why God had to act to give man the ability to repent and believe. Without God's grace, man would never be able exercise his will to confess and repent.

Paul puts our condition and God's grace together when he first described man as *"dead in your trespasses and sins"* and *"by nature children of wrath."*[401] As we've seen, this is man's natural spiritual condition. But then in the following verse there is one of the most powerful and enticing statements in the Bible. Paul continues, *"But God . . ."* It's like a great big traffic cop in the sky walks out in front of all humanity who are walking blindly to their natural destiny in hell and stops the flow of traffic.

> But God, being rich in mercy, because of His great love with which He loved us, even when we were dead in our transgressions, made us alive together with Christ (by grace [there's the first mention of that word] you have been saved), and raised us up with Him, and seated us with Him in the heavenly places in Christ Jesus, so that in the ages to come He might show the surpassing riches of His grace [second mention] in kindness toward us in Christ Jesus.[402]

You can almost feel Paul hammering the theme of grace home as he continues, *"For by grace you have been saved . . ."*[403] STOP! That is the third time *"grace"* is mentioned. Do you see what

---

[401] Ephesians 2:1, 3
[402] Ephesians 2:4-7
[403] Ephesians 2:8

grace has done? Grace took us when we were spiritually dead and *"made us alive together with Christ"*[404] Then grace *"raised us up and seated us with Him in the heavenly places in Christ Jesus . . ."*[405] All the verbs used in this text are past tense, telling us that God's work doesn't depend on our response.

Grace changes the heart and destiny of the sinner. Grace doesn't judge him because Christ has been judged in his place. Grace is greater than the works of the law because we can't keep the law. Grace changes us from striving to achieve righteousness through our works to resting in Christ because of His work.

And how do we engage God's grace? Paul continues, telling us salvation comes *"through faith, and that not of yourselves, it is the gift of God."*[406] Even our ability to repent and believe is not our own. This gift is given to us *"because the gift of the Holy Spirit has been poured out on the Gentiles also."*[407] This is God's gracious, proactive means of saving men and women from every ethnic group in the world.

Paul finishes with doctrinal precision, *"not as a result of works, so that no one may boast."*[408] Going to church, confessing your sins to a priest, carrying a Bible, helping the poor, even the act of believing, are all good works which cannot gain salvation. Repeat—salvation cannot be gained by good works!

Just think of what we see here. God is *"rich in mercy,"*[409] that is, He is abundant in the attribute that withholds punishment when it is due. Why does He do this? It's *"because of His great love."*[410] You will never be loved like this by anyone else. God's love isn't measured by the loveliness of the object loved. Nor is it based

---

[404] Ephesians 2:5
[405] Ephesians 2:6
[406] Ephesians 2:8
[407] Acts 10:45
[408] Ephesians 2:9
[409] Ephesians 2:4
[410] Ibid.

on being returned. Paul said, *"But God demonstrates His own love toward us, in that while we were yet sinners, Christ died for us."*[411]

Grace is the force that drove Martin Luther to his knees. For years he thought faith was a work. He had always seen *"the righteousness of God"*[412] as an attribute of the sovereign Lord by which He judged sinners—not something sinners could ever possess. He described the breakthrough that put an end to the Dark Ages in history:

> I saw the connection between the justice of God and the statement that "the just shall live by his faith." Then I grasped that the justice of God is that righteousness by which *through grace and sheer mercy God justifies us through faith* [italics added]. Thereupon I felt myself to be reborn and to have gone through open doors into paradise. The whole of Scripture took on a new meaning, and whereas before the 'justice of God' had filled me with hate, now it became to me inexpressibly sweet in greater love. This passage of Paul became to me a gate to heaven.[413]

REPENT

Man's part in salvation can be summed up in two words—repent and believe. Salvation begins with God, but God moves each sinner to do certain things. Without this gracious work of God and the response of the sinner, no one would be saved.

The first word we will focus on is repent. This is absolutely impossible without the grace of God that changes the heart of the sinner. When Peter explained to skeptical Jewish believers how God had saved Gentiles in the house of a Roman centurion named Cornelius, Luke records, *"When they heard this, they quieted down and glorified God, saying, 'Well then, God has granted to*

---

[411] Romans 5:8
[412] Romans 1:17
[413] Roland Bainton, *Here I Stand* (New York: Abingdon, 1950), 65.

the Gentiles also the repentance that leads to life.'"[414] Repentence is a gift from God but it is also a required response of the human heart.

It's good to start here because this is where Jesus started. When Jesus began His earthly ministry, the first message that He preached was *"Repent, for the Kingdom of heaven is at hand."*[415] Luke observes that Jesus' objective was *"to call... sinners to repentance."*[416] Jesus also said, *"I tell you, no, but unless you repent, you will all likewise perish."*[417] In essence, this is the gospel in one word.

A *"false addition to faith?"*

But repentance must be clearly defined. Some fail to do this. One well-known Bible teacher said repentance is "a false addition to faith."[418] A prominent pastor said, "The Bible requires repentance for salvation, but repentance does not mean to turn from sin, nor a change in one's conduct . . . Biblical repentance is a change of mind or attitude concerning either God, Christ, dead works or sin."[419]

Another pastor attempts to clarify the issue by pointing out the differences between what he called *free grace* and *Lordship* theories of salvation. In attacking the Lordship position, he notes that it either "front loads" the gospel with unbiblical demands, or it "back loads" the gospel with unrealistic, legalistic expectations after salvation.

His theory is based on his view of repentance. Like others who advocate a free grace model, he states that repent means

---

[414] Acts 11:18

[415] Matthew 3:2

[416] Luke 5:32

[417] Luke 13:5

[418] Charles C. Ryrie *Balancing the Christian Life* (Chicago: Moody Press, 1969), 177.

[419] Michael G. Corcoris, *Lordship Salvation – Is It Biblical?* (Dallas: Redencion Viva, 1983).

"[C]learly, 'to change one's mind or perspective.'"[420] Unfortunately, he didn't dig a little deeper into the meaning of the word. If he had, he would have come to a different conclusion.

The biblical view

The word used for repent is the Greek word *metanoia*. This comes from two words, *meta*, which means "to perceive afterwards," and *nous*, which mean "the mind, the seat of moral reflection."[421] But we can't leave it there.

Indeed, two of the most prominent word study sources used in intensive Bible study among New Testament scholars agree that repentance means more than simply to change one's mind. The *New International Dictionary of New Testament Theology*, edited by Colin Brown says,

> In fact the predominantly intellectual understanding of *metanoia* as change of mind plays very little part in the NT. Rather the decision by the whole man to turn round is stressed. It is clear that we are concerned neither with a purely outward turning nor with a merely intellectual change of ideas.[422]

The second trusted resource is *The Theological Dictionary of the New Testament*, edited by Gerhard Kittel. Kittel explains repentance this way:

> God's definitive revelation demands a final and unconditional decision on man's part. It demands radical conversion, a transformation of nature, a definitive turning from evil, a resolute

---

[420] Jeremy White, *The Gospel [un]Cut: Learning to Rest in the Grace of God* (Bloomington, IN: Westbow Press, 2012), 32.

[421] W.E. Vine and F.F. Bruce, *Vine's Expository Dictionary of Old and New Testament Words* (Old Tappan NJ: Revell, 1981), 279.

[422] J. Goetzmann, "Μετάνοια," ed. Lothar Coenen, Erich Beyreuther, and Hans Bietenhard, *New International Dictionary of New Testament Theology, vol. 4,* (Grand Rapids, MI: Zondervan Publishing House, 1986), 358.

turning to God in total obedience. . . . It affects the whole man, first and basically the centre of personal life, then logically his conduct at all times and in all situations, his thoughts, words and acts.[423]

The pastor I referred to above who holds to the *free grace* model of salvation is mistaken when he concludes that the Lordship model is in error because it "is actually an inclusion of works as part of the gospel, making Christianity essentially no different from any other legalistic religion."[424] He further states,

[O]ffering salvation as a free gift based on faith alone while also demanding that true 'saving faith' *must* produce a litany of observable evidence (without which you have no right to rest assured you are saved) is essentially a bait-and-switch scam if there ever was one![425]

This is a gross misrepresentation of those who hold to the Lordship salvation position. Those who hold this position *do not* believe that works front load the gospel with demands to perform some works *before* one can be saved. Neither do they *demand* a "litany of observable evidence" to be exhibited *after* one is saved.

Those who hold the Lordship position would agree with Jesus. And Jesus simply said, *"Every tree that does not bear good fruit is cut down and thrown into the fire. So then, you will know them by their fruits."*[426] Fruit is the result, not the demand.

The bottom line is that true repentance produces spiritual fruit. But that doesn't mean that works alone hold the key to heaven. Jesus anticipated this when He added, *"Not everyone who says to Me, 'Lord, Lord,' will enter the kingdom of heaven, but he*

---

[423] J. Behm, "Metanoia" in Gerhard Kittel, ed., *Theological Dictionary of the New Testament* (Grand Rapids: Eerdmans, 1967), 4:1002-1003.

[424] White, *The Gospel* [un]Cut, 32.

[425] Ibid., 34.

[426] Matthew 7:19-20

who does the will of My Father who is in heaven will enter."[427] It seems obvious from the teaching in the New Testament that repentance means more than merely "to change the mind."

John the Baptist

John the Baptist amplifies Jesus' teaching on repentance by giving us some clear illustrations. He shows us clearly that repentance is not merely a changing of the mind, but a change of direction in life. This is crucial distinction.

Before Jesus even began His public ministry, John was sent by God to prepare the way for Jesus' ministry. John preached "*a baptism of repentance for the forgiveness of sins.*"[428] He preached out in the desert, not in the Temple in Jerusalem, stressing the radical difference in his message.

Matthew says that crowds of people were coming out to the desert to hear him and be baptized by him. The Sadducees and Pharisees, the spiritual leaders of Judaism in Jerusalem at the time, were among the crowds. But they weren't coming to repent. John could see right through them. After calling them a *"brood of vipers"*[429] John told them they needed to *"bear fruits in keeping with repentance . . ."*[430] Some might think, "Wow! Kind of harsh John." But John was simply pointing out that the Pharisees' actions didn't match up with their words. Repentance demands fruit.

Others who were there asked, *"[W]hat shall we do?"*[431] That is, what does true repentance look like? John explained, *"The man who has two tunics is to share with him who has none; and he*

---

[427] Matthew 7:21
[428] Luke 3:3
[429] Luke 3:7
[430] Luke 3:8
[431] Luke 3:10

who has food is to do likewise."[432] Repentance meant a meaningful sharing of material possessions *followed* saving faith.

There were also some tax collectors there. They were hated by the Jews because they were Jews who had sold out to Rome and, in turn, been given the privilege to set the tax rates according to their own whims. When these men asked what they should do, John replied, "*Collect no more than what you have been ordered to.*"[433] For them, repentance changed the way they conducted their business.

Likewise, some Roman soldiers asking about repentance were told, "*Do not take money from anyone by force, or accuse anyone falsely, and be content with your wages.*"[434]

The message is very clear. The religious leaders were told their repentance was false because it bore no fruit while two despised groups in Jewish society were told that repentance demanded a change to the very core of their identity. Crooked tax collectors were to be honest, and cruel soldiers were to be compassionate. Talk about changing your life! This was not a mere changing of their mind. But notice, *none of this was demanded before salvation.* This all came after they repented.

Doesn't this make sense? If someone says they are truly repentant over something they've done, isn't it reasonable to think they would stop doing it. Paul said, "*How shall we who died to sin still live in it?*"[435]

In a section on sin and repentance from his book *Loving God*, Chuck Colson tells the story of Mickey Cohen. Cohen was a member of the mob who was supposedly saved at a Billy Graham crusade. When he was told that a Christian needed to separate from sinful activities practiced in the mob, he seemed incredulous. He said,

---

[432] Luke 3:11
[433] Luke 3:13
[434] Luke 3:14
[435] Romans 6:2

You never told me that I had to give up my career. You never told me that I had to give up my friends. There are Christian Movie Stars, Christian Athletes, and Christian Business Men. So what's the matter with being a Christian gangster? If I have to give all that up—if that's Christianity—then you can count me out.[436]

Would the *free grace* people say Mickey was saved even if he remained a gangster for the rest of his life? Repentance is more than a theoretical walk in the park. It demands a change of heart and a change in life. Paul said, *"For the sorrow that is according to the will of God produces a repentance without regret, leading to salvation, but the sorrow of the world produces death."*[437] Repentance brings about radical change in the behavior of the sinner because it changes their heart. Anything less than that is false hope.

Turning from sin

True repentance today makes the same demands. Rosaria Champagne Butterfield was a tenured lesbian professor at Syracuse University. But through an incredible series of events that showed the gracious hand of God in her life, she came to understand the radical nature of repentance that dismantled her world. She writes,

> The Bible told me to repent, but I didn't feel like repenting. Do you have to feel like repenting in order to repent? Was I a sinner, or was I, in my drag queen friend's words, sick? How do you repent for a sin that doesn't feel like a sin? How could the thing that I had studied and become be sinful? How could I be tenured in a field that is sin? How could I and everyone that I knew and loved be in sin? In this crucible of confusion, I

---

[436] Chuck Colson, *Loving God* (Grand Rapids, Michigan: Zondervan, 1983), 94.

[437] 2 Corinthians 7:10

learned something important. I learned the first rule of repentance: that repentance requires greater intimacy with God than with our sin. How much greater? About the size of a mustard seed. Repentance requires that we draw near to Jesus, no matter what. And sometimes we all have to crawl there on our hands and knees. Repentance is an intimate affair. And for many of us, intimacy with anything is a terrifying prospect.[438]

Repentance is costly. For Butterfield it meant losing her friends, her identity, and eventually, her job. You can't say you repent and continue to live the life you once lived. The convicting power of the Spirit of God won't let the true believer do that.

BELIEVE

The other primary word that describes man's part in salvation is believe. Jesus said, *"The time is fulfilled, and the kingdom of God is at hand; repent and believe in the gospel."*[439] That sums it up— repent and believe.

So, what does it mean to "b*elieve in the gospel?"* It must be important because the word *believe* is used 36 times in Matthew, Mark, and Luke, and an amazing 107 times in John. The word *faith* is exactly the same word in the original language as *believe*, and it is used 40 times in Matthew, Mark, and Luke, though John doesn't use it at all. Both *believe* and *faith* convey complete trust in a person or object. This is not merely a feeling. Saving faith is based on certain objective facts.

Confess with your mouth

Paul refers to this when he says, *"[I]f you confess with your mouth Jesus as Lord, and believe in your heart that God raised Him*

---

[438] Rosaria Champagne Butterfield, *The Secret Thoughts of an Unlikely Convert: An English Professor's Journey Into Christian Faith*, (Pittsburgh, PA: Crown & Covenant Publications, 2012), 21-22.

[439] Mark 1:15

from the dead, you will be saved."[440] There are two conditions given for saving faith—"*confess with your mouth Jesus as Lord,*" and "*believe in your heart that God raised Him from the dead.*"

To confess something means "to say the same thing." The word for "Lord" is *kurios*. It means "master of, having authority, sovereign."[441] This contradicts the *free grace* model of salvation. One cannot be saved without confessing Jesus as Lord. It is illogical to conceive of salvation that is based on faith in Jesus' saving work on the cross but reject His Lordship over our lives.

In fact, that's impossible. When Jesus said "*[R]epent and believe in the gospel,*"[442] both words are imperatives, or commands. When the Philippian jailer asked Paul and Silas, "*Sirs, what must I do to be saved?*" They answered, "*Believe in the Lord Jesus and you will be saved.*"[443] This was also a command.

The picture of Jesus sitting in heaven begging people to "accept Him into their hearts" is prominent today. It conjures up the image of a mediocre middle school student waving his hand wildly in the air and begging "pick me, pick me, pick me" next for the baseball game. This makes God out to be a beggar while man is casting the deciding vote.

But this is not the God of the Bible. This is not seen in the commands to be saved or in the call to "*confess Jesus as Lord.*" In speaking to the sophisticated intellectuals on Mars Hill in Athens, Paul said that "*God is now declaring to men that all people everywhere should repent . . .*"[444] indicating God's command to repent was for everyone.

The word often used to describe this is *Lordship*. This strikes at the heart of the free grace people mentioned earlier. They say

---

[440] Romans 10:9

[441] Ceslas Spicq and James D. Ernest, *Theological Lexicon of the New Testament, vol. 2.* (Peabody, MA: Hendrickson Publishers, 1994), 341.

[442] Mark 1:15

[443] Act 16:30-31

[444] Acts 17:30

that faith in Jesus as our Savior is the only qualification necessary for salvation. Surely, Jesus is our Savior, as we see from the 24 times the word is used in the New Testament.

But the word *Lord* is used 670 times, providing weight to the demands of Lordship by the sheer number of times it's used. The argument that we "make Jesus our Lord" some time *after* salvation just doesn't hold water. Jesus *is* Lord whether we recognize it or not.

In trying to hold on to the core of the gospel (a noble thing), the *free grace* people instead have ended up teaching a truncated gospel—one that leaves confessing Jesus as Lord out of the picture. This has produced thousands of people who "made a profession of faith" when they were young, only to walk away later in life. It has also produced churches that are filled with people who need to be entertained and told how wonderful they are because pastors are afraid to offend them by talking about their sin.

In contrast, Scripture indicates that before one confesses Christ they have not done one thing to seek or obey Him.[445] Confessing Christ is not for the weak of heart. It is not merely trying to be a better person. That's like re-arranging the deck chairs on the Titanic. Confessing Christ is the equivalent of spiritual death. Paul said, "*[O]ur old self was crucified with Him, in order that our body of sin might be done away with, so that we would no longer be slaves to sin . . .*"[446]

The "*old man*" is our self, our will, our agenda, our ambitions and dreams. This doesn't mean we stop sinning. No, we still live in our fleshly bodies that continue to demand their own way. But when we come to Christ the "old man" dies, and we see the greater beauty of Jesus and recognize that He is the only One who can free us from sin.

---

[445] Romans 3:10-11
[446] Romans 6:6

Tullian Tchividjian said it well, "Only the gospel of Jesus Christ can truly save you. The gospel doesn't make bad people good; *it makes dead people alive.*"[447]

Spiritual death isn't easy, but it's the only way to achieve spiritual life. Jesus said, "*I came to set a man against his father, and a daughter against her mother, and a daughter-in-law against her mother-in-law; and a man's enemies will be the members of his household.*"[448]

At times that can be incredibly difficult. Rosaria Champagne Butterfield comes to our aid again:

> I often wonder: God, why pick me? I didn't ask to be a Christian convert. I didn't "seek the Lord." Instead, I ran like the wind when I suspected someone would start peddling the gospel to me. I was intellectually—and only intellectually—interested in matters of faith and I wanted to keep it that way. How did a smart cookie like me end up in a place like this?
>
> In the pages that follow, I share what happened in my private world through what Christians politely call conversion. This word—conversion—is simply too tame and too refined to capture the train wreck that I experienced in coming face-to-face with the Living God. I know of only one word to describe this time-released encounter: impact. Impact is, I believe, the space between the multiple car crash and the body count.[449]

That's why confession is an outward act. You can't hide the effects of a redemptive encounter with Jesus. That's why it's so important to tell someone when you get saved and then follow it up by being baptized and joining a good Bible-teaching church. We don't hide our wedding announcements or birth announcements.

---

[447] Tullian Tchividjian, *Surprised by Grace*, (Wheaton, Illinois: Crossway, 2010), 56-57.

[448] Matthew 10:35-36

[449] Butterfield, *The Secret Thoughts of an Unlikely Convert*, xi.

Why would we hide our spiritual birth announcement? Jesus said, *"Therefore everyone who confesses Me before men, I will also confess him before My Father who is in heaven. But whoever denies Me before men, I will also deny him before My Father who is in heaven."*[450] That's a sobering thought that should melt away the fear of even the introvert who wants to follow Jesus.

Believe in your heart

The second instruction Paul gives is to *"believe in your heart that God raised Him from the dead."*[451] If confessing is the outward act of a repentant heart, believing is an inward one. Obviously, this refers to certain historical facts about the crucifixion and resurrection of Jesus. It implies belief in the historicity of the person named Jesus. It means that the historical and theological facts of the crucifixion are accepted.

You *can't believe* in Muhammad, Buddha, Gandhi, Joseph Smith, Mary Baker Eddy, Charles Taze Russell, or any other self-proclaimed prophet or god and be a Christian. But you *can be* from any tongue, tribe, color, nation, socio-economic group, or ethnic background on the face of the earth and be a Christian. That's because the unifying factor is belief in Jesus and Him alone for the salvation of your soul.

The crowning event of this belief is *"that God raised Him from the dead."*[452] Talk about faith! After all, whoever heard of someone coming back from the dead? It's never happened before or since. But the overwhelming historical evidence from key eyewitnesses tells us that it did happen. Books like *Evidence That Demands a Verdict* by Josh McDowell, and *The Case For Christ* by former Chicago Tribune investigative reporter Lee Strobel are very helpful in examining this evidence. For skeptics who'd like to apply their professional skills while analyzing data, *Cold Case*

---

[450] Matthew 10:32-33
[451] Romans 10:9
[452] Ibid.

Christianity by former homicide detective, J. Warner Wallace might fit the bill.

Believing this message is our part of the process that God uses to save us. We hear the gospel and God gives us the gift of faith to believe it. We are then, *"sealed in Him with the Holy Spirit of promise, who is given as a pledge of our inheritance, with a view to the redemption of God's own possession, to the praise of His glory."*[453] Salvation is God's gracious work from start to finish.

When Jesus was called to the burial crypt of his friend Lazarus who had been dead for three days, He told Mary and Martha, Lazarus' two sisters, what He was going to do. Then He said, *"I am the resurrection and the life; he who believes in Me will live even if he dies, and everyone who lives and believes in Me will never die. Do you believe this?"*[454] Do you?

Reckoned as righteous

What happens when we believe? We receive our answer to this in the first book of the Bible. God had told Abraham that he would be the father of a great nation. But Abraham had a hard time believing that since he was childless. The Lord took him outside and told him to look at the stars, saying *"[S]o shall your descendants be."*[455]

What would you do? Abraham *"believed in the Lord; and He reckoned it to him as righteousness."*[456] In other words, God made Abraham righteous simply because he believed God's promise regarding his future. But notice this was *applied* righteousness, not *earned* righteousness. Abraham didn't do anything, he just believed.

Paul taught the same thing in the New Testament when he quoted this verse and fleshed it out a little bit. He noted, *"For if*

---

[453] Ephesians 1:13-14
[454] John 11:25-26
[455] Genesis 15:5
[456] Genesis 15:6

Abraham was justified by works, he has something to boast about, but not before God. For what does the Scripture say? 'Abraham believed God, and it was credited to him as righteousness.'"[457]

The word for credited means "reckon, think, credit."[458] Some translations translate it as "count," but I like the word "credited" better. It paints a financial picture of God placing something of inestimable value into our spiritual bank account when we were spiritually broke. God credits our account with His righteousness, goodness, justice, and holiness when our account shows nothing but lies, cheating, hate, greed, jealousy, self-centeredness, pride, and deceit. That's like Jeff Bezos or Bill Gates depositing his entire estate in our bank account in exchange for a garbage can!

This strong connection between faith and righteousness is seen two verses later when Paul explains, *"But to the one who does not work, but believes in Him who justifies the ungodly, his faith is credited as righteousness . . ."*[459] You see the same emphasis in Romans 4:6, 8, 9, 10, 11, 22, 23, and 24. The theme of God crediting our account with His righteousness that is activated by our faith is dominant throughout this passage.

Some call this the *imputation* of God's righteousness. We see this clearly in Paul's second letter to the church in Corinth when he explains that God has *"reconciled"* (another financial term) the account of all who believe in Him in faith with His account, *"not counting their transgressions against them"* so that we are credited with His righteousness.

He finished this by saying, *"He (God) made Him who knew no sin (Jesus) to be sin on our behalf, so that we might become the righteousness of God in Him."*[460] What an exchange! He didn't merely

---

[457] Romans 4:2-3

[458] J. Eichler, "Λογίζομαι," ed. Lothar Coenen, Erich Beyreuther, and Hans Bietenhard, *New International Dictionary of New Testament Theology, vol. 3*, (Grand Rapids, MI: Zondervan Publishing House, 1986), 822.

[459] Romans 4:5

[460] 2 Corinthians 5:21

cover our sin, He became sin on our behalf so that He would receive the punishment for our sin so that we could receive His righteousness.

We have absolutely nothing to offer to God that He needs or wants. Our achievements, wealth, reputation, intellect, or religious works don't mean anything to God when it comes to the salvation of our soul. We come to Him destitute and leave with the applied righteousness of God credited to our spiritual account.

Luther said the same thing. In his famous book called *Bondage of the Will*, he discussed the nature of freewill with Erasmus. He contended,

> But a man cannot be thoroughly humbled, until he comes to know that his salvation is utterly beyond his own powers, counsel, endeavors, will, and works, and absolutely depending on the will, counsel, pleasure, and work of another, that is, of God only. For if, as long as he has any persuasion that he can do even the least thing himself towards his own salvation, he retains a confidence in himself and does not utterly despair in himself, so long he is not humbled before God . . . . But he who . . . [depends] wholly upon the good will of God, he totally despairs in himself, chooses nothing for himself, but waits for God to work in him; and such an one is the nearest unto grace, that he might be saved.[461]

That's why Abraham had *"nothing to boast about"* meaning that he had no works that merited salvation and even his faith was non-meritorious. Faith is not the work of salvation, it is simply the channel through which salvation flows.

Ultimately, we have nothing to boast about because this is all the work of God through the power of the Holy Spirit. The apostle

---

[461] Martin Luther, trans. Henry Cole, *Bondage of the Will* (Lafayette, IN: Sovereign Grace Publishers, Inc., 2001), 30.

Paul reminds us, "*a natural man does not accept the things of the Spirit of God, for they are foolishness to him; and he cannot understand them, because they are spiritually appraised.*"[462] Without the saving and sanctifying work of the Holy Spirit, we would remain in our natural fleshly state, unable to comprehend the spiritual things of God.[463] Jesus taught that the Holy Spirit gives life, while man's efforts accomplish nothing.[464] Spiritual cleansing and renewal happens only through the power of the Holy Spirit.

One might say that Luther lived a long time ago and they saw things differently. That's true to an extent because it's obvious that styles and technology change. But the heart of man doesn't. That remains the same. Your heart is unsaved unless you repent and believe. J.I. Packer appeals to you this way:

> To the question, 'what must I do to be saved?' The old gospel replies: believe on the Lord Jesus Christ. To the further question, 'what does it mean to believe on the Lord Jesus Christ?' its reply is: it means knowing oneself to be a sinner, and Christ to have died for sinners; abandoning all self-righteousness and self-confidence, and casting oneself wholly upon him for pardon and peace; and exchanging one's natural enmity and rebellion against God for a spirit of grateful submission to the will of Christ through the renewing of one's heart by the Holy Ghost. And to the further question still, how am I to go about believing on Christ and repenting if I have no natural ability to do these things? it answers: look to Christ, speak to Christ, cry to Christ, just as you are; confess your sin, your impenitence, your unbelief, and cast yourself on his mercy; ask him to give you a new heart, working in you true repentance and firm faith; ask him to take away your evil heart of unbelief and to write his law within you, that you may never henceforth stray from him.

---

[462] 1 Corinthians 2:14
[463] John 3:6,
[464] John 6:63

Turn to him and trust him as best you can and pray for grace to turn and trust more thoroughly; use the means of grace expectantly, looking to Christ to draw near to you as you seek to draw near to him; watch, pray, and read and hear God's Word, worship and commune with God's people, and so continue till you know in yourself beyond doubt that you are indeed a changed being, a penitent believer, and the new heart that you desired has been put within you.[465]

Have you repented of your sins? Have you confessed Jesus as Lord? Do you believe that God raised Him from the dead? If you do, you will be saved because God's grace has been extended to you. You will experience new life on earth, and the blessings of heaven to come. This is the future of the believer as we will see in the next chapter.

---

[465] James I. Packer and Mark Dever, *In My Place Condemned He Stood* (Wheaton, Illinois: Crossway Books, 2007), 138.

CHAPTER THIRTEEN

"Remember that what you possess in this world will be found at the day of your death and belong to someone else; what you are will be yours forever."[466]
—*Henry Van Dyck*

Post Tenebras Lux

What is the result of yielding to God?

C arol Rhodes is a friend of both authors. She has a unique perspective on God's sovereignty. Can God's jurisdiction really be part of a divine economy when tragedy strikes in a three-part series? We asked her to share her grief-filled experiences and what it has meant as she relates to her heavenly Father.

At first reviewing this book, it seemed to me to be the law enforcement version of "Who's on First." Why would they ask me to contribute? Then it hit me—this one chapter encapsulates four years of my life. Years that would progressively lead me to question all I had counted on as foundational truth.

My security began in 1971 when, after 30 years of searching found its culmination in the realization that God was real—not a wishful delusion—and was readily available through

---

[466] John MacArthur, *Nothing But the Truth: Upholding the Gospel in a Doubting Age* (Wheaton, IL: Crossway Books, 1999), 98.

a relationship with His Son, Jesus Christ. My life was radically changed as I experienced more and more of the wonder of God's goodness and love.

No longer overwhelmed with the insecurities inherent in my roles as wife and mother of three sons and a citizen of a world continually in chaos, I looked for and found, guidance and peace in God's Word and found I could rely on my prayer-answering Lord to be faithful in any and all circumstances. With this as my firm foundation, I was now, unknowingly, ready to learn much more about this God I loved and served.

Oct. 5, 2005. Together with the love of my life since high school, we sat down with a doctor to address my husband's lack of energy. Within two hours we were referred to an oncologist. We were shocked, but God was not and within the deepest part of me I knew that there would be no healing and that the end would be quick. My prayer for my husband was two-fold: that he would have no fear and that he would experience the overwhelming presence of a good God.

But well-meaning people began to deluge me with urgent suggestions: miracle drugs, faith healers, cancer centers, declaration prayers denouncing Satan, claiming healing. I began to fear that I was praying incorrectly, so I asked the Lord for a sign and that's exactly what I got! In a dream I saw myself looking down on a large gathering of people and one of them held up a large hand-lettered sign. On it was printed, "THIS IS WHAT GOD HAS CHOSEN." I knew from that point on my original prompting from the Lord was correct and I could relax into my original prayer.

Eight weeks from the first pronouncement of cancer, my husband of almost 46 years was gone and life as I had known it would never be the same.

As I struggled to find my footing over the next months I searched for God's perspective—and three thoughts began to take shape:

1. Grief, as awful as it is, is also an affirmation of love. The opposite of love isn't hate—it's apathy. I had loved and been loved. The cost of loving is pain at the loss. But would I have wanted to live never experiencing love?

2. God had stepped in when I needed Him by giving me truth to hang onto at the beginning of that eight-week journey. I might not be happy about what was happening, but I had my marching orders—pray and serve my husband. When my focus began to waiver and I grew fearful and doubting, the Lord graciously reminded me THIS IS WHAT I HAVE CHOSEN.

3. Months after Rick's passing I realized the cryptic message that got me through that journey was also a message for my new life. Widowhood was what God had chosen for me. No accident, I had a new calling.

Fast-forward 20 months. It was a warm summer Texas day. My Bible study was scheduled to begin the next week and all the leaders gathered to prepare for the kick-off. After glad-to-see-you-again hugs, we gathered together for a time of prayer and praise. One woman after another began to sing the chorus of her favorite praise song. Sweet female voices harmonized as we joined each woman in praise. When it was my turn to lead I began singing "My Peace I Give Unto You." Evidently, I was the only one who knew the words because I sang the entire chorus by myself! We all laughed about my unexpected solo as we began our planning session.

During the morning break I was surprised to see the youngest of my three sons appear at the door. From the look on his face I knew something was terribly wrong. Once outside, he choked out the words, "Kevin's gone." My middle son had been instantly killed in a car accident as he was coming home from work. My sweet son—a faithful husband with sons of his own, compassionate, fun-loving, Godly—was gone. As I followed my youngest son home, I said, "God, this morning when I left home I had three sons." His response was immediate. "You still do." Eternal life is a reality.

Nevertheless, I was once again catapulted into grief. The precious memories I had of Kevin were mixed with disappointment, pain and confusion. Why Kevin? I could understand the loss of a husband, while gut-wrenchingly sad, still somehow understandable. Death is inevitable the older we get but Kevin was 44 years old! Where's the sense in that?

Slowly, as though through a thick cloud, I once again began to see the truth I so wanted to avoid—the world isn't fair. Greed and prejudice and hatred cause pain and suffering for the innocent and a distracted teenage driver can mow down a greatly loved son.

The God I ran to for solace reminded me that He knew just how I felt—He, too, had lost an innocent Son to a largely uncaring world. But He was still in control and one day, I would see my son again. The song I had sung by myself was, in reality, a song He was singing to me:

"My peace I give unto you.

It's a peace that the world cannot give,

It's a peace that the world cannot understand

Peace to know, peace to live

My peace I give unto you."

I have learned that God's peace isn't the absence of grief. For a Christian, peace is the companion of grief. I was learning lessons about the character of God that I suppose could only come through a breaking heart.

Then the bottom fell out. Four years later, almost to the day my husband had been diagnosed with cancer, the source of my youngest son's terrible leg pain was found—again, cancer.

A few months earlier a spot on his skin had been removed and at that time he was told that it was a melanoma, but they removed it all and not to worry.

Dana continued with the hectic schedule of husband, father of three young children, and business owner despite growing pain in his leg. Throughout the summer, he went to the chiropractor, got massages, took prescriptions for pain and muscle aches—nothing helped. Finally, his general practitioner ordered a full body scan. What had appeared to be a single skin lesion had by this time metastasized to his whole body.

I went numb. This could not be happening again—it was unthinkable. I refused to even consider the loss of this greatly loved "child." God would not, could not allow this to happen! Dana, deep dimples, a charmer from birth, optimistic, confident, generous, and kind began a fight for his life.

He asked if he and his family could move in with me into my large home. I saw this as a gift from God. I was able to keep a semblance of order and provide the supervision and love that the kids (12, 9, and 5) needed while his wife threw herself into caring for him.

It wasn't long before a hospital bed was needed. Days were filled with treatments that seemed almost worse than the disease itself.

People were wonderful. The church provided endless meals, friends stepped up to the bat with the kids, a physician friend came at noon a number of times to hydrate him just because it made him feel better—no charge, prayers from people we didn't even know were lifted to the throne room of heaven.

I was caught up in the eye of a hurricane—devastation swirled around me while I helplessly watched. But I knew the One who had control. The only Physician who had the power to heal. The God who had sustained me through the loss of Rick and the loss of Kevin.

I pleaded, I begged, I nagged. God, heal my son. Don't let this happen—You can't let this happen.

Dana grew worse. His hair fell out, he could no longer get up from the bed, the cancer had invaded his brain, further robbing us of the wonderful person he was.

Now the numb was wearing off, and I was angry. God was letting this happen. Where was He? At night I would go outside in the dark, away from the house and yell into the heavens. "Don't do this! Don't take my son! Don't make my precious daughter-in-law a widow. Don't take the father of my grandchildren!"

Dana got sicker, weaker, thinner. Now I was really mad. Whose fault was this? The dermatologist who said not to worry? Dana who didn't follow up? The MD who for so long just ordered painkillers? The radiologist? The oncologists?

But I knew the only One with ultimate power and control, and He was holding out. So, I upped the ante. I threatened. "God, if you let him die I will never speak to You again."

He died. January 10, 2010 Dana died. I stood there holding his hand watching him breathe and realized the next breath didn't come. He died.

And, so did I. Oh, I took my next breath but something in me died. It seems like the story should end there. I wanted to end there. Three quarters of my family were gone and the God that I had trusted and relied on had failed me.

I went on with life, fulfilling obligations, putting on a happy face, comforting others—it's easy for me to bury feelings. I think it was Norm Wright who said, "You can bury feelings, but you must realize you bury them alive and there will be a resurrection."

Weeks went by; maybe months, and I attempted to keep my promise never again to speak to God. But how do you just instantly ditch the habit of decades; how do you cut off the best Friend you ever had?

I thought of John the Baptist, his whole life single-focused on elevating Jesus, now in prison. He begins to question.

If Jesus is who John has always believed He is, why is this happening? John sends a message to Jesus. "Are You really the Messiah?" Jesus sends back a cryptic answer—look at all I've done (Matthew 11:1-6).

What kind of an answer is that?! John is going to die for goodness sake! John is left with the same questions I was struggling with. I realized this is not an uncommon occurrence in Scripture.

After some straight talk (John 6) to a large group of followers, Jesus finds only a small handful still with Him. He looks at Peter and challenges him about his commitment. I can see Peter weighing the options then responding (my paraphrase) "Where else can I go? I've seen too much to walk away now."

That was me. I'd had too many years with Jesus to turn my back on Him now—like Peter, I'd seen too much. But in reality, not enough. I had naively thought I knew Him. But in truth, I had made Him into a small and manageable god that I could understand and arrogantly, command.

Now I had a decision to make. Could I still trust and worship and obey a God I didn't always understand, a God who didn't fit into my Sunday school image, a God with an agenda that often differs from mine?

Humbled by my smallness, exhausted from my raging internal battle, I bowed the knee. I prayed, and He was there.

Someone asked me a while back if I wish I had known all that was going to transpire at the beginning of my four-year journey. After a little thought, I told her that I realized I DID know. Not the details but Jesus' words to His disciples that they could expect trouble in this world.

Little girls are taught that living happily ever after is our expectation/right and anything that differs is a deviation from the "plan." But the truth is that we live in a fallen world but as believers in the One who overcame death we also live with the hope of eternity on this side. His grace is more than sufficient, and His strength is truly manifested in our weakness.

Do I wish those four years and the ones following could be a do-over? You bet! But looking back over the decades I've been a child of God, I can see He has taken my prayers seriously—to be closer to Him, to know His power, to share His heart for others, to die to self, to live by faith and not by sight—and He is in the process of answering those prayers. I just had no idea the cost on this side of eternity.

—Carol Rhodes

Carol's story is more extreme than most of us will ever face. But, like Job, it gives us a glimpse into God's jurisdiction in extreme cases. It points to spiritual realities that are not seen in the natural world. But these realities are what keep Carol going. It's what brings meaning to life, even in the darkest hour.

The promise of heaven means sin is eradicated, justice is done, love runs free, and God's sovereign plan of the ages comes to fruition. That's what gives Carol hope. That's what tells her that the death of her husband and sons isn't the end of it. Heaven is what gives the hope of life restored and fulfilled. Heaven is more than theology; it's biography. It is everything we hope for in earthly relationships and more, so much more.

Of course, there are many myths about heaven. Most people think that we will all become angels when we die or that magically we will all get there somehow. Others envision some kind of "soul sleep" or holding tank where one is kept until they enter into heaven. These are nothing but fanciful imaginations with no basis in reality.

Neither is there any such thing as purgatory. This is a Catholic doctrine that was not practiced until the twelfth century. It was invented as a theoretical place for the temporal punishment for "venial" (non-mortal) sins that can be purged by indulgences paid by loved ones on earth to prepare them for heaven. These doctrines of the Catholic Church are not found anywhere in the Bible.

There is also no second chance. Those who think that somehow God will forgive all the rebellion and rejection of His name do not know the Bible. The writer of the book of Hebrews spells it out clearly, telling us *"it is appointed for men to die once and after this comes judgment . . ."*[467]

FIRST FRUITS

Perhaps the place to start is by noting that Jesus preceded us in death, resurrection, and entrance into heaven. This provides enormous hope for believers in the face of death. When I was in high school, my friends and I got a kick out of walking through graveyards at night. "Don't be scared," we would joke, "I'm right behind you." There was a lot of bluster until we got to the gate and we were ready to begin our escapade. We all thought it was kind of exciting except for one guy who always said, "You go first," like he meant it.

Jesus went first. Paul tells us *"Christ has been raised from the dead, the first fruits of those who are asleep."*[468] Just as Jesus was physically resurrected three days after His crucifixion, so every person who believes in Him and confesses their sin will experience the same kind of resurrection body that Jesus has. No other religious leader has ever had the audacity to suggest he can do that.

The phrase *"first fruits"* was an agricultural term designating the first part of the crop to come in. When you plant something, you wait for the first sprig of green to pop up knowing that there will be many others. That's part of the promise of heaven for all who know Jesus.

---

[467] Hebrews 9:27
[468] 1 Corinthians 15:20

But obviously we can't contemplate entering His presence in our present bodies. Paul tells us why. He says, *"there are also heavenly bodies and earthly bodies, but the glory of the heavenly is one, and the glory of the earthly is another."*[469] That is, earthly and heavenly bodies are different in what they can accomplish. The very best that earthly specimens can produce in art, music, athletics, medicine, or technology are all brutally extinguished in death. But the glory of heaven is that the very best of God's creative powers will be exhibited in every person in heaven.

GLORIFIED BODIES

Unlike our physical body on this earth, we will have a resurrected body that will have the same characteristics as Jesus' resurrected body. Jesus' body after the resurrection was not some kind of gaseous cloud or spirit being. It was physical, but it was more than physical. He exhibited all the physical characteristics of His earthly body but without limitations.

For example, when the women came to the tomb on Sunday morning after the crucifixion, they were met by an angel who said, *"Why do you seek the living One among the dead? He is not here, but He has risen."*[470] The rest of the women ran to tell the disciples, but Mary stayed behind. As she was weeping, a man stood in front of her. Through her tears she thought it was the gardener, but when He said, *"Mary,"* she instantly recognized Him. It was Jesus! She recognized his voice just like we recognize the voice of a loved one calling our name in the dark of night.

Many others saw Jesus and recognized Him too. As Mary and the other women were running from the empty tomb back to the upper room where the disciples were, *"Jesus met them and greeted them. And they came up and took hold of His feet and worshiped Him."*[471] Later in the day, Jesus miraculously appeared to the

---

[469] 1 Corinthians 15:40
[470] Luke 24:5-6
[471] Matthew 28:9

disciples in the upper room where the doors were locked tight. At first, they thought, *"they were seeing a spirit."*[472] Wouldn't you? Knowing this, Jesus said, *"See My hands and My feet, that it is I Myself; touch Me and see, for a spirit does not have flesh and bones as you see that I have."*[473]

Then He asked them for something to eat. Luke tells us that when they gave Him a boiled fish *"He took it and ate it."*[474] Why was eating so important in these post-resurrection appearances? To prove He wasn't a ghost!

Jesus repeated His appearance to the disciples a week later when "doubting" Thomas was there. When the disciples told Thomas about Jesus' appearance to them he replied that he wouldn't believe unless he could place his finger in the nail prints of Jesus' hand. When he finally did see Jesus and Jesus offered him a chance to do just that, Thomas declined. Instead, he simply exclaimed, *"My Lord and My God."*[475] This shows clearly that, not only was Jesus alive, but Thomas believed Jesus was God.

All told, Paul tells us that after His resurrection Jesus *"appeared to Cephas, then to the twelve. After that He appeared to more than five hundred brethren at one time, most of whom remain until now, but some have fallen asleep; then He appeared to James, then to all the apostles; and last of all, as to one untimely born, He appeared to me also."*[476] That's quite a list of eyewitnesses.

These appearances left no doubt about the physical nature of Jesus' resurrected body. It's clear that He appeared "in a glorified, celestial body that was not bound by limitations of an ordinary earthly body."[477] M.J. Harris explains,

---

472 Luke 24:37
473 Luke 24:39
474 Luke 24:43
475 John 20:28
476 1 Corinthians 15:5-8
477 Norval Geldenhuys, *The Gospel of Luke, New International Commentary on the New Testament* (Grand Rapids: Eerdmans, 1951), 640.

The resurrection of Jesus was not his transformation into an immaterial body, but his acquisition of a "spiritual body" which could materialize or dematerialize at will. When, on occasion, Jesus chose to appear to various persons in material form, this was just as really the "spiritual body" of Jesus as when he was not visible. . . . In his risen state Jesus transcended the normal laws of physical existence. He was no longer bound by material or spatial limitations.[478]

A PLACE FOR YOU

Now that we've affirmed Jesus' glorified body, the next logical question is "Where did He go when He died?" For Christians the question is, "Where do we go when we die?" Is it the same place as "paradise" that Jesus referred to when He assured the thief on the cross that he would be with Him when he died? Is it the same as "Sheol" in the Old Testament?

The truth is that Scripture doesn't give us an exact location for heaven. The thing we do know is that it is in the presence of the Lord. Paul taught that for Christians to be *"absent from the body"* is to be *"at home with the Lord."*[479] Paul also assures us that some day when the Lord returns to the earth for his own, those who have already died as Christians will be resurrected first and then *"we who are alive and remain will be caught up together with them in the clouds to meet the Lord in the air, and so we shall always be with the Lord."*[480]

Even though Paul doesn't explain exactly where we will "be," we do know that heaven is a specific place. The apostle John records that at one point, Jesus had gathered His disciples and told them that he would soon be leaving them. He was referring to His impending crucifixion, but the disciples didn't know that.

---

[478] M. J. Harris, *From Grave to Glory: Resurrection in the New Testament* (Grand Rapids: Zondervan, 1990), 142-43.

[479] 2 Corinthians 5:8

[480] 1 Thessalonians 4:17

They grew fearful, especially when Jesus said, *"Where I go, you cannot follow Me now; but you will follow later."*[481]

Jesus answered them in some of the most tender words in the New Testament. Of course, it would have been absolutely impossible for Jesus to tell them about the crucifixion and the resurrection at that time. They wouldn't have understood. Neither would they have understood about Jesus' reference to heaven when He replied to their panic by saying,

> Do not let your heart be troubled; believe in God, believe also in Me. In My Father's house are many dwelling places; if it were not so, I would have told you; for I go to prepare a place for you. If I go and prepare a place for you, I will come again and receive you to Myself, that where I am, there you may be also.[482]

There's something incredibly comforting about Jesus' words. Perhaps His imagery of *"my Father's house"* conjures up images of the comfort and security of the house we grew up in. The paintings of Thomas Kinkade bring this to mind. Kinkade was known as the "painter of light" for his beautiful paintings of houses, churches, and village scenes that evoked memories of the warmth of home. Many of his paintings were at dusk or shortly after nightfall when the warmth of the light he painted illuminated the darkness with a call to come home.

But this is more than that. It's interesting that He changes the terminology from the Father's *"house"* to preparing a *"place."* The word for *"house"* means a building or a dwelling place. The word for *"place"* means "location." Our residence in heaven is not limited to a house. It's more like an outdoor estate where walls are not needed for protection from the elements or to keep criminals out.

---

481 John 13:36
482 John 14:1-3

Ultimately, heaven is too wonderful to be explained in words. But we can gain further insight into what the "place" will be like in Revelation, the last book of the Bible. The description offered there is brief, but helpful. There we find:

1. We will dwell in a completely new heaven and earth which God will create after He destroys the first heaven and earth.[483]

2. God will reside there with us, with no remnant of previous sin or corruption.[484]

3. We will reside in a new city of Jerusalem that will be 1,500 miles cubed. The city will be comprised of a foundation of a dazzling array of precious stones, streets of translucent gold, and twelve gates named after the twelve apostles each made of a single pearl.[485]

4. There will no need for a temple because God and the Lamb will be the temple and there will be nothing unclean which will ever enter the city, thus eradicating a need for sacrifice.[486]

5. The brilliance of the glory of God will remove any need for light.[487]

6. The gates of the city will never be closed, allowing for the free-flowing entry of the citizens of heaven who will be made up of all the nations of the earth who bring the treasures of their divine productivity into the city as tribute.[488]

7. Our bodies will be like Jesus' resurrected body, unbound by the earthly constraints of gravity and atmosphere.[489]

---

[483] Revelation 21:1; 2 Peter 3:10
[484] Revelation 21:4, 9
[485] Revelation 21:10-21
[486] Revelation 21:22,27
[487] Revelation21:23
[488] Revelation 21:24-25
[489] Revelation 21:24-26

8. We will be nourished by the water of life and the tree of life, lost in the Garden of Eden but now restored, which will furnish life-giving enjoyment and sustenance.[490]

Heaven is everything we would expect it to be and more. It is everything that earth isn't. It is perfect, complete, fulfilling, and forever. What a place He has prepared for us!

NO MORE SUFFERING

As glorious as these truths are, perhaps the most compelling hope of heaven is the lack of suffering and pain. The crying, the pain, the sadness, the disease, the gnawing hunger, the humiliation, the financial struggle, the broken relationships, the fear of death, and death itself are gone. They are all gone!

The apostle John taught this in explicit language in the last book of the Bible when he was explaining the glories of heaven. John tells us *"He will wipe away every tear from their eyes; and there will no longer be any death; there will no longer be any mourning, or crying, or pain; the first things have passed away."*[491]

The pain of this world is seen acutely at the time of death. Whether it comes "naturally" at an advanced age, or as an unwelcome intruder through war, disease, or some unforeseen "accident," it is never welcome. Anyone who has witnessed death even at a distance realizes the incredible draw toward heaven.

A PERSONAL APPLICATION

I (Jon) have lived through the incredible pain of holding our three-year-old son Charlie in my arms just moments after the doctors pronounced him dead. He had fallen into our pool the previous day and, despite the heroic efforts of the doctors and nurses, it was an uphill, losing battle to save him.

---

[490] Revelation 22:2
[491] Revelation 21:4

After seeing that "all his numbers were in the wrong place," they placed him into a 72-hour coma with the hope that the swelling in his brain would go down enough to survive. The doctors advised us to go home and get some sleep, in preparation for a long vigil. When a call came early the next morning we rushed back to the hospital only to be told that Charlie had died a minute before we got off the elevator.

We were ushered into his room as they removed the various wires and tubes attached to his body. I picked up his lifeless little body and held him in my arms as I walked to the window. I gazed "out there" into the sky as the first wave of grief washed over me. It was a surreal moment. As I held the physical remains of my son, the realization that the "real" Charlie was not in his body but "out there" in heaven somewhere was overwhelming. That's because Jesus is the *"first fruits"* of all who die in Him.

By the way, the Bible assures us that this applies to all children who die. King Jeroboam sinned greatly against God, but his infant son received the promise of heaven because *"there is found something good toward the Lord God"*[492] in him. Likewise, God said, *"You slaughtered My children"*[493] when addressing the horrible practice of child sacrifice practiced by pagan nations surrounding Israel.[494] Even though they had pagan parents, God regarded them as His.

When the whole generation of adults died in the wilderness and were denied entrance into the Promised Land because of their sin, God brought their children into the land because they *"have no knowledge of good and evil."*[495] In like manner He ushers children and those who don't have the mental capacity to discern good and evil into heaven because of His gracious provision. Like

---

[492] 1 Kings 14:13
[493] Ezekiel 16:21
[494] Ibid.
[495] Deuteronomy 1:39

David when he lost his infant son I too can say, *"I will go to him, but he will not return to me."*[496]

If you want to dig deeper into this subject, I highly commend the little book *Safe In the Arms of God* by John MacArthur.[497] It is the only book that I've ever run across that is totally devoted to the subject of the death of a child and is thoroughly biblical and very helpful. I wish I had found it sooner.

ACCIDENTAL C0-LOCATION OF ATOMS?

The purveyors of wisdom in our world offer no hope at all for times like this. Bertrand Russell, an atheist philosopher of the early 20th century said, *"[M]an is the product of causes that had no prevision of the end they were achieving. That his origin, his growth, his hopes and fears, his loves, his beliefs, are but the outcome of accidental co-locations of atoms."*[498]

If that's true, then why do we have such a visceral attachment to an "accidental co-location of atoms?" Why is there such deep, gut wrenching grief associated with dying? I believe it's because no one can really live with Russell's assessment, no matter what they say.

When I was in college, I took an evening biology class from an atheist professor who boasted that human beings are merely protoplasm. One evening at our break, a group of students was discussing a campus rapist who was on the loose. Knowing that the professor and his wife had just welcomed a baby daughter, a student asked the professor what he would do if a rapist ever raped his daughter. The professor replied vehemently that he would emasculate the rapist. I asked him why, since his daughter

---

[496] 2 Samuel 12:23

[497] John MacArthur, *Safe in the Arms of God: Truth From Heaven About the Death of a Child* (Nashville, Tennessee: Thomas Nelson, 2003).

[498] Bertrand Russell, *Mysticism and Logic* (New York: Norton, 1929), 47-48.

was just protoplasm. He just glared at me. He knew his daughter was more than mere protoplasm.

ONE WHO IS WORTHY

There will be no sadness in heaven because there will be no sin. There will be no crying and suffering, no hospitals or cemeteries, no broken bones and no broken hearts. All of these *"first things"* will be completely eradicated in God's perfect provision.

But, "how does that occur?" one might ask. The last book of the Bible provides a profound and moving description of Jesus taking on Himself the pain and suffering of the world in achieving heaven for us.

A gigantic 4K TV screen could not begin to capture the electric scene in heaven. John sees an emerald like brilliance of the rainbow around the throne of God with flashes of lightening and peals of thunder emanating from it, the sparkling ruby-red and white diamond appearance of the throne laid out on the brilliant transparent crystal-like floor surrounding it, with God sitting regally on the throne with a scroll in His hand surrounded by a comprehensive host of angelic beings.

John continues, *"I saw in the right hand of Him who sat on the throne a book written inside and on the back, sealed up with seven seals."*[499] The book was a scroll in God's possession that had writing on the front and back. This was the customary method of recording contracts in the Roman Empire. Wills, contracts and title deeds were folded and signed multiple times, depending on the length of the document. Each page was folded over and sealed with the official wax seal of an official witness. A Roman will had to be sealed by at least seven seals in order to be considered authentic.[500]

---

[499] Revelation 5:1

[500] Robert L. Thomas, *Revelation 1-7: An Exegetical Commentary, vol. 1,* (Chicago: Moody Press, 1992), 377.

Since the book was in God's possession, it pictures His last will and testament or His title deed to the earth. It incorporates His instructions regarding what would happen on the earth in the following chapters of Revelation. An angel appears and asks, *"Who is worthy to open the book and to break its seals? And no one in heaven or on the earth or under the earth was able to open the book or to look into it."*[501] No one was found who had the authority or power to break the seals, thus holding the rights of God's inheritance captive until the book could be opened.

With no one to open it, John was overwhelmed with grief. He continues, *"Then I began to weep greatly because no one was found worthy to open the book or to look into it..."*[502] He wept because God's decree for all mankind was locked up in the book. The thought of life without God's explanations and instructions was horrifying.

W.A. Criswell paints a picture of all mankind looking on, weeping with John at the unexpressed, hidden instructions of God. He writes:

> [John's tears] represent the tears of all God's people through all the centuries. Those tears of the Apostle John are the tears of Adam and Eve, driven out of the Garden of Eden, as they bowed over the first grave, as they watered the dust of the ground with their tears over the silent, still form of their son, Abel. Those are the tears of the children of Israel in bondage as they cried unto God in their affliction and slavery. They are the tears of God's elect through the centuries as they cried unto heaven. They are the sobs and tears that have been wrung from the heart and soul of God's people as they looked on their silent dead, as they stand beside their open graves, as they experience in the trials and sufferings of life, heartaches and disappointments indescribable. Such is the curse that sin has laid upon

---

[501] Revelation 5:2-3
[502] Revelation 5:4

God's beautiful creation; and this is the damnation of the hand
of him who holds it, that usurper, that interloper, that intruder,
that alien, that stranger, that dragon, that serpent, that Satan-
devil. "And I wept audibly," for the failure to find a Redeemer
meant that this earth in its curse is consigned forever to death.
It meant that death, sin, damnation and hell should reign forever and ever and the sovereignty of God's earth should remain
forever in the hands of Satan.[503]

But what ecstatic relief we find in the next verse when an el-
der who represents the church which is in heaven steps in and
says, "*Stop weeping; behold, the Lion that is from the tribe of Judah,
the Root of David, has overcome so as to open the book and its seven
seals.*"[504]

Someone was found with the authority and power to open the
book. And His authority and identity were very clear. In the Old
Testament, we are told that the line of Jewish kings would not
depart from the tribe of Judah.[505] Likewise, the "*Root of David*"
is used by Isaiah to designate the coming Messiah.[506] This clearly
refers to Jesus.

If there was any doubt about the identity of the One with the
authority to open the book, it is erased when John continues,
"*And I saw between the throne (with the four living creatures) and
the elders a Lamb standing, as if slain, having seven horns and seven
eyes, which are the seven Spirits of God, sent out into all the earth.*"[507]

As John continues to look, he sees a lamb with seven horns
that speak of His complete power, seven eyes that speak of His

---

[503] W. A. Criswell, *Expository Sermons on Revelation: Five Volumes Complete
and Unabridged in One*, (1966, repr., Grand Rapids, Michigan: Zondervan
Publishing House, 1981) 3:69-70.

[504] Revelation 5:5

[505] Genesis 49:10

[506] Isaiah 11:1

[507] Revelation 5:6

complete knowledge, and seven Spirits of God that depict His complete dominance over the whole earth.

And this lamb is standing, showing life, but He is standing "*as if slain*," depicting death. Who else could this be but Jesus Christ, slain for the sins of mankind? Can there be any doubt?

When He moves to take the scroll from the hands of God the representatives of mankind in heaven are holding "*bowls full of incense which are the prayers of the saints.*"[508] This is the same scene described by the prophet Daniel in the Old Testament.[509] It's the culmination of recorded history of man on the earth. And it's the beginning of the ultimate work of salvation and the initial stages of the preparation of the earth for the coming kingdom of God.

It's no wonder that this prompts a second spontaneous outburst of praise before the execution of judgment seen in the following chapters. John had previously described twenty-four elders, representative of the completed work of the raptured church already in heaven singing, "*Worthy are You, our Lord and our God, to receive glory and honor and power; for You created all things, and because of Your will they existed, and were created.*"[510]

Now we see the "*myriads of myriads, and thousands of thousands*" of angels joining in the chorus praising Jesus for His sacrificial death that made Him worthy as they proclaimed, "*Worthy is the Lamb that was slain to receive power and riches and wisdom and might and honor and glory and blessing.*"[511]

It would be hard to imagine a more powerful and emotion-packed scene. Heaven is not merely an academic subject to be debated. Heaven will be the personal joy of every person who repents of their sin and believes that the work of Christ on the cross covers their sin and prepares a place in heaven for them.

---

[508] Revelation 5:8
[509] Daniel 7:13-14
[510] Revelation 4:11
[511] Revelation 5:12

Death is not the final act. For those who know Christ, death is the gate to heaven. The final act on earth will be when God wraps up human history and begins the unending years of unequaled joy in His presence. This will happen,

> [I]n the twinkling of an eye, at the last trumpet; for the trumpet will sound, and the dead will be raised imperishable, and we will be changed . . . But when this perishable will have put on the imperishable, and this mortal will have put on immortality, then will come about the saying that is written, 'Death is swallowed up in victory. O death, where is your victory? O death, where is your sting?' The sting of death is sin, and the power of sin is the law; but thanks be to God, who gives us the Christ.[512]

Did you catch the part about "immortality?" Those who follow Christ will never die! Man's quest for immortality is found only at the cross. The *"sting of death"*[513] is removed because sin is removed. Sin is *"swallowed up in victory"*[514] because of the victory Jesus gained at the cross!

The greatest enemy of man is not economic deprivation, a lack of education, war, disease, or even death. The greatest enemy of man is his sinful heart. We can't do anything about the maladies that afflict humanity as we walk across the stage of life.

But we can do something about the cause of death. The thing that empowers the final sting of death is sin. That doesn't mean that we don't still sin. We are still in the flesh, and even though we are saved, our flesh still pulls at our will for self-gratification.

But every sin of every Christian is covered at the cross so that *"there is now no condemnation for those who are in Christ Jesus."*[515]

---

[512] 1 Corinthians 15:52, 54-57
[513] 1 Corinthians 15:56
[514] Ibid.
[515] Romans 8:1

Paul again tells us, that *"our citizenship is in heaven, from which also we eagerly wait for a Savior, the Lord Jesus Christ; who will transform the body of our humble state into conformity with the body of His glory, by the exertion of the power that He has even to subject all things to Himself."*[516]

Songwriter Bill Gaither wrote a beloved song a number of years ago titled, *Because He Lives*. The last verse catches the significance of heaven:

> And then one day, I'll cross death's river.
> I'll fight life's final war with pain.
> And then, as death gives way to vict'ry,
> I'll see the lights of glory and I'll know he reigns.[517]

Shout if you want! Sing if you want! Jump up and down if you want! If you're not moved by this, you're either not a believer or you're in a coma.

The sting of death is gone because He lives! Carol has a living hope that gives the proper context to her suffering on this earth. She will see Rick and Kevin and Dana again in heaven. I will see my son Charlie again. Every believer who has lost a loved one who is saved will see them again in heaven.

And they will be more alive than they ever were on earth because they will have all the characteristics of the resurrected Jesus, and they will never die again. More importantly, we will see Jesus! That's why the sting is gone!

Seventeenth century Puritan pastor Richard Baxter put pen to paper and captured some of the majesty of the ultimate jurisdiction of God. It is our sincere hope that this book has brought you to trust in His eternal rule so that you might enjoy your eternal rest in heaven with Him. Baxter described it:

---

[516] Philippians 3:20-21

[517] Bill Gaither, *Because He Lives*, Sony/ATV Music Publishing LLC, Warner/Chappell Music, Inc., CAPITOL CHRISTIAN MUSIC GROUP.

Doubtless as God advances our senses, and enlarges our capacity, so will he advance the happiness of those senses and fill up with himself all that capacity . . . . We shall then have light without a candle, and perpetual day without the sun . . . . We shall then have enlightened understandings without Scripture, and be governed without a written law; for the Lord will perfect his law in our hearts, and we shall be all perfectly taught of God. We shall have joy, which we drew not from the promises, nor fetched home by faith or hope. We shall have communion without sacraments, without this fruit of the vine, when Christ shall drink it new with us in his Father's kingdom and refresh us with the comforting wine of immediate enjoyment. To have necessities, but no supply, is the case of them in hell. To have necessity supplied by means of the creatures, is the case of us on earth. To have necessity supplied immediately from God, is the case of the saints in heaven. To have no necessity at all, is the prerogative of God himself.[518]

The phrase *"post tenebras lux"* (after darkness, light) became the unofficial rallying cry of the Protestant Reformers of the 16th century. It was utilized by John Calvin's adopted city of Geneva and imprinted on their coins. It also spans the length of the massive Repentance Wall in Geneva today.

The phrase referred to the end of a thousand-year reign of spiritual darkness as the gospel of Jesus Christ was hidden in the councils and creeds of the Catholic Church. As the Reformers re-discovered the Bible as the ultimate authority for the church, the light of the gospel was freed once again, and the world was changed.

"Post tenebras lux" can also be used to describe the brilliant consummation of history in the last chapters of the book of Revelation. Death and sin will be banished forever. The darkness

---

[518] Richard Baxter, abridged by Benjamin Fawcett, A. M., *The Saints Everlasting Rest* (New York, n.d.), 31, 71-72.

of disease, pain, war and suffering of the previous world are completely absent. Loved ones separated by death will be reunited. Eternal beauty and order will dominate every corner of the new heaven and earth.

And there will be no need for light because all heaven will be illuminated with the presence of Jesus. John explains that the glorious light of Jesus Himself will shine throughout heaven and there will be *"no need of the sun or of the moon to shine on it, for the glory of God has illumined it, and its lamp is the Lamb."*[519] Such is the final jurisdiction of God. Darkness will be banished. And all the inhabitants of heaven will bask in the eternal light of Jesus Christ. Post tenebras lux indeed!

---

[519] Revelation 21:23

About the Authors

Dr. Jon McNeff is pastor emeritus of NorthCreek Church in Walnut Creek, California where he also serves as associate dean of the distance location site for Master's Seminary. Before this, Jon served NorthCreek Church as senior pastor for twenty-four years. He also served churches in Cypress and Rolling Hills Estates, California, totaling forty-three years in ministry.

Jon has a Bachelor of Arts in music from Long Beach State University. He also has a Master of Divinity in systematic theology and a Doctor of Ministry in pastoral counseling, both from Talbot School of Theology. He has been married to his wife Anne since 1972. They have three adult children and eight grandchildren.

Jon's belief in the inerrancy and sufficiency of Scripture has fueled his commitment to build the church through consistent expository preaching, Christ centered worship, small group discipleship, biblical counseling, and proclaiming the gospel of Jesus Christ both locally and globally.

Lt. Jim McNeff (ret.) is a partner and managing editor of *Law Enforcement Today* where he has worked since 2016. Previous to this, he served in law enforcement for thirty-one years. He retired as a police lieutenant after twenty-eight years with the

Fountain Valley Police Department in Orange County, California. Prior to that, he served the 3902 Security Police Squadron in the United States Air Force, assigned to the 1st Air Command and Control Squadron at Offutt Air Force Base, Nebraska.

Jim holds a Bachelor of Science in criminal justice from Southwest University and graduated from the Sherman Block Supervisory Leadership Institute as well as the International Association of Chiefs of Police (IACP) course, Leadership in Police Organizations. He authored *The Spirit behind Badge 145* as well as *Justice Revealed*. He has been married to his wife Jamie since 1983. They have three adult children and three grandchildren. You can see more at his website, www.badge145.com.

Index

Printed in the United States
By Bookmasters